Flat Belly Cookbook

FOR DUMMIES

A Wiley Brand

Flat Belly Cookbook

FOR DUMMIES®
A Wiley Brand

by Erin Palinski-Wade, RD, CDE, LDN;
Tara Gidus, MS, RD, CSSD, LDN; and
Kristina LaRue, RD, LDN, CLT

FOR DUMMIES®
A Wiley Brand

Flat Belly Cookbook For Dummies®

Published by: **John Wiley & Sons, Inc.**, 111 River Street, Hoboken, NJ 07030-5774, www.wiley.com

Copyright © 2014 by John Wiley & Sons, Inc., Hoboken, New Jersey

Published simultaneously in Canada

For general information on our other products and services, please contact our Customer Care Department within the U.S. at 877-762-2974, outside the U.S. at 317-572-3993, or fax 317-572-4002. For technical support, please visit www.wiley.com/techsupport.

Wiley publishes in a variety of print and electronic formats and by print-on-demand. Some material included with standard print versions of this book may not be included in e-books or in print-on-demand. If this book refers to media such as a CD or DVD that is not included in the version you purchased, you may download this material at http://booksupport.wiley.com. For more information about Wiley products, visit www.wiley.com.

Library of Congress Control Number: 2013948007 ⟨641.5⟩

ISBN 978-1-118-69266-0 (pbk); ISBN 978-1-118-69257-8 (ebk); ISBN 978-1-118-69265-3 (ebk); ISBN 978-1-118-69276-9 (ebk)

Manufactured in the United States of America

10 9 8 7 6 5 4 3 2 1

Contents at a Glance

Recipes at a Glance

Meat

Seafood

Comfort Foods

Soups

Salads

Sides

Snacks

Desserts

Smoothies

Cocktails

Vegetarian and Vegan

Slow-Cooker Meals

Kid-Friendly Meals

Table of Contents

Introduction

· ·

Are you completely satisfied with your waistline? Do you have a toned, flat stomach? If not, you're not alone. Most people aren't happy with their stomachs and want flatter, firmer midsections. But many of them don't know where to start. That's where this book comes in! If you're looking for a blueprint to the flat belly of your dreams, you're in the right place.

Having excess belly fat is not only undesirable for cosmetic reasons, but also incredibly dangerous to your health. In fact, wide waistlines may just be one of the biggest health concerns in the United States. Why? Because they indicate an excessive amount of *visceral fat* (also known as *belly fat*), which is the most dangerous fat for your health. Belly fat has been associated with an increased risk of heart disease, diabetes, cancer, and even dementia! So, slimming your midsection is important not just to look better in your bathing suit, but also to improve your health long term!

How can you go about slimming your belly? Does shedding belly fat mean sacrificing all your favorite foods and saying goodbye to flavor? Absolutely not! That's why we've written this book. *Flat Belly Cookbook For Dummies* is your blueprint to success. Throughout this book, you find the steps you need to take in order to shed excess fat and keep it off for good — all while eating the foods you love (and never thought possible while on a weight loss plan). And even better, you won't feel hungry and you'll never feel deprived! Think losing weight means giving up on foods like pasta, chocolate, and even cocktails? Think again! In this book, we show you just how to incorporate all these decadent options as part of a meal plan you can actually stick with.

You don't need to be a chef to follow the recipes in this book. In fact, even if you've never set foot in the kitchen before, we have you covered. Throughout this book, we offer tips and tricks to make cooking a breeze. And we keep your time in mind, too. This book is packed full of quick meal and recipe options, so even the busiest person can find success.

About This Book

Fad diets and cookie-cutter diets don't work. If they did, the United States wouldn't be facing the obesity crisis it's currently in. So, what *does* work?

Individualizing your weight loss plan. Just like no two individuals are exactly the same, no two paths toward weight loss goals should be exactly the same either. That's what sets the Belly Fat Diet plan apart from other weight loss plans you may have tried in the past. The plan we cover in this book provides unique weight loss paths based on your sex, age, and even personality, to help you custom-tailor your weight loss plan to your individual needs. Plus, this book provides realistic, practical tips and advice. We know that you're crunched for time, under stress, and facing real-world problems. Your food choices aren't always your main priority. That's why this book takes away the guesswork and simplifies your weight loss plan so you can reach your goals and maintain them permanently!

This book not only helps you decode food labels, identify belly fat–fighting nutrients, and plan your meals, but also provides more than a hundred mouth-watering recipes that will satisfy all your cravings. In fact, you won't feel like you're following a weight loss plan at all!

As you're reading this book, keep in mind that sidebars (text in gray boxes) and anything marked with the Technical Stuff icon (see "Icons Used in This Book," later) are skippable.

Within this book, you may note that some web addresses break across two lines of text. If you're reading this book in print and want to visit one of these web pages, simply key in the web address exactly as it's noted in the text, pretending as though the line break doesn't exist. If you're reading this as an e-book, you've got it easy — just click the web address to be taken directly to the web page.

Finally, here are a few things to keep in mind when it comes to the recipes. Unless otherwise specified,

- Eggs are large.
- Pepper is freshly ground black pepper.
- Butter is unsalted.
- Flour is all-purpose unless otherwise specified.
- Sugar is granulated unless otherwise noted.
- All herbs are fresh unless dried herbs are specified.
- All temperatures are Fahrenheit. (Refer to the Appendix for information about converting temperatures to Celsius.)
- Vegetarian recipes are marked by a small tomato icon (like the one to the left) in the Recipes in This Chapter lists.

Foolish Assumptions

We don't make too many assumptions about you (you know what they say about assuming), but we do assume a few things:

- ✔ You're trying to lose weight and shed unwanted belly fat.
- ✔ You've made the commitment to begin making lifestyle changes to improve your overall health and lose weight.
- ✔ You enjoy food and don't want to sacrifice great taste in order to achieve your goal weight. (Don't worry — you don't have to!)
- ✔ You have a hectic schedule and are often on the run. Although you want to eat healthy and get in better shape, life can often get in the way.

Icons Used in This Book

Throughout this book, you'll notice *icons* (small images in the margins that are designed to call your attention to specific pieces of information). Here are the icons we use in this book and a key to what they mean:

When you see the Tip icon, you're sure to find helpful tips and practical advice to help flatten your midsection and promote long-term weight loss.

We use the Remember icon when we mention information that's worth, well, remembering. Typically, these paragraphs help you stay on track to achieve your long-term weight loss goals.

When we mention a food or nutrient that may pack on belly fat or identify a common obstacle to weight loss, we grab your attention with the Warning icon.

We use the Technical Stuff icon when we share information that's interesting but not essential to your understanding of the subject at hand. If you're in a hurry, you can skip anything marked with this icon.

Beyond the Book

In addition to the material in the print or e-book you're reading right now, this product also comes with some access-anywhere goodies on the web.

Check out the free Cheat Sheet at www.dummies.com/cheatsheet/flat bellycookbook for the top five ways to flatten your abs, tips on maintaining your weight loss long term, and more.

Where to Go from Here

If you're a seasoned dieter, you may have tried unsuccessfully in the past to shed belly fat for good. But like most people trying to lose weight, you may have hit a road block or two on your journey to your long-term goals. Most likely, you have a specific area or two that you struggle with, such as eating on the run or dealing with hunger. Instead of reading through this book in order, page by page, you can skip right to the areas you need to focus on the most. So, look over the Table of Contents and see what topics seem the most relevant or interesting to you. Then turn right to them!

If you're just starting out and you aren't sure what belly fat is or how to tell if you have too much, start by reading Chapter 1, where you find all the belly fat basics. If you already know the dangers of an elevated waistline and just want to know how to get started shedding unwanted pounds and inches, head to Chapter 4 to learn about the Belly Fat Diet plans and which is best for you. And if you're familiar with the Belly Fat Diet and you're looking for new and delicious recipes that work within your plan, head to Parts II through IV to dive into the more than 100 belly fat–burning recipes this book serves up.

Part I

Getting Started with the Belly Fat Diet

In this part . . .

- Understand the anatomy of belly fat and the associated health dangers.
- Identify whether you have excess belly fat.
- Discover which Belly Fat Diet plan is right for you.
- Find superfoods that fight off belly fat.
- Decode a food label to maximize your Belly Fat Diet plan results.

Chapter 1

Wrapping Your Mind around Belly Fat

You've heard it in the news and possibly seen it in the mirror. *Belly fat* seems to be the latest buzzword. But what exactly is it? How do you know if you have too much? And is belly fat really any different from fat in other parts of your body? The truth is that belly fat, also known as *visceral fat,* is, indeed, much different from fat in other areas. In fact, belly fat is considered the single most harmful form of fat in your entire body! Having a high level of belly fat has been linked to heart disease, high blood pressure, metabolic syndrome, type 2 diabetes, and even certain cancers. And here's some surprising news: You don't have to be overweight to have too much belly fat. Even people at their ideal body weight can have too high a percentage of body fat, specifically in the midsection. Even at a normal body weight, if your waistline expands by 4 inches over time, this can increase your risk for stroke by as much as 15 percent!

Throughout this chapter, we explain what belly fat is, where excess belly fat comes from, the health consequences of having too much belly fat, and how to determine if you have too much. When you understand belly fat and how you accumulate it, you can start taking action to reduce it in order to improve your overall health, appearance, and energy levels!

What Is Belly Fat?

To understand belly fat, first you need to understand the various types of fat in your body. The body contains three distinct types of fat:

- ✔ **Triglycerides:** Triglycerides make up about 95 percent of all the fat in your body. This is the fat that circulates in your bloodstream and provides a source of energy to your body.

- ✔ **Subcutaneous fat:** Subcutaneous fat is the layer of fat that lies right below the skin's surface, between the skin and the abdominal wall. This is the fat that you can pinch with your fingers. It's also typically the fat that you aim to reduce for cosmetic reasons.

- ✔ **Visceral fat:** The last type of fat in your body is visceral fat, or what is often referred to as belly fat. This fat hangs below the muscles of your abdomen where it's in close proximity to most of your vital organs. And that's what makes this fat so dangerous. Because of its location, visceral fat is the easiest source of energy for your internal organs, providing them with a constant, steady stream of energy while at the same time exposing them to toxic hormones and chemicals. And that's one reason that this fat is so deadly.

Figure 1-1 illustrates where subcutaneous fat and visceral fat are located. As you can see, subcutaneous fat is the outermost layer of fat and sits on top of abdominal muscles. Below the abdominal muscle is where visceral fat lies. Even though you can't pinch this fat or see it with your eyes, chances are, if you have a large amount of subcutaneous fat, you also have an excessive amount of visceral fat. And as the figure shows, this dangerous fat surrounds all the organs in the abdominal cavity.

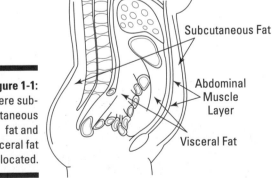

Subcutaneous Fat

Abdominal Muscle Layer

Visceral Fat

Figure 1-1: Where subcutaneous fat and visceral fat are located.

Illustration by Wiley, Composition Services Graphics

Fat cells don't just passively hang around and provide stored energy. Research has found that fat cells are actually *metabolically active,* meaning that they secrete hormones and chemicals that can impact every organ in your body. When you're at a healthy body weight and you have a healthy level of body fat, the chemicals and hormones secreted by fat cells are healthy. They help to regulate appetite and insulin levels, and even help you to burn stored fat. But when you have too many fat cells or your fat cells become larger in size than normal (which can happen in people who are overweight or have excess body fat), your fat cells are producing more hormones and chemicals than your body needs, which, over time, can impact your health, increase inflammation in your body, and increase your risk for diseases such as diabetes, heart disease, and cancer.

So, excessive fat anywhere in your body can be damaging, but what makes visceral fat the most dangerous fat is that it's thought to produce an even larger amount of harmful chemicals than subcutaneous fat does. Because visceral fat is so close to your organs, excess visceral fat can cause some serious damage throughout your body. In addition, visceral fat surrounds your organs and, over time, can place excess pressure on them, virtually strangling the organs and putting stress on their ability to function correctly.

Why Does Belly Fat Develop?

In order to successfully shed belly fat once and for all, it helps to know the reasons that you accumulated excessive belly fat in the first place. Once you know where this belly fat is coming from and why, you can begin to make the changes needed to get rid of it for good!

Excessive accumulation of belly fat doesn't come from just one place or one behavior. Many factors can impact belly fat. Of course, what you put into your mouth plays a major role, but other factors also can increase or decrease your level of belly fat, including your lifestyle (for example, your stress level and how much sleep you get) and hormones. In this section, we cover all these factors.

Diet

How and what you eat can play a major role in the amount of belly fat you accumulate. By limiting your intake of belly-bloating foods and transitioning to alternatives that can actually slim your waistline, not only can you lose body weight, but you can significantly reduce your waistline.

Here are some of the biggest dietary contributors to belly fat, along with some slimming alternatives:

✔ **Simple sugars:** If you sprinkle sugar on your cereal or sip on soda, sweetened teas, and fruit drinks, you're providing your body with a large amount of simple sugars. Simple sugar is sugar in its simplest form — your body can use this sugar for energy with very little effort. Unfortunately, because simple sugars are so easily utilized by your body for energy, they can lead to rapid spikes in blood sugar. This, in turn, triggers a rapid increase in insulin, which signals your body to store more fat (especially belly fat).

Avoid simple sugars by choosing low-sugar and sugar-free beverages whenever possible. Instead, opt for water, naturally flavored seltzer, or unsweetened ice teas. To sweeten foods, use seasonings such as cinnamon instead of added sugar.

✔ **Refined carbohydrates:** Foods that are made with enriched and white flours are called *refined carbohydrates*. Your body digests these carbohydrates rapidly, leading to spikes in both insulin and blood glucose levels (see "Insulin," later in this chapter).

Instead, choose 100 percent whole-grain options. You can identify these by looking for the first ingredient listed on the label — it should contain the word *whole* (such as *whole oat flour* or *whole wheat flour*).

✔ **Unhealthy fats:** Eating a meal that contains fat doesn't necessarily mean that you'll increase your body fat. However, certain types of dietary fat *do* encourage the increase of belly fat. Saturated fats (which are found in high-fat animal proteins, butter, cream, and so on) and trans fats (which are found in many processed and commercial baked and fried goods) can have very negative impacts on overall health. A diet high in these fats can increase inflammation, increase your risk of heart disease and diabetes, and of course, pack on the belly fat!

These fats can have such an impact on belly fat that a study out of Johns Hopkins University found the amount of fat surrounding your abdomen is directly proportional to the amount of saturated fat you take in through your diet.

On the flip side, unsaturated fats — specifically, monounsaturated fats (found in olive oil, almonds, avocados, and so on) and omega-3 fatty acids (found in fish, walnuts, flaxseeds, chia seeds, and so on) — have been found to *decrease* belly fat. By replacing saturated fats and trans fats with monounsaturated fats and omega-3 fatty acids, you can improve your overall health, as well as reduce your waistline.

✔ **High-sugar, high-fat drinks:** What you drink may be just as important for shedding belly fat as what you eat. Drinks can seem harmless, but they actually can cause significant damage to your health and your waistline. In fact, consuming excessive fluid calories may be the most damaging thing you can do to your belly. Drinking your calories in the form of soda, juice, whole milk, and coffee loaded with creamers and sugar can set off a cascading effect of elevated blood glucose and insulin levels, resulting in an increased amount of belly fat storage. What's even worse is that fluids don't keep you full in the same way that solid foods do. So, now you've consumed calories, but you're still hungry. This combination can lead you to eat more, resulting in weight gain.

Instead of consuming high-sugar, high-fat drinks, opt for low-sugar, low-calorie beverages such as water, seltzer (even naturally flavored seltzers), unsweetened teas and coffees, and low-fat milk.

Diet isn't just about *what* you eat, it's also about *how* you eat. Have you ever thought, "I'll just skip breakfast so I can limit my total daily calories and lose weight"? If so, did this strategy work for you? Most likely, no. Although you may save a few calories by skipping a meal, this strategy will eventually back-fire and lead to your gaining even more weight and belly fat. Why? Because skipping meals can lead to excessive hunger. Think about the last time you were extremely hungry. Were you craving a salad, or did you want to down a bag of chips followed by a few slices of pizza? Usually, when you get too hungry, your mind doesn't want healthier food options. Instead, you start to crave foods high in unhealthy fats or rich in refined carbohydrates. You may also eat faster than you normally would, causing you to miss the signs that you're full, which can result in overeating.

Plus, skipping meals can confuse your body. Your body begins to wonder when the next meal is coming, or if it's coming at all. Now, instead of burning up stored fat for energy, it protects you by slowing down your metabolism to *conserve* energy, in case potential famine or starvation is on the horizon. In addition, your body works to store more fat to save up additional energy reserves in case the next meal never comes. Although this strategy would be helpful if you truly were in danger of starvation, when you intentionally skip meals, it can prevent you from losing weight and belly fat.

The best strategy for belly fat loss and weight loss is to eat a balanced meal or snack every three to four hours. This way, you avoid excessive hunger and food cravings, and keep your metabolism functioning at its peak.

Lifestyle

According to the U.S. Centers for Disease Control and Prevention (CDC), as of 2011, 36 percent of all American adults over age 20 are now obese with another 33 percent classified as being overweight. In addition, the CDC also states that 17 percent of children are now classified as obese. That means that more than half the country is above their ideal body weight, and our children are well on their way. So, what's causing so many people to gain weight and keep them from being able to lose it? There isn't a simple answer, but many lifestyle factors play a role in the obesity epidemic.

Over the past few decades, people's schedules have been getting busier, work demands have been getting higher, and many people work longer hours while struggling to make ends meet in an uncertain economy. (It's no wonder stress levels are high!) You may feel as though you don't have a minute to sit and relax, or even breathe, between juggling work, family, and your other responsibilities. And when you're overscheduled, you may not find the time to exercise or to prepare a healthy meal. Instead, you may pull into a drive-thru and eat your meal in front of the computer or TV. This can cause you to eat foods rich in refined carbohydrates, saturated fats, and sodium — the perfect recipe for increased belly fat.

Another side effect of an overscheduled, stressful lifestyle is lack of sleep. Maybe you're staying up late to meet a deadline or you can't fall asleep at night because your mind is racing with thoughts of the bills you need to pay and all the things you need to do tomorrow that you didn't get done today. Getting too little sleep can have a major impact on your overall health. Inadequate sleep raises stress hormone levels, can slow metabolism, and can even increase hunger — a combination that is sure to result in increased belly fat!

Hormones

Many, many hormones are constantly cycling through your body each and every day. However, when some of these hormones are out of balance, it can trigger your body to start storing fat, specifically in your midsection. This can lead to an accumulation of excessive subcutaneous fat, as well as visceral fat. Insulin and stress hormones, such as adrenaline and cortisol, are the main hormones that impact belly fat.

Insulin

When you eat, your digestive system breaks down food into small particles that can be used for fuel in your body. Carbohydrates are broken down into simple sugars called *glucose,* which is the primary source of energy for every cell in your body. Glucose is then absorbed in your bloodstream, creating a rise in blood glucose levels. To allow your body's cells to take glucose from the bloodstream and use it as energy, your pancreas produces a hormone called *insulin.* Insulin picks up the glucose and transports it into your cells. The glucose is either used for energy immediately or stored as an energy reserve for later.

If you eat a food that is rapidly digested (meaning that it's quickly converted into glucose), this can cause a spike in blood glucose levels, resulting in a rapid rise in insulin. The insulin then works to quickly move glucose into your body's cells. When the glucose isn't immediately needed for energy, it's stored away in your fat stores as an energy reserve. If you start to store more and more of this extra energy and never get around to burning it, you end up with fat cells that are increasing in size. Insulin's favorite place to store excess energy is right in your midsection, which results in an increased amount of belly fat.

The amount of insulin circulating in your body and storing fat largely depends on the food choices you make. Foods high in refined carbohydrates and simple sugars, such as candy, white bread, and sugary beverages, spike blood glucose and insulin levels, resulting in an increased amount of belly fat storage. On the other hand, lean proteins, healthy fats, and fiber help to slow the amount of glucose released into the bloodstream. These foods help to keep blood glucose levels consistent throughout the day, which protects against spikes in insulin.

By eating a diet rich in lean proteins, vegetables, whole grains, and healthy fats, you can work to stabilize your blood glucose and insulin levels, helping to reduce the amount of belly fat you store.

Stress hormones

If you want to achieve a flat stomach once and for all, you must gain control over the amount of stress in your life. During times of stress, your body goes into "fight-or-flight" mode, as it gears up to protect you against a predator or other physical stress. (This response was very helpful when we were cavemen, but it's not quite as helpful for the kinds of stresses most of us face today.) When you're under stress, your body increases its production of a stress hormone called *adrenaline,* which then signals your body's fat cells to release stores of fatty acids to be used as energy.

The problem is, when stress comes from a non-physical source, such as from your boss rather than a mastodon, the fatty acids aren't burned off. Instead, the adrenal glands release the hormone *cortisol* to collect and store the unused fatty acids. Unfortunately, cortisol doesn't always bring these fatty acids back to the cells they came from. Instead, it tends to favor storing fat right in your abdomen. So, if this cycle repeats itself on a regular basis because you're under a lot of stress, more fat is mobilized and relocated right to your waistline.

What Does Belly Fat Mean for Your Health?

Who doesn't want to look great in a bathing suit and be happy with the man (or woman) in the mirror? But the quest to banish belly fat isn't just skin deep. Belly fat is the most dangerous fat in your body. And having even just a small amount of excess belly fat can have a significant impact on your overall health. Elevated levels of belly fat can cause inflammation throughout your body and increase your risk for everything from heart disease to metabolic syndrome to diabetes to cancer. Belly fat has such a dramatic impact on health that a study out of Europe found that increasing your waist circumference by just 2 inches (even if you're within a healthy weight range) can increase the risk for mortality in women by 13 percent and in men by 17 percent! As you can see, getting your waistline under control is vital to taking charge of your health and improving your overall wellness and longevity.

Heart disease

If you want to have a healthy heart, slimming your waistline is essential. Research has found that a large waistline can increase your risk for high blood pressure, heart disease, and even stroke. The link is so strong that a recent study out of Johns Hopkins University found that losing belly fat was directly correlated with an improvement in the flexibility of arteries, allowing for improved blood flow and reducing strain on the heart.

So, why does belly fat wreak such havoc on the heart? Studies have found that visceral fat produces specific proteins that can cause damage within the body. These proteins can cause contraction in blood vessels, elevating blood pressure. Additionally, they can trigger chronic inflammation, which can lead to a buildup of plaque in the arteries. In addition, a large waistline can contribute to metabolic syndrome, a condition of early-stage insulin resistance that can dramatically increase your risk for heart disease (see the "Metabolic syndrome" section, later).

High blood pressure

Blood pressure is the measurement of the blood's force against the wall of the arteries. When weight is elevated, excess fat can place additional pressure on the walls of your arteries, increasing blood pressure. When blood pressure is elevated, your organs — such as your heart and your kidneys — have to work harder. If blood pressure isn't controlled, it can significantly damage these vital organs, which is why achieving and maintaining a healthy body weight is so critical to your health.

Metabolic syndrome

Excessive amounts of visceral fat in your body can increase the amount of free fatty acids circulating in your bloodstream. This can lead to elevated triglyceride levels, as well as a decline in HDL ("good") cholesterol levels. In addition, excessive levels of belly fat can also increase *insulin resistance,* a condition that occurs when the cells of the body have a decreased ability to respond to insulin. All these factors can increase your risk of developing metabolic syndrome.

Metabolic syndrome is the umbrella term for a combination of disorders that, when combined, can indicate a high risk for the development of heart disease, diabetes, and stroke. The more risk factors you have, the higher your risk for disease. In fact, having metabolic syndrome can make you twice as likely to develop heart disease and five times as likely to develop diabetes than someone without any risk factors.

There are five main risk factors that are looked at when determining if someone has metabolic syndrome. Displaying at least three of the five risk factors qualifies you as having this condition. The risk factors are

- **A large waistline:** Men should have a waist circumference less than 40 inches; women, less than 35 inches.

- **Elevated triglyceride levels:** Triglyceride levels should be less than 150 mg/dL.

- **Low HDL cholesterol levels:** Men should have HDL levels of at least 45 mg/dL; women, at least 50 mg/dL.

- **Elevated blood pressure levels:** Normal blood pressure is considered 120/80 mmHg.

- **Elevated fasting blood glucose:** Normal fasting blood glucose is less than 100 mg/dL.

As you can see, not only is excessive belly fat a risk factor for metabolic syndrome, but having an increased amount of this fat can increase your chances of developing many of the other risk factors that qualify you for having metabolic syndrome.

Diabetes

As belly fat increases, so does insulin resistance. As your cells become more and more resistant to insulin, sugar from the food you eat is unable to enter the cells freely. Instead, insulin, which carries the sugar from your bloodstream into your cells for energy, is essentially locked out. This means that although you're producing insulin, it can't do its job correctly, which results in rising blood sugar levels. When blood sugar levels increase outside the normal range and stay elevated, this increases your risk of developing type 2 diabetes.

Cancer

Fat cells are not just stored energy; they're also metabolically active. This means that they're constantly producing hormones and chemicals that can impact your body. One of the hormones that fat cells produce is estrogen. The more fat cells you have, and the larger those fat cells are, the more estrogen they produce. This means that individuals who are overweight and have excessive body fat will have higher levels of circulating estrogen in their bodies than people who are at a normal body weight.

Although estrogen can be beneficial to the body, high levels of estrogen can promote tumor growth in the breasts. It can also increase the risk of colorectal cancer in both men and women.

Are You at Risk?

Your body weight on a scale doesn't tell the whole picture when it comes to visceral fat. In fact, even individuals who are at their ideal body weight can have too much belly fat. And a person who would be classified as "overweight" by looking at the scale alone may actually have a large amount of muscle mass and a lower percentage of body fat. Bottom line: The number on the scale tells you nothing about visceral fat or your risk for medical complications.

Now, we're not saying to throw away the scale completely. But just keep in mind that the scale doesn't tell the whole story when it comes to belly fat. Other numbers, such as body mass index and waist circumference, will give you a much more accurate measure of your true risk when it comes to belly fat.

Calculating your body mass index

Body mass index (BMI) is a formula that uses your body weight and your height to help you determine if you're at a healthy weight, underweight, overweight, or obese. BMI can be a good indication of body fat in most people, but, just like the scale, it's not perfect. People with large amounts of muscle mass, such as elite athletes and bodybuilders, can have an elevated BMI but a low percentage of body fat.

BMI does *not* measure body fat directly, but it is the most practical and affordable method in an office or home setting for determining whether you're overweight or at risk for becoming overweight. If your BMI falls outside the ideal range, you can use the additional measurement methods in this chapter to determine if you have excessive visceral fat.

To determine your individual BMI measurement, use the chart in Figure 1-2. You need to know your height in inches and your weight in pounds. Look at the left side of the chart and find your height in inches. Then find your body weight in pounds. Finally, find where these two numbers intersect and drag your finger toward the top of the chart to see the corresponding BMI. Table 1-1 tells you what that number means (that is, whether you're in the healthy range or whether you're under- or overweight).

If you can't find your BMI on this chart, or if you just prefer online calculators, check out the one offered by the National Heart, Lung, and Blood Institute: www.nhlbisupport.com/bmi.

Ideally, you want to keep your BMI within the healthy range, because a BMI outside this range can significantly increase your risk of developing weight-related health conditions.

BMI (kg/m²)	19	20	21	22	23	24	25	26	27	28	29	30	35	40
Height (in.)	Weight (lb.)													
58	91	96	100	105	110	115	119	124	129	134	138	143	167	191
59	94	99	104	109	114	119	124	128	133	138	143	148	173	198
60	97	102	107	112	118	123	128	133	138	143	148	153	179	204
61	100	106	111	116	122	127	132	137	143	148	153	158	185	211
62	104	109	115	120	126	131	136	142	147	153	158	164	191	218
63	107	113	118	124	130	135	141	146	152	158	163	169	197	225
64	110	116	122	128	134	140	145	151	157	163	169	174	204	232
65	114	120	126	132	138	144	150	156	162	168	174	180	210	240
66	118	124	130	136	142	148	155	161	167	173	179	186	216	247
67	121	127	134	140	146	153	159	166	172	178	185	191	223	255
68	125	131	138	144	151	158	164	171	177	184	190	197	230	262
69	128	135	142	149	155	162	169	176	182	189	196	203	236	270
70	132	139	146	153	160	167	174	181	188	195	202	207	243	278
71	136	143	150	157	165	172	179	186	193	200	208	215	250	286
72	140	147	154	162	169	177	184	191	199	206	213	221	258	294
73	144	151	159	166	174	182	189	197	204	212	219	227	265	302
74	148	155	163	171	179	186	194	202	210	218	225	233	272	311
75	152	160	168	176	184	192	200	208	216	224	232	240	279	319
76	156	164	172	180	189	197	205	213	221	230	238	246	287	328

Figure 1-2: Find your BMI using this chart.

Illustration by Wiley, Composition Services Graphics

Table 1-1	BMI Categories and Risk	
BMI	*Weight Status*	*Risk*
Less than 18.5	Underweight	Increased risk
18.5–24.9	Healthy weight	Low risk
25.0–29.9	Overweight	Increased risk
30.0–39.9	Obese	High risk
40.0 or more	Severe obesity	Very high risk

Source: National Heart, Lung, and Blood Institute

Even if your BMI puts you in the healthy range, you may still have too much visceral fat. So, be sure to assess your risk using every method outlined in this chapter to get a clear picture of where you stand.

Getting out the tape measure

In the fight against belly fat, there is one measurement that you should become very familiar with: your waist circumference. According to the National Institutes of Health, an elevated waist circumference is associated with an increased risk of high cholesterol, high blood pressure, diabetes, and heart disease. Even if you're at a healthy body weight, having a large waistline can still significantly increase your disease risk. This is why being aware of your waist circumference, in addition to your BMI (see the preceding section), is so important.

If your BMI is normal, but your waist circumference is elevated, you still need to work to reduce your overall body fat — specifically, belly fat — to improve your health. On the other hand, if you have an elevated BMI, but your waist circumference is normal, this could mean you carry a large amount of lean muscle mass, but have reduced levels of body fat, indicating a low risk. If you're not sure about your risk, talk to your doctor.

Measuring your waist circumference isn't exactly the same as the measurements you would take for determining your clothing size. Instead, follow these steps for the most accurate waist measurement:

1. **With your fingers, locate the top of your hipbone.**

2. **Place a tape measure around your bare stomach, just above your upper hipbone (as shown in Figure 1-3), and check the number.**

Keep the tape measure snug, but don't pull so tight that it compresses the skin. Breathe normally and relax your abdomen — no sucking in your stomach!

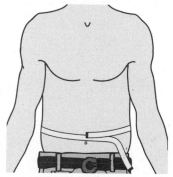

Figure 1-3:
Measuring waist cir-
cumference.

Illustration by Wiley, Composition Services Graphics

The safest levels of visceral fat are indicated by a waist circumference of less than 35 inches for women and less than 40 inches for men.

In addition to your waist circumference, another very important measurement is *waist-to-hip ratio* (a measurement that compares the size of your hips to the size of your waist). The larger your waist is in relation to your hips, the more likely you are to have an excessive level of visceral fat, increasing your risk of disease. Waist-to-hip ratio is especially important to individuals who have a healthy BMI, because it can be an excellent way to determine if you're storing too high a percentage of your body weight in your abdomen.

To measure your waist-to-hip ratio, follow these steps:

1. **Measure your hips at the widest part of your buttocks.**

2. **Using the waist circumference measurement you took earlier, divide your waist measurement by your hip measurement.**

   This number is your waist-to-hip ratio. For example, if you have a waist measurement of 35 inches, and a hip measurement of 42 inches, you would divide 35 by 42 and get 0.83.

Use the chart in Table 1-2 to check your level of risk based on your waist-to-hip ratio.

Table 1-2	Waist-to-Hip Ratio and Risk	
Male Waist-to-Hip Ratio	*Female Waist-to-Hip Ratio*	*Health Risk*
0.95 or below	0.80 or below	Low
0.96–1.0	0.81–0.85	Moderate
1.1 or above	0.86 or above	High

Getting a checkup

After you've determined your BMI, waist circumference, and waist-to-hip ratio (see the previous sections), you have a pretty good idea if you have too much visceral fat or are at risk for having too much. There are a few additional numbers you want to be aware of to assess your overall risk for disease. We cover those numbers in this section.

Knowing your numbers and your risks isn't meant to be scary or upsetting. Whether you have a high risk or a low risk, *knowing* your risk is important so that you can begin to make the diet and lifestyle changes necessary to improve your health for a long and happy life!

Cholesterol

Technically, you want a blood lipid panel, but if you tell your doctor you want your cholesterol tested, this is what you'll get. This measurement includes your total cholesterol, high-density lipoprotein (HDL), low-density lipoprotein (LDL), and triglycerides. Table 1-3 tells you what the numbers mean in terms of risk.

Table 1-3	Understanding Your Cholesterol Levels	
Blood Lipid	*Range*	*Risk Category*
Total cholesterol	Less than 170 mg/dL	Very low
	170–199 mg/dL	Low
	200–239 mg/dL	Moderately high
	240 mg/dL or above	High
LDL cholesterol	Less than 100 mg/dL	Very low
	100–129 mg/dL	Low
	130–159 mg/dL	Borderline high

Blood Lipid	Range	Risk Category
	160–189 mg/dL	High
	190 mg/dL or above	Very high
HDL cholesterol	60 mg/dL or above (men and women)	Very low
	40–59 mg/dL (men) or 50–59 mg/dL (women)	Low
	Less than 40 mg/dL (men) or less than 50 mg/dL (women)	High
Triglycerides	Less than 150 mg/dL	Low
	150–199 mg/dL	Moderate
	200–499 mg/dL	High
	500 mg/dL or above	Very high

Having elevated levels of total cholesterol, LDL cholesterol, and triglycerides can increase your risk for developing heart disease. On the contrary, you want to have higher levels of HDL cholesterol, which acts almost like a garbage truck in the body, scooping up cholesterol and transporting it back to the liver, where it can be removed from the body. Higher levels of HDL cholesterol protect against heart disease, as well as certain cancers.

Have your blood lipids checked annually or more often if they're not where they should be.

Blood pressure

Hypertension (high blood pressure) can increase your risk for heart disease, stroke, and even diseases of the kidney. Because you can't "feel" an elevated blood pressure, you need to have your blood pressure checked at least once a year, more often if it's high.

Blood pressure is a combination of two measures: systolic and diastolic. You don't need to know what those words mean, but just know that the systolic number is the one on top (or the first number), and diastolic is the one on the bottom (or the second number). For example, in a blood pressure of 120/80 (pronounced "120 over 80"), 120 is the systolic number and 80 is the diastolic number.

Table 1-4 shows the categories for blood pressure in adults.

Table 1-4	Blood Pressure in Adults	
Category	*Systolic Number (The Number on Top)*	*Diastolic Number (The Number on the Bottom)*
Normal	Less than 120 mmHg	Less than 80 mmHg
Pre-hypertension	120–139 mmHg	80–89 mmHg
Stage 1 hypertension	140–159 mmHg	90–99 mmHg
Stage 2 hypertension	160 mmHg or above	100 mmHg or above

Source: National Heart, Lung, and Blood Institute

Blood glucose

Having an elevated blood glucose level can be an indication of insulin resistance, as well as diabetes. Because uncontrolled blood glucose levels can lead to serious health conditions, including heart disease, kidney disease, circulatory problems, and even blindness, you should be screened for high blood glucose once a year, more often if it's high.

If you find that your blood glucose level is elevated, making dietary changes, increasing physical activity, and shedding excess belly fat can significantly reduce insulin resistance and improve blood glucose control. Table 1-5 shows the normal range for fasting blood glucose.

Table 1-5	Understanding Blood Glucose Levels
Fasting Blood Glucose Levels	*Category*
Normal	70–99 mg/dL
Pre-diabetic	100–126 mg/dL
Diabetic	127 mg/dL or above

Putting it all together

Your BMI, waist circumference, waist-to-hip ratio, cholesterol, blood pressure, and blood glucose all are risk factors that can determine your odds of developing long-term health consequences, such as diabetes and heart disease. By being aware of the areas that are increasing your risk, you can start to make the dietary and lifestyle changes necessary to reduce these risks and improve your long-term health.

As you start to follow the meal plans outlined throughout this book, you'll notice your BMI, waist circumference, and waist-to-hip ratio begin to drop, and your health risks will dramatically decrease. Use Table 1-6 to analyze your current health risks, as well as to help you see the decline in health risks as you work toward achieving your flat-belly goals!

Table 1-6	Health Assessment Levels
Number of Health Assessment Levels above Normal	*Health Risk*
0	Low
1–2	Moderate
3–4	High
5 or more	Very high

Chapter 2

Introducing the Belly Fat–Burning Lifestyle

In This Chapter

▶ Introducing the Belly Fat Diet

▶ Understanding why the Belly Fat Diet works

▶ Incorporating the Belly Fat Diet into your daily life

*N*ow that you have an understanding of what belly fat is and where it comes from, it's time to start taking action. Chapter 1 introduces you to belly fat, how to determine if you have too much of it, and the health dangers associated with this deadly fat. Throughout this chapter, we tell you what the Belly Fat Diet is and why it works, so you can dive right in and shed this unhealthy fat once and for all. We also give you tips for incorporating this weight loss plan into your life so you see how small, simple changes can add up to big results!

Getting to Know the Belly Fat Diet

The Belly Fat Diet has four main facets that will help you achieve amazing results quickly and easily. In this section, we break them down so you can get started with your plan today!

Diet is a four-letter word

You may have noticed that we use the word *lifestyle* not *diet* in this chapter's title. Wonder why? Because diets don't work! We're talking about diets in the traditional sense, where you go on a very restrictive meal plan for a set amount of time, only to return to your old habits and undo all your hard work. We don't want you to diet. We don't want you to invest your time, money, and hard work into doing something that will only give you temporary results. What good is it if you can achieve your goal weight for one month, only to regain the weight? That certainly won't help your health or your self-esteem. Sure a restrictive diet may help you shed pounds quickly, but it won't teach you how

to make real changes that you can stick with to maintain your results. And worst of all, being too restrictive can lead to a slower metabolism, which can not only lead to your regaining the weight you lost, but also make it harder to re-lose this weight again in the future.

So, join us in saying "no" to diets for good! Instead, this book shows you how to lose weight in a healthy way, one in which you can enjoy all foods and, most important, manage and maintain your ideal weight for good. The plan we outline in this book improves not just your waistline, but your health as well.

Eating more to lose more

Your eyes aren't deceiving you. This heading does say to eat *more* to lose more, not eat less! And who doesn't love that? Knowing that we should eat more of something always makes us happy! But we want to be clear: This isn't a recommendation to eat more of *all* foods. That's a surefire recipe for excessive weight gain and increased belly fat. But you do want to begin eating more of the foods that actually help you to shed belly fat. Some foods are such potent belly fat fighters that by eating more of them, you can actually increase your body's ability to shed overall body fat, as well as target stubborn belly fat and rid yourself of it once and for all. In fact, when you view the meal plans in Chapter 4, you'll even notice that one food group is *unlimited!*

So, why does eating more of certain foods fuel fat burning? Certain foods and food groups, such as vegetables, are loaded in fiber, low in calories, and packed full of belly fat–fighting nutrients. This allows these foods to keep you full for long periods of time without expanding your waistline. And by staying full, you can keep cravings and excessive hunger at bay, helping to prevent less-healthy food choices.

One of the secrets of the Belly Fat Diet is its focus on high-volume, low-calorie foods. This means foods that are extra filling, but surprisingly low in calories. In fact, on this plan, you most likely eat more food than you've ever eaten before. Except this time, by making the right food choices, you'll see the number on the scale do gown and your waistline shrink before your eyes. All without ever feeling hungry and while finally getting rid of annoying food cravings once and for all!

Timing your meals

Part of the recipe for success with the Belly Fat Diet is to make sure you don't skip out on meals. Waiting too long in between meals or skipping meals all together is weight loss sabotage. That's because it sets you up to have erratic blood glucose levels and excessive hunger, and triggers intense cravings. And the cravings that occur aren't for the foods you want to eat for a flat belly. Instead, the cravings that occur are typically for refined carbohydrates and foods rich in unhealthy saturated and trans fats — the foods that are the worst for your health and waistline.

In addition, skipping meals can result in your eating too quickly at your next meal or snack. Why does that matter? Because it actually takes 20 minutes for your stomach to get the signal to your brain that you've eaten enough and you're satisfied. Eat too quickly and you'll miss this signal all together, resulting in your eating more than you truly need and going from satisfied to stuffed after a meal.

To help yourself slow down when eating and to prevent cravings and excessive hunger, be sure to eat on a regular basis and stick to a consistent schedule. Not only will this allow you to regulate your appetite, but small, frequent meals and snacks actually boost your metabolism, helping you to shed pounds and inches even faster! For the best results, we recommend not going more than three to four hours between meals or snacks. Don't stress if this seems like it may not work with your schedule or you don't have time to eat that often. These meals and snacks don't need to be elaborate or time consuming. For instance, if you eat breakfast at 8 a.m., but you won't be able to eat lunch until 2 p.m., instead of waiting it out until you're starved by lunchtime, at 11 a.m., grab a low-fat string cheese or a handful of walnuts. These easy options are fast and portable, and most important, they keep excessive hunger away.

Now, you may be saying, "I don't need to eat every four hours. I go all day without eating until dinner, and I don't feel hungry." That may *seem* true, but think about it: When you walk in the door at night, are you grabbing whatever you can get your hands on as a snack before dinner is ready? Do you finish your dinner in record time? If so, these are signs that you're excessively hungry. When you're distracted and busy during the day, you can miss your body's subtle cues that you're starting to get hungry. When your day winds down and you're less busy, that's when it hits you — you feel like you're starving! When you ignore the signals your body is sending you until you can't ignore them any longer, you'll typically find yourself reaching for the wrong foods, experiencing cravings for less-than-healthy options, and speed-eating.

Try the following guidelines when planning out your meals and snacks throughout the day:

- ✔ Eat breakfast within an hour after waking.
- ✔ Plan a light meal or snack every three to four hours.
- ✔ Aim to have your last meal or snack at least one to two hours before going to bed, to allow time for adequate digestion.

You may have heard that you shouldn't eat after a certain time of night (for instance, after 7 p.m.), because doing so can lead to weight gain. This advice is more of a myth than a fact, and it really depends on how late you stay up at night. Eating late at night won't in and of itself cause you to gain weight, but if you eat when you're tired or distracted, such as snacking while watching your favorite TV show, you may end up eating more than your body truly needs. In addition, eating too close to bed can impact digestion, disrupt your sleep, and even cause heartburn. So, make sure you plan at least one to two hours between your last meal or snack and the time when you'll hit the hay.

Finding the best nutrients for a flat belly

Sure, when you're trying to flatten your belly and lose weight, there are foods you want to avoid. Highly processed foods rich in refined carbohydrates, saturated and trans fats, and sodium can really bloat your midsection. But research has found that by eating more of certain nutrients, you can actually shed belly fat quicker and easier.

The recipes and meal plans in this book incorporate many of these nutrients for you, so you don't have to even think about them. But when you create your own meals or develop your own belly fat–burning recipes, aim to incorporate the following nutrients on a regular basis to really blast away that belly fat once and for all:

- ✔ Monounsaturated fats
- ✔ Omega-3 fatty acids
- ✔ Vitamin C
- ✔ Potassium
- ✔ Fiber
- ✔ B vitamins
- ✔ Calcium

Realizing that it's a lifestyle, not another diet

We don't want you to think of the Belly Fat Diet as a diet to go on and off. Instead, it's important to focus on making lifestyle changes. That's because lifestyle changes are changes you'll make *for life*. If you implement these changes now and stick with them for good, not only will you achieve your ultimate goal weight, but you'll stay there! So, instead of thinking about this plan as a fad diet to go on and off, focus on making small, gradual changes over time.

One of the main reasons you want to focus on making small, gradual changes is to keep from becoming too restrictive with yourself or from becoming overwhelmed. Think about the last time you tried to do too many things at once. Maybe you decided to take on a home renovation at the same time that you were making a job change. Were you completely successful at either project? When you take on too many things at once, you can't really put all your thought and focus into any one area. So, what happens? You don't really succeed at anything because you're trying to do a little bit of everything. It's the same thing with weight loss. If you try to grocery shop and cook every meal from scratch while exercising two hours a day, that leaves little time for you to do anything else. And it leads to burnout. Now you're discouraged that you weren't able to do everything you set your mind to, you feel like a failure, and ultimately, you may give up. Instead, it's much better to just make one or two small changes every day, such as eating one less meal away from home or getting in ten extra minutes of physical activity. It's much better to take three months to lose 15 pounds than to lose 15 pounds in one month, only to gain it right back the next month.

Screwing up is okay. In fact, it's a great thing! It's *such* as great thing that we actually *want* you to screw up from time to time! Now, you may think we're crazy, but screwing up actually teaches you some very important lessons. If you eat perfectly 100 percent of the time while losing weight, what happens when you get to your goal weight and would like to occasionally indulge? Will you know how to indulge from time to time while maintaining your weight if you never indulged at all while losing weight? Would being so perfect make you feel a bit deprived and lead to your overdoing less-than-healthy food choices as soon as you achieved your weight loss goals?

We've worked with thousands of clients and helped them to achieve their ultimate goal weight and maintain it, and do you know who our most successful clients are? Not the ones who are perfect 100 percent of the time. The "perfect" dieters burn out, get off track, and struggle to motivate themselves to try to lose weight again. The ones who learn how to occasionally treat themselves while also transforming some of their favorite junk foods into belly-friendly options with simple recipe adjustments not only lose weight faster, but also keep it off. And they enjoy the process!

The non-diet diet

The Belly Fat Diet isn't a diet at all. In fact, we don't even like the word *diet.* Think about it: Diets tend to be something you'll go "on" only to go back "off" again in the future. And what happens when you go "off" your diet? Typically you go right back to the old behaviors that caused you to gain excess belly fat in the first place. And what's the point in that? You get to your goal weight and stay there for a few days, only to regain back everything you worked so hard to lose. Well, that's not going to happen this time! That's because the number-one thing we want you to remember about the Belly Fat Diet is that it's a *lifestyle,* not another diet.

One of the secrets of the Belly Fat Diet and one of the main reasons it differs from almost all the other weight loss plans out there, is that it isn't a short-term fix. As you read this book, we show you how to make small, gradual lifestyle changes that, just like they sound, you can stick to for life. That means no more starving yourself for a month only to go back to old habits or binge on junk food due to deprivation. Instead, we show you how to make dietary changes that will keep you feeling full and satisfied. You won't even have to give up your favorite foods! Instead, we show you how to make simple changes to your current meal plan that will instantly slim your waistline, drop excess pounds, and allow you to maintain the results permanently!

If you remember nothing else from this book, remember that deprivation doesn't work! It actually leads to weight *gain* due to increasing hunger, cravings, and possible binge eating from being too restrictive. That's why the Belly Fat Diet teaches you how to enjoy your foods while losing weight. Throughout this book, you enjoy delicious recipes that you would never think would actually promote weight loss. In addition, we show you how to transform all your favorite meals and snacks into great-tasting, belly fat–blasting alternatives.

The Principles Behind the Plan: Seeing Why the Belly Fat Diet Works

Have you ever started to follow a weight loss plan only to wonder why you were eating a certain way or avoiding a certain food? Staying motivated with a weight loss plan can be difficult if you don't know *why* you're doing what you're doing. For that reason, we devote this section to explaining why we developed the Belly Fat Diet and exactly how and why it works on promoting not just weight loss, but specifically fat loss from your midsection. This way, when you see that your meal plan calls for you to eat a large amount of one food group or to limit your intake of certain nutrients, you'll understand the science behind it, which makes it easier to stay on track.

Reducing insulin response

If you've tried losing weight before, but you couldn't overcome constant hunger or strong food cravings, you may have experienced an insulin response that triggered increased appetite and cravings.

After you eat a food that contains carbohydrates, such as bread or fruit, your body breaks down the carbohydrates into glucose, which is used for energy in your body. Insulin is the hormone that carries glucose from the bloodstream to your cells for energy (see Chapter 1). However, when you eat a food that causes a spike in blood glucose, that glucose spike is followed by a spike in insulin levels. When the glucose has all been transported out of the bloodstream and into your cells, you're left with excess levels of insulin circulating in your bloodstream. Your brain senses this elevated level of insulin and realizes you need more glucose to enter your bloodstream to prevent your blood glucose from dropping too low. So, your brain sends out the message by causing you to feel hunger and crave carbohydrates. As you can see, this can become a vicious cycle where you eat a refined carbohydrate and then crave more not long after eating. This cycle can lead to weight gain, and most important, to your storing dangerous amount of belly fat.

The Belly Fat Diet identifies the food sources that can elevate insulin levels and gets you to begin transitioning away from these foods and filling up on whole grains, lean proteins, fresh produce, and healthy fats to balance blood glucose and insulin levels. This balance prevents those pesky carbohydrate cravings and increased hunger, allowing you to take in fewer calories while feeling satisfied, resulting in weight loss success!

Reducing stress hormones

In Chapter 1, we explain how emotional and physical stressors can lead to the release of stress hormones, such as cortisol and adrenaline, in your body. These stress hormones mobilize fatty acid stores, and if those fatty acid stores go unused, they're deposited in your midsection.

The good news is, you can consume nutrients that will help decrease the amount of circulating stress hormones in your body, which in turn helps to protect against an accumulation of excess belly fat. The Belly Fat Diet focuses on increasing your intake of nutrients such as vitamin C and omega-3 fatty acids, which can reduce the amount of circulating stress hormones in your body.

Following the Belly Fat Diet can not only decrease your level of stress hormones, but also impact *neurotransmitters* (chemicals in the brain that transfer signals throughout your nervous system), impacting your mood as well. Transitioning to a diet rich in whole grains and healthy fats, as well as eating at regular intervals throughout the day, can have a direct impact on these brain chemicals.

If you're making the wrong food choices, eating too much or too little, or waiting too long between meals, your mood and your stress levels can be impacted. The wrong food choices or an imbalance of nutrients in your body can lead to imbalances in neurotransmitters, which can cause moodiness, irritability, concentration issues, and even insomnia. The balance provided on the Belly Fat Diet will help you to take in the right nutrients, in the right amounts, to help keep your neurotransmitters in balance, preventing a rise in stress levels, while helping you to feel great!

Regulating blood glucose

Even if you're making the right food choices, you may still experience strong food cravings and hunger, which may occur due to rapid fluctuations in blood glucose levels. And you know what happens when you get too hungry? More than likely, you reach for the wrong foods. Most people don't crave salads when they're starving. More than likely, you'll start to crave high-fat or high-sugar foods. If you allow yourself to eat in a way that lets you become excessively hungry on a regular basis, you'll experience intense food cravings often, which can be hard to fight off.

So, what leads to these intense cravings? These cravings are typically the result of waiting too long to eat in between meals or snacks. In addition, if you choose meals or snacks made up of quickly digesting foods (like refined carbohydrates), that can also lead you to feel hungry soon after eating. To help you prevent these intense cravings, the Belly Fat Diet has you plan out your meals and snacks to prevent excessive hunger. This not only helps to keep blood glucose levels in check, but also helps to boost your metabolism, allowing you to burn more calories throughout the day and promoting weight loss.

In addition, the Belly Fat Diet shows you what foods to choose to keep yourself feeling satisfied and full for hours, instead of just minutes. These foods are rich in slowly digested nutrients, such as fiber and protein, as well as provide a limited blood glucose response. When the blood glucose response to a food or meal is minimal, it prevents a rapid rise and fall in blood glucose and insulin, which can protect against food cravings.

Living the Flat Belly Lifestyle

You want the changes that you begin making today to become a part of your life for years to come. Viewing this approach as a lifestyle, not a diet, prevents a pattern of *yo-yo dieting* (weight loss followed by weight re-gain, over and over again). By focusing on small, gradual changes that you can stick with, you can make these changes part of your normal, daily routine. This helps prevent any sliding back into old habits and behaviors that led to your gaining excess belly fat in the first place. If you focus on making small, gradual changes that you can stick with, these changes will become part of your typical routine, or lifestyle, and you won't revert back to your old way of life.

One of our favorite aspects of the Belly Fat Diet is that it isn't a one-size-fits-all approach to weight loss. Not everyone has the same mind-set, the same goals, or even the same personality type when it comes to improving health and losing weight. Some people may want to jump right in and make multiple lifestyle changes at once. Others may want to gradually wade their way in by making a small change here and there over time. And the Belly Fat Diet allows for both approaches! You can follow it in multiple ways, using the meal plans in Chapter 4.

In this section, we offer tips for making the Belly Fat Diet part of your lifestyle, not just another diet you'll stick to for a month and then go off.

Committing yourself to change

After you've become motivated to lose weight, the first step is to commit yourself to making the lifestyle changes necessary to reach your goal. Of course, that's easy to say, but it isn't always easy to do. However, before you start to feel overwhelmed or stressed about committing yourself to change, remember that this book walks you through this process and shows you the easiest ways to begin making changes starting today, so you can rid yourself of excess belly fat once and for all.

One of the biggest factors that can impact your ability to commit to change is your level of motivation. Typically, you start out with all the motivation in the world. But after a few days or weeks, you may find your motivation dwindling. And without motivation, sticking with the changes you've started to make can be difficult. Here's an exercise that can help you think about why you're making these changes in the first place and boost your motivation:

1. **Take out a pen and a piece of paper and ask yourself the following question: Why do I *truly* want to lose weight?**

   Write down all your reasons for wanting to lose weight. Think long and hard about all the reasons you want to commit to losing weight and keeping it off. Sure, you want a flat stomach and you want to look better in clothes. But what else will losing weight help you achieve? Will it increase your energy levels? Will it allow you to improve your health so you can be there for your children and grandchildren? Will your self-confidence improve, knowing that you were able to achieve a goal? No matter how small the reason for wanting to lose weight seems, write it down.

2. **Now look at your list. Read it over. Memorize it. And most important, carry it with you at all times.**

   If you want, make copies of the list so you can keep them at home, at the office, in the car, and so on.

3. **Whenever you're tempted to veer off your weight loss plan and revert to your old habits, look at your list and focus on why you're putting in all the hard work.**

   Constantly reminding yourself of not only what you're aiming to achieve, but also *why* you want to achieve it, can help you stay motivated throughout the process.

Another powerful tool in the fight to stay committed to change is visualization. Visualization allows you to use the power of your mind to call upon a vivid image of you at your goal weight. To make this work, close your eyes and picture yourself at your ultimate goal weight. Call upon all your senses to make this image as realistic as possible. Are you finally fitting in your favorite outfit? How does it look on your body? How do your clothes feel against your skin? Are they comfortable instead of too snug? How do you feel on the inside? Are you full of energy instead of feeling tired and sluggish? Can you hear the comments people are making about how terrific you look and your noticeable improvement in energy? Take a few minutes to focus on this image and burn it into your memory. Now, when you hit a roadblock with your weight loss plan or you're faced with temptation, step back for a moment, close your eyes, and picture this image again. What's worth more to you: achieving this ideal image where you look and feel great or the short-term satisfaction of indulging in a tempting treat?

These tools aren't foolproof, but even if they help you to resist temptation and keep you motivated 80 percent of the time, you'll be well on your way to achieving your weight and health goals.

Taking the first steps to a flatter belly

To get started with flattening your belly and improving your health, look at where you are today, and then look at what changes you can start to make. No matter how healthy you eat, there is always room for improvement. And the same goes for lifestyle behaviors. You can always exercise more, sleep better, reduce stress, and so on. That's why it's important to never strive to be perfect with your diet and lifestyle changes. Perfection is impossible — even the healthiest person can always do more.

So, why not start where you are and work on small improvements? To start, for three days, write down every single food and beverage you consume and how much you had. Don't forget to write down any seasonings and condiments you add to foods, such as salt, butter, or oils. In addition, write down any and all exercise and physical activity you get every day, how many hours you sleep each night, and rank your stress level on a scale of 1 to 10 (with 10 being the highest).

At the end of those three days, scrutinize the data you've gathered. Circle all the foods, beverages, and behaviors that may be negatively impacting your health and your waistline. For instance, circle any foods that contain the following belly bloaters:

- ✔ Saturated fats
- ✔ Trans fats
- ✔ Refined carbohydrates
- ✔ Simple sugars
- ✔ Excess sodium

Also, look for days that lack any belly fat–fighting nutrients. For instance, circle days on which you had

- ✔ Fewer than two servings of fruits and vegetables
- ✔ Fewer than two servings of whole grains
- ✔ Fewer than two servings of healthy fats (monounsaturated fats or omega-3 fatty acids)
- ✔ Fewer than 25 grams of fiber

Look for any behaviors that may contribute to excessive belly fat, such as lack of sleep (less than seven hours per night), high stress levels (a ranking of 7 or above), or lack of physical activity (less than 30 minutes per day).

Now when you look at your list, you can easily identify areas of your current diet or lifestyle that may be contributing to gains in weight and belly fat. And you can start to address these areas by making small, gradual changes over time.

If you don't know what behaviors caused you to gain weight and belly fat in the first place, how can you fix them?

For an easy way to track the foods you eat, try sites such as Lose It! (`www.loseit.com`) and MyFitnessPal (`www.myfitnesspal.com`). Both of these sites also have smartphone apps that allow you to track what you eat when you're on the go.

Managing stress

In the preceding section, when you ranked your stress level, was it 7 or above every day? If so, your stress level may be having a negative impact on your overall health, not to mention your waistline. Even if you ranked your stress level as mild to moderate, you may still be experiencing high levels of stress at times, without even noticing it. And when stress increases, so do those pesky stress hormones, such as cortisol and adrenaline, that can pack on pounds and increase belly fat.

Stress isn't always a bad thing. In fact, the stress response in your body is there to protect you. A certain level of stress can even be healthy — it can help you to be more productive, increase focus, or even give you an energy boost. But at a certain point, stress goes from being helpful to being harmful. And when stress levels rise and stay elevated for days at a time, it can spell trouble. Excess stress can impact your mood and your overall health, and it can dramatically expand your waistline.

Stress plays such an important role in belly fat that if you don't gain control over your stress levels, it can be almost impossible to achieve and maintain a flat stomach. But don't let this leave you feeling defeated! Even if you're constantly under high levels of stress day in and day out, there are simple things you can begin doing, starting today, to lower your stress, decrease the amount of stress hormones circulating in your bloodstream, and lose belly fat!

Stress can impact everyone in different ways. And sometimes, stress can creep up on you until it just feels normal and you may not even notice the impact it's having on your health and your body. To help you identify the most common stressors you face each and every day, ask yourself the following:

- ✔ What part of your daily routine do you find the most stressful or agitating?
- ✔ How do you typically react to stress? Do you get angry? Do you shut down? Do you feel agitated inside?
- ✔ How many times in a typical day do you feel that you get angry, anxious, or agitated?
- ✔ Do you typically try to multitask to the point of exhaustion?
- ✔ Do you tend to run late to appointments and meetings?
- ✔ Do you feel upset or anxious when things don't go as perfectly as you planned?

The answers to these questions allow you to see what causes your daily stress, how often you're stressed, and how you can best manage your overall stress to improve your body weight and well-being.

Keep an eye out for signs of *stress overload,* a point at which stress levels become damaging both to your mental and physical well-being. The symptoms of stress overload can be mental and emotional, physical, or behavioral. Here are the symptoms to watch for:

- ✔ Mental and emotional
  - • Decreased concentration
  - • Forgetfulness

- Negative thinking
- Constant racing thoughts and worry
- Moodiness
- Agitation
- Feeling overwhelmed

✔ Physical

- Muscle aches and pains
- Rapid heart rate
- Gastrointestinal changes, such as constipation and/or diarrhea

✔ Behavioral

- Eating too much
- Eating too little
- Insomnia
- Sleeping too much
- Sleeping too little
- Isolating from others
- Using substances, such as alcohol or cigarettes, to relax

The more symptoms you have, the closer you are to experiencing dangerous levels of stress overload. Having more than two or three of these symptoms means it's time to start working on managing and reducing your overall stress levels.

If you've identified that you have high levels of stress every day and if you're experiencing symptoms of stress overload, you need to begin taking action to gain control of your stress. Here are three easy-to-implement strategies that can reduce stress almost immediately:

✔ **Deep breathing:** Deep breathing is simple to do and can cut stress almost immediately. When you breathe slowly and deeply, it signals to your brain to relax, helping to reduce your heart rate, lower stress hormones, and provides a calming effect.

To get started, follow these steps:

1. **Sit or lie in a comfortable position, and place one hand on your chest and the other hand just below your ribs on your stomach (see Figure 2-1).**

Figure 2-1:
Deep
breathing.

Illustration by Wiley, Composition Services Graphics

   2. Take a deep breath in through your nose and into your belly.

   You should feel the hand on your stomach move, but the hand on your chest should remain still.

   3. Exhale through pursed lips (like when you're trying to whistle).

   You should feel the hand on your stomach go in as you breathe out.

   4. Repeat five to ten times, breathing in deeply and slowly.

✔ **Progressive muscle relaxation:** Progressive muscle relaxation involves slowly tensing and relaxing muscle groups to help you relax and fight stress. Tensing and then relaxing each muscle forces you to become aware of physical sensations, allowing you to release tension.

Here's how to do it:

   1. Starting with your toes, tense the muscles for 5 to 10 seconds.

   2. Relax for 30 seconds.

   3. Repeat Steps 1 and 2 with your legs, your buttocks, your hands, your arms, your chest, your neck, your face, and your scalp, working your way up the body.

✔ **Exercise:** Physical activity increases the flow of blood to your brain, and blood carries with it essential oxygen and energy (in the form of glucose). As you concentrate intensely in times of stress, the neurons in your brain produce more and more waste products, which can build up and cause a "foggy thinking" effect. When blood flow to the brain increases, it washes away this waste buildup, allowing you to think more clearly. In addition, exercise releases *endorphins,* which are feel-good chemicals in the brain that help to lift your mood and combat stress. So, to reduce stress, take a walk, hop on your bike, get on the treadmill, go for a hike — just get moving!

For even more tips on managing stress, check out *Stress Management For Dummies,* 2nd Edition, by Allen Elkin (Wiley).

Getting support for your lifestyle changes

If you've ever tried to improve your eating habits or lose weight in the past, you know how important the support of those around you is. Even if you have all the best intentions and stock your home with all the belly fat–blasting foods you can find, resisting fried foods and sweets is difficult if your family is eating them right next to you. Ideally, when you're trying to make better food choices, everyone around you will eat the same way. Although the recipes in this book are delicious and can appeal to every member of your family, they still may not convert entirely to your new lifestyle. But even if they aren't making the same food choices as you, your family and friends can be supportive of your efforts to help you stay on track.

Getting your family on the flat belly bandwagon

If you want to be successful with your weight loss goals, your best bet is to not keep your efforts a secret. When you let your family know that you're aiming to eat healthier, you may be surprised by how supportive they can be. When you're healthier and more energetic, and you feel better about yourself, everyone around you feels better as well. So, why *wouldn't* your family want you to keep up with your efforts?

The principles of the Belly Fat Diet are healthy for everyone, regardless of whether he or she needs to lose weight. Even if your family doesn't make all the dietary and lifestyle changes you're making, they can still be supportive of your efforts in a variety of ways. For example, instead of stocking the fridge with ice cream, as a family you can vow to go out for a small cone once a week and keep fresh fruit on hand for a sweet fix while at home. If your family loves to eat out, maybe together you can decide on restaurants to frequent that offer more belly-friendly options.

In addition, enlist your family to help you become more physically active. Exercising alone can be boring, but when you make a game out of it with other people, you don't even realize that you're exercising. Get outside together and throw around a baseball, go for a walk, or even play a game of tag! It doesn't matter what you do to get moving — just move more and have fun with it!

Finding support among your friends

Sharing with friends that you're trying to lose weight and improve your overall health can be difficult. You may worry that they've seen you try before only to go back to old habits or fall off track within a few weeks. You may think they don't have much confidence in you. Even if this is true, sharing your goals with friends can still help you to be successful this time around.

Every past attempt at weight loss that failed was a learning experience. Think about *why* you weren't successful in previous attempts. Did you get hungry too quickly? Were you too restrictive with yourself? Did you forget to plan ahead to have healthy options on hand? By identifying the past slip-ups that caused you to get off track with your weight loss goals, you know what areas you need to devote the most time and energy to in order to succeed this time.

This is where friends can be helpful! If you know that your past attempts at weight loss failed because you allowed yourself to get too hungry too often, friends and co-workers can help remind you throughout the day not to go more than four hours without a meal or a snack. They can also help to remind you to drink your water, which can help with feeling full. Have you struggled with the motivation to get active? Instead of calling your friends to chat on the phone or meeting at a bar or coffee shop, arrange a time to meet for a walk and catch up. If you have a sedentary job, recruit co-workers to join you for a lunchtime walk.

When you share your weight loss and health goals with those around you and let them know what steps you need to take to make you successful, you'll end up with a strong team of cheerleaders that will help you to stay motivated while you achieve your weight and waistline goals!

Improving your body image

One of the worst things you can do when you're trying to lose or maintain weight or trying to improve your health is to participate in negative self-talk. This is where you carry on a dialogue in your head where you talk down to yourself, beat yourself up, or cast doubt on your abilities to achieve an optimal body weight. Be on the lookout for this negative self-talk. Just because you have weight or body fat to lose doesn't mean you have to beat yourself up about your body. Doing so will only lead to shame, which is never productive. Shame doesn't motivate people to succeed.

Instead, focus on the positives. What do you love about your body? How does you body help you during the day? For instance, you may say "My legs are strong, and they allow me to run or walk" or "My arms allow me to carry my baby." Think about the words and phrases you say to yourself throughout the day. Are these words building your self-esteem or are they eroding it away?

You didn't get to where you are right now overnight. And as much as you may want to, you can't achieve your goals overnight either. There are no quick fixes — you'll get the most out of your Belly Fat Diet journey and stay motivated throughout the process when you speak to yourself kindly and remind yourself just how much you've accomplished and how proud you are of yourself. Your body will thank you for it!

Chapter 3

Identifying Belly-Blasting Superfoods

*W*hen you're trying to reduce your waistline, you may think the solution is just to reduce your overall caloric intake. Taking in less calories than you burn each day can, indeed, promote weight loss. But you don't just want to lose weight — you also want to target belly fat so you can shed pounds and inches from your midsection. And in the journey toward a flat stomach, not all calories are created equal. Certain foods help to maximize the amount of belly fat you burn, while others store belly fat and hang onto it, making it almost impossible to achieve flat abs.

Throughout this chapter, we help you identify the best foods for a flat belly, as well as the ones that can keep you from achieving your goals.

The Power of Protein

One of the best ways to burn off belly fat without feeling hungry is with protein. However, not all proteins are created equal. When it comes to protein, there are two main forms:

✔ **Plant-based proteins:** Proteins that come from — you guessed it — plants, such as lentils and soybeans. Plant-based proteins are typically low in fat and high and fiber, making them belly-friendly choices.

✔ **Animal proteins:** Proteins that come from animal sources, such as chicken or fish. Some animal proteins are high in saturated fats, which can increase body-wide inflammation, increasing both belly fat and disease risk. Other animal proteins are leaner, such as fish and white-meat poultry; they contain less unhealthy fat and can even contain beneficial fats, such as omega-3 fatty acids.

On your Belly Fat Diet plan, protein sources are divided into three categories:

- **Lean protein:** Approximately 30 to 40 calories per ounce, and 3 g of fat or less per ounce
- **Medium-fat proteins:** Approximately 45 to 55 calories per ounce, and 5 g of fat per ounce
- **High-fat proteins:** Approximately 80 to 100 calories per ounce, and 8 g of fat per ounce

As you can probably guess, the best proteins for your waistline and health are the lean proteins — these proteins are the ones you want to make up the majority of your protein choices. Medium- and high-fat protein options should be selected less often (once a week or less), to prevent you from taking in large amounts of unhealthy saturated fats and excessive calories. See Chapter 4 for lists of various forms of proteins and the categories in which they fall, as well as how to count them in your Belly Fat Diet plan.

Now that you have a better understanding of the types of protein and which are best for you, let's take a deeper look at just how protein can help you to shed unwanted pounds and belly fat once and for all.

The muscle and metabolism connection

Your body can't make its own protein, which is why getting enough protein from your diet is so essential. Your body's main source of protein is its muscle mass. If you don't consume enough protein to meet your body's needs, your body will have to pull protein from your muscles, breaking them down.

Muscle makes up a large component of your metabolism — it burns much more calories pound per pound than fat tissue. So, if you begin to lose muscle mass, your metabolism will start to slow. That means that even if you eat the exact same amount of calories as you always have, you'll start to gain weight just because you're burning fewer calories because you have less muscle mass!

Bottom line: Consuming enough protein helps ensure that your body doesn't have to break down your muscles to get the protein it needs.

The hunger connection

Unlike food rich in carbohydrates, which are digested quickly, protein takes about three times as long to break down and digest, which helps you feel satisfied longer. And that's the main goal when it comes to following a weight loss plan you can stick with — you don't want to allow yourself to become too hungry! If you get too hungry, that can lead to food cravings, eating rapidly, and making less-than-belly-friendly food choices. On the other hand, eating foods that provide you with a sense of satiety (like protein foods) can control your appetite, allowing you to make healthy food choices and prevent cravings.

Consuming a source of lean protein at each meal is very beneficial when you follow your Belly Fat Diet plan. It prevents you from becoming too hungry in between meals and snacks and straying off course.

Plant-based proteins, such as lentils and soybeans, are just as effective at fighting off hunger pangs as animal proteins are.

The Role of Whole Grains in Fighting Belly Fat

Did you know that some grains can help you fight belly fat, while others can actually make you store more? There are two main types of carbohydrates:

- ✔ **Refined:** Refined carbohydrates have been processed in such a way that many of the healthy nutrients contained in the food naturally are stripped out. When it comes to grains, the bran and germ (two layers of the grain) have been removed, and what's left is the starchy endosperm (a third layer of the grain), which has less fiber and overall nutritional value. Because refined carbohydrates provide you with carbohydrates but little in the way of protein or fiber, digestion occurs rapidly and the carbohydrates in the grain are quickly converted into glucose (sugar). This results in a rapid rise in blood glucose, followed by a rise in insulin to bring the sugar into your cells. Excess insulin circulating in your body results in your body storing more and more belly fat (see Chapter 2). White bread and white rice are examples of refined carbohydrates.

- ✔ **Unrefined:** Unrefined carbohydrates haven't been processed the way refined carbohydrates have. In the case of grains, a whole grain is one that still contains all its original three layers: the bran, endosperm, and germ. The fact that the whole grain has these three layers means it's loaded with fiber, vitamins, minerals, and antioxidants, in addition to the carbohydrates. Whole grains still trigger an insulin response, but because these grains are rich in fiber and protein, the insulin response is reduced. This leads to less insulin circulating in the bloodstream and less belly fat being stored. Whole grains fall into the unrefined category. They're rich in nutrients that fight belly fat.

In the past, you may have followed a low-carb diet and been convinced that all carbs are the bad. But carbohydrates are essential for many reasons, especially energy. Glucose is the main source of energy for your brain and body. If you reduce your carbohydrate intake too much, you may notice a decline in energy levels and even problems concentrating and thinking clearly.

In addition to energy, whole grains provide numerous other benefits, including the following:

- ✔ Reduced risk of heart disease, stroke, and type 2 diabetes
- ✔ Reduction in digestive system and hormone-related cancers
- ✔ Help maintaining digestive system regularity
- ✔ Help achieving and maintaining a healthy body weight

Not only do whole grains provide health benefits, but they also can help to battle pesky cravings, which can sabotage weight loss efforts. Unrefined carbohydrates are digested slower than refined carbohydrates, which provides you with a greater feeling of satiety and helps to regulate appetite. When you select whole grains, your appetite is controlled for longer and cravings are minimal to nonexistent due to the decreased insulin response — a recipe for weight-loss success!

Now that you know all the wonderful health benefits whole grains provide and the impact they can have on slimming your waistline, it's important that you know how to identify these wonder grains so you can be on your way to achieving your goal weight and waistline. There are two main ways to identify whole grains:

- ✔ **Look at the product packaging.** If you see the words *100 percent* followed by a grain on the product packaging such as "100 percent whole wheat," you're getting all parts of the grain or a whole-grain product.

- ✔ **Examine the ingredient list.** The first ingredient is what makes up the majority of the food. For grains, the first ingredient should use the word *whole,* such as "whole wheat flour" or "whole rye flour." If the first ingredient is not a "whole" ingredient, but you see one farther down the list, you can't be sure of the proportion of whole grain in the product, and it may not be your best choice.

Foods that list the following ingredients first are refined carbohydrates and should be limited:

- Unbleached flour
- Wheat flour (without the word *whole* in front of *wheat*)
- Semolina
- Multigrain
- Durum wheat
- Enriched flour
- Bran flour (without the word *whole* in front of bran)
- Mixed grain
- Cornmeal

The Link between Dairy and Belly Fat

You may be surprised to hear this, but consuming dairy products on a regular basis can actually help you to shed excess belly fat. Dairy is rich in *whey,* which is a protein that helps promote the formation of lean body mass (muscle mass that helps to boost metabolism). In addition, because dairy is rich in protein, it can help to regulate appetite and help you feel full longer, preventing cravings and helping you control your portion sizes.

Dairy doesn't just help with appetite. A study published in *Obesity Research* found that obese individuals who consumed a dairy-rich diet lost more body fat (specifically belly fat) than other individuals consuming the same number of overall calories but following a low-dairy diet. In fact, the results were so significant that the dairy group lost almost double the amount of fat and weight!

So, why is dairy so beneficial to belly fat? It may be due to the calcium-rich properties of milk products, because calcium plays a critical role in how fat is stored and broken down in the body. Dairy products also contain *arginine,* an amino acid that has been shown to promote fat loss while preserving lean body mass. Finally, dairy products contain *conjugated linoleic acid* (CLA), a fatty acid that has been associated with promising weight loss research in animal studies.

When it comes to using dairy to shed belly fat, not just any dairy will do. As you've probably seen in the grocery store, the amount of dairy options available can be overwhelming. Should you choose full fat, no fat, low fat, organic? To simplify things, use the following easy guidelines when choosing dairy:

✔ **Look for low-fat options.** Full-fat dairy is rich in saturated fat, which can trigger inflammation as well as negatively impact heart health. CLA isn't found in fat-free dairy, so opt for low-fat instead.

✔ **Look for dairy sources from grass-fed cows.** These cows have a more favorable composition of their milk than grain-fed cows, including five times more CLA. Some organic milk comes from grass-fed cows, but not all, so be sure to read the label.

If you can't tolerate dairy, don't despair! Using non-dairy alternatives is perfectly acceptable on your Belly Fat Diet plan. Options such as almond milk, soy milk, coconut milk, and hemp milk are all good options. However, opt for unsweetened varieties whenever possible. If you do pick a sweetened variety, pick a brand with 10 g of sugar or less per cup and avoid brands that contain high-fructose corn syrup in the ingredients.

Non-dairy alternatives are great if you can't tolerate dairy or if you're a vegan, but if you don't have dietary restrictions, you may want to opt for the real thing instead: Non-dairy alternatives may be fortified with calcium, but they don't contain arginine or CLA.

Fruits for a Flat Belly

When you're striving to lose weight and improve health, an essential ingredient you don't want to overlook is fruit. Fruits provide you with antioxidants, phytochemicals, fiber, and carbohydrates. In addition, they give you a feeling of "sweet satisfaction," helping to reduce your cravings for sweets, such as candy, which have a negative impact on your waistline.

In addition to the health benefits of fruit, this sweet food group is also needed for sustainable weight loss. In fact, fruit plays such an important role in body weight that research has actually found that individuals who eat multiple servings of fruit on a regular basis were able to lose more weight than those who ate large amount of vegetables each day with little to no fruit intake.

Fruit can also play a role in the fight against stress. A study out of Germany found that when you consume a diet rich in vitamin C, stress hormones such as cortisol and adrenaline (the ones that can pack on belly fat) return to normal levels more quickly after a stressful situation. This means that a diet rich in vitamin C can lower the amount of stress hormones circulating in your body, protecting against excess belly fat storage. You can find vitamin C in many fruits, including grapefruit, kiwifruit, oranges, papayas, and strawberries.

Some fruits contain an added layer of belly fat–fighting abilities. Eating these fruits on a regular basis can help to maximize your results as you follow your Belly Fat Diet plan:

- **Blueberries:** Blueberries contain one of the highest antioxidant levels of all foods, making it a powerful inflammation fighter. In addition, an animal study found that when rats consumed just 2 percent of their daily calories from blueberries, they were able to significantly decrease levels of visceral fat over a period of three months! In addition, blueberries have been associated with a reduction in food cravings, helping to further promote weight loss.

- **Tart cherries:** These cherries aren't the same as sweet cherries you often eat raw. Instead, tart cherries can be fresh or dried. These tart treats are rich in anthocyanins, which have been found to help increase belly fat losses. In fact, a University of Michigan study found adding cherry powder to food led to a 9 percent reduction in body fat in mice.

- **Grapefruit:** The research on the link between this fruit and belly fat has been very promising. A study released in the *Journal of Medicinal Food* found grapefruit to be a powerful fat burner. In addition, a study out of Vanderbilt University found that when obese adults consumed half a grapefruit or 4 ounces of 100 percent grapefruit juice before three main meals, they experienced a significant decrease in both body weight and waist circumference. Grapefruit also contains diuretic properties, helping to beat bloat associated with water retention, further slimming your midsection.

Many medications interact with grapefruit and grapefruit juice. Discuss consuming this fruit with your doctor or pharmacist if you're taking a prescription medication to avoid any adverse interactions.

- **Pomegranate:** Similar to blueberries, this sweet and sour fruit contains a very high level of antioxidants. In addition, pomegranates are rich in the polyphenol catechin, which has been found to help increase the body's ability to burn fat, as well as boost metabolism!

Fruit has many health benefits and can be a potent belly fat fighter. However, you *can* have too much of a good thing. Although fruit is rich in many vitamins and minerals, it's also rich in natural sugars. These sugars are fine to consume, but eating too much fruit can promote weight gain. Chapter 4 outlines just how much fruit you should have each day to promote the waistline-slimming benefits without overdoing it!

Vegetables That Slim the Waistline

Among the best weapons you have in the fight against weight gain and belly fat are vegetables, which are loaded with a great amount of volume and leave you feeling full, with very few calories (thanks to their high fiber and water content).

Picture this: You feel very hungry and sit down to a plate of food. The plate is filled with one small dinner roll that you scarf down. Do you feel satisfied? Probably not? Now imagine that you're just as hungry, but the plate of food you have this time is filled with 6 cups of lettuce topped with sliced carrots, cucumbers, and tomatoes. It takes you almost 20 minutes to eat all these vegetables. Do you feel satisfied now? Guess what? This giant plate of salad had the same calorie content as that measly little dinner roll, but for the same amount of calories, one filled you up and the other left you feeling as though you had barely eaten.

Vegetables allow you to eat a large volume of food and feel satisfied, all while helping you to reduce your overall caloric intake, promoting weight loss. And they do this without leaving you hungry or feeling deprived! That's why vegetables are *unlimited* on your Belly Fat Diet plan. In fact, we want you to eat vegetables — lots of vegetables! The more, the better. In Chapter 4, you see that you have a minimum amount of vegetables to consume each day (because eating too few can leave you feeling hungry), but there is no maximum.

Vegetables are packed with vitamins, minerals, and antioxidants. Some of these nutrients (such as catechins and anthocyanins) actually fight fat, while others fight oxidative stress, helping to reduce inflammation.

When you eat vegetables, be sure to include variety. All vegetables have great health benefits, but if you eat the same few vegetables over and over, you may miss out on essential nutrients. For that reason, you want to fill your plate with color and strive to incorporate vegetables of different colors on a regular basis. Each vegetable color comes with its own distinctive health benefits. For instance, orange vegetables are rich in cancer-fighting beta-carotene, which can also improve eye health and decrease inflammation. Dark green leafy vegetables are an excellent source of stress-fighting vitamin C along with folic acid, which is critical for protein digestion and metabolism. And even white vegetables such as cauliflower and onions have health benefits — they have the disease-fighting chemical allicin, which may help reduce overall cholesterol and blood pressure levels, as well as fight off inflammation in the body.

Starchy vegetables: Only in moderation

All vegetables are great for your health, but not *all* vegetables are unlimited on your Belly Fat Diet plan. Starchy vegetables are full of nutrients and belly fat–fighting chemicals, but they have a higher carbohydrate and calorie content than other vegetables. For this reason, they would lead to weight gain if you consumed huge amounts of them.

On your Belly Fat Diet plan, starchy vegetables fall into a different food group than the other vegetables (see Chapter 4). They're in the same food group as bread, pasta, and rice because they contain an equivalent amount of carbohydrates. The vegetables that fall into this starch category are

- Beans and lentils
- Corn
- Peas
- Plantains
- Potatoes
- Sweet potatoes
- Yams
- Winter squash (for example, acorn, butternut, pumpkin, and spaghetti)

Focus on Fat

Believe it or not, eating fat can *fight* fat instead of causing you to store more of it. Can this really be true? The answer is yes! Dietary fat can actually help you to shed pounds and belly fat. But it's not just *any* fat that makes a difference — it has to be the right types of fat. You want to work on incorporating mostly monounsaturated fats and omega-3 fatty acids into your diet on a regular basis to benefit from their fat-fighting abilities.

So, how do these fats actually help your body to ditch excess inches around your midsection? To start, both of these fats contain powerful anti-inflammatory properties. In addition, omega-3 fatty acids have been shown to reduce the levels of circulating stress hormones in your body, which, when elevated, can store additional belly fat. And, just like proteins, fats take longer to digest, helping you to feel full longer and decrease cravings, which can help you to take in fewer calories throughout the day.

Following are good sources of monounsaturated fats:

- Almond butter (natural)
- Almonds

- Avocado
- Cashews
- Olive oil
- Olives
- Peanut oil
- Peanut butter (natural)
- Peanuts
- Sesame oil

Following are good sources of omega-3 fatty acids:

- Chia seeds
- Cod
- Eggs (omega-3 variety)
- Flaxseeds
- Halibut
- Salmon
- Sardines
- Scallops
- Seaweed
- Soybeans
- Tofu
- Walnuts

Before you run out and add all the fats you can find to your meals and snacks to boost the burning of belly fat, you need to know which fats are actually *damaging* to your waist and health. These are fats that you want to limit or avoid to prevent weight gain, the accumulation of belly fat, and damage to your health:

- **Saturated fats:** Saturated fats have been linked with an increased risk for heart disease and elevated cholesterol levels, but most important, they may increase inflammation in the body. These fats are mainly found in animal proteins, so a diet rich in high-fat dairy, red meats, and processed meats will be high in saturated fat. To ensure that you don't take in too much of these damaging fats, your total intake of saturated fats should be less than 10 percent of your daily calorie intake.

✔ **Trans fats:** Trans fats are the most damaging fats to both your waistline and your health. Avoid them as much as possible. Trans fats lurk in processed foods such as fried foods, pastries, baked goods, biscuits, muffins, and even some brands of microwave popcorn. Not only can these fats increase inflammation and pack on belly fat, but they can lower your healthy cholesterol levels, raise your bad cholesterol levels, and significantly increase your risk for heart disease. In fact, research has shown that even 2 g of trans fats per day can have a negative impact on your health, so avoiding them is very important. Be on the lookout for foods that list partially hydrogenated oils in the ingredients list — this is a sign that the food contains trans fats.

Drinks: The Good, the Bad, and the Ugly

The foods you eat aren't the only things that impact your waistline. Drinks can play an important role in belly fat as well. Sugary drinks such as sodas and sweetened lemonades and teas pack on the pounds and spike insulin levels, resulting in excess belly fat. On the flip side, some beverages have the ability to help you burn belly fat — and if you're not drinking them, you're missing out!

One of the best beverages for your belly is green tea. This tasty drink is packed full of disease-fighting antioxidants, which can protect your cells from damage. In addition, green tea can also help to fight off excess stress hormones, helping to cut down on belly fat storage. And given that green tea is one of the least processed teas, it's rich in a catechin called epigallocatechin-3-gallate (EGCG), which has been found to boost metabolism and reduce overall body fat, specifically belly fat!

Many beverages such as coffee and tea contain caffeine, which can play a role in helping to shed belly fat. Caffeine can provide your body with a slight metabolism boost, helping you burn more calories throughout the day. But don't get carried away — at a certain point, too much caffeine can actually *impede* your weight loss efforts. Excessive intake of caffeine can have a negative impact on health. In high amounts, it can cause feelings of agitation, affect concentration, and even disrupt your sleep cycle — all things which can actually increase your stress levels and the production of stress hormones and even slow your metabolism! So, as with most things, moderation is key. Limit your intake of caffeine to no more than 300 mg per day (about the amount in two or three cups of coffee).

Alcohol can be a major source of weight gain and increased belly fat when consumed in excess. It's a source of *empty calories* (calories that provide little to no nutrient value and limited fullness). In addition, alcohol can actually *increase* your appetite, leading to overeating.

You don't need to eliminate alcohol on your Belly Fat Diet plan. Some alcohol, such as wine, can have health benefits. Red wine, for instance, is a great source of resveratrol, which has anti-inflammatory properties and may be beneficial to heart health.

In order to slim your waistline, keep an eye on the quantity of alcohol you consume. If you do choose to drink alcohol, follow these simple guidelines:

- ✔ **Your best choice for alcohol is red or white wine, a wine spritzer, or light beer.**

- ✔ **If you have a mixed drink, avoid high-calorie mixers such as soda.** Instead, try mixing your drink with club soda or seltzer with a splash of juice for flavor.

- ✔ **Drink alcohol at the end of the meal instead of before eating.** Alcohol can stimulate appetite and lower inhibitions, resulting in your making less healthy food choices or eating larger portions.

- ✔ **Limit the amount you consume per day.** On your Belly Fat Diet plan, you may enjoy up to one serving of red or white wine per day. If you choose to drink another form of alcohol or have more than one serving of wine, count each additional serving as *two* fat servings.

Here's what constitutes a serving of alcohol:

- • Beer: 12 ounces
- • Wine: 4 ounces
- • Liquor: 1.5 ounces

Belly Bloaters to Avoid

We outline many foods and drinks in this chapter that can help to shrink your belly. But many foods also have the potential to bloat your belly as well. Some can bloat your belly almost instantly by increasing gas in your digestive tract, causing your abdomen to look distended — this condition can be uncomfortable, but it's only temporary. When you have an event coming up where you want your midsection to look as slim as possible, it's usually best to avoid these foods for a few days beforehand.

Other foods may contain ingredients such as saturated fats and refined carbohydrates that can pack on the pounds and cause your body to accumulate belly fat, gradually expanding your waistline over time. These foods can hurt your health, so limit or avoid them all together.

Here are some of the biggest belly bloaters and where they're found:

- **Sugar alcohols:** These are sugar substitutes that are only partially digested in your body. Because of this, they provide fewer calories per gram than regular sugar. They can also cause uncomfortable gastrointestinal side effects such as bloat, gas, and diarrhea, all of which can cause your belly to look and feel distended. You find sugar alcohol mostly in sugar-free snack foods, gums, and candies — if you see ingredients such as xylitol, sorbitol, and maltitol, you've found sugar alcohols.

- **Carbonated beverages:** Carbonation is mostly just water and typically calorie free, so it seems innocent enough. Even though this beverage certainly won't pack on actual pounds, it can really bloat your belly. Because the carbonation comes from gas blended with water, when you drink this beverage, the gas can "puff out" your stomach, making it appear distended and bigger than it really is. This puffiness will only last for a few hours, but even so, avoid carbonated drinks on days when you want to look your slimmest.

- **High-sodium foods:** Salt doesn't stand out as a belly bloater because it's calorie free. But excess sodium causes your body to hold onto excessive water weight, which leaves you feeling bloated and makes it hard to have a flat, toned midsection. Excessive sodium intake can do more damage than just making you look bloated, though. In addition to the negative impact sodium has on your waistline, it can also increase blood pressure and stiffen arteries. For that reason, you should aim to keep your daily sodium intake under 2,000 mg (or under 1,500 mg per day if you have high blood pressure).

- **Refined carbohydrates:** Refined carbs are everywhere you look — white rice, white pasta, sugary cereals, enriched-flour crackers, the list goes on and on. These grains have been processed and stripped of the outermost and innermost layers of grain, leaving all the carbohydrates and calories, but little of the protein, fiber, and nutrients. This processing allows these grains to be digested rapidly, providing little in the way of fullness after eating. In addition, this rapid digestion leads to spikes in blood sugar and insulin levels, causing additional fat storage right where you want it least — your belly!

Enjoy grains, but choose whole grains instead. Reach for brown rice over white rice, whole wheat pasta over white, and popcorn over snack chips. With a few simple changes to your grain selection, you can reduce cravings and hunger and avoid the belly fat–storing insulin spikes that accompany refined grains.

✔ **Processed meats:** Meats such as bacon, sausage, and hot dogs are high in sodium and saturated fats. Because sodium causes your body to retain excess water, this alone can bloat your belly. But combine that with a high intake of inflammation-promoting saturated fat, and you have a recipe for excess belly fat. Limit processed meats to special occasions and occasional treats to prevent a negative impact on your health and your belly. If you do choose to have them more often, look for lower-fat options made with turkey or chicken breast over beef and pork varieties. But keep in mind that these lower-fat options typically contain just as much sodium as the original options, so don't overdo it!

✔ **Soda:** Although this popular beverage is a staple in most restaurants and homes, it's a very potent belly bloater! Not only does it contain gas-producing carbonation, but the real danger lies in its main ingredient: sugar! Soda is a very rich source of empty calories. And worst of all, these calories don't provide any fullness, leaving you just as hungry as you were before you drank them. In addition to excess calories, soda provides a spike in blood sugar followed by an insulin spike, leading to excessive belly fat storage.

Diet soda isn't the solution. In addition to including temporarily bloating carbonation, diet sodas are loaded with artificial sweeteners, which are a foreign chemical to your body. If you take in too much of an artificial ingredient, such as artificial sweeteners, it may increase inflammation, which stores fat. In addition, some studies have linked diet soda with an increase in hunger and cravings, which can make staying on track with your meal plan a challenge. If you love carbonation, stick to naturally flavored seltzer. Or try a splash of 100 percent fruit juice in water for a refreshingly flavorful alternative.

Chapter 4

The Belly Fat Diet Plans

1n the previous chapters, we tell you where belly fat comes from and the foods and nutrients that can blast away this dangerous fat. In this chapter, we put it all together in a meal plan that offers quick results and that you can maintain long term. Your individual Belly Fat Diet plan shows you how to effectively balance your meals and snacks throughout the day to prevent hunger, boost metabolism, and slim your waistline, once and for all.

Finding the Right Plan for You

One of the things that makes the Belly Fat Diet plan so different from all the other "diets" and weight loss plans out there is that it isn't a one-size-fits-all approach. Everyone has different needs when it comes to losing weight and shedding belly fat, and that's why the cookie-cutter approach that many plans use just doesn't work. Instead, you can pick which plan is the best fit for you based on your personality, lifestyle, how much weight you have to lose, and even how quickly you want to lose it.

In addition, when you achieve your goal weight, we want to make sure you understand want it takes to stay at this weight long term. No more yo-yo dieting! Instead, the Belly Fat Diet devotes a whole plan to maintaining your results. And, if you're already at a healthy body weight, but you just want to slim your waistline a bit and improve your overall health, you can start with the Maintenance Plan as well. In this section, we give you an overview of each of these plans, the philosophy behind each, and who is the most appropriate person for each plan.

The Turbo-Charged Plan

If you want to see results immediately and you tend to be a bit impatient about weight loss, this plan may just be the one for you! If you've tried to lose weight time and time again with little to no results, and you feel that your metabolism is slower than a snail, the Turbo-Charged Plan may be the best option for you, as well.

Of all the Belly Fat Diet plans, this plan is the most rigid and requires a high level of dedication — for this reason, it's not for everyone. The goal of this plan is to help the "resistant dieter" — the person who struggles to lose 1 to 2 pounds even when following a weight loss plan to the letter. This plan may also be the one for you if you want to see progress quickly and you tend to be impatient about getting weight off.

If you exercise more than 30 minutes most days of the week or if you start this plan and find you're losing more than 2 pounds per week (which leads to loss of muscle mass and not just body fat, which can slow metabolism), transition to the Moderation Plan instead; it'll help you continue to reach your weight loss goals and keep the weight off for good.

The Turbo-Charged Plan is best suited for

- ✔ People who have experienced little to no success with previous weight loss programs, even when following them exactly

- ✔ People who are *sedentary* — sitting most of the day with limited physical activity

- ✔ People over the age of 40, especially pre- and post-menopausal women

- ✔ People who believe their metabolism has slowed with age

- ✔ People who are short in stature (women under 5'2", or men under 5'6")

- ✔ People who tend to be impatient when trying to lose weight and want to see quick results to stay motivated

The following people should *not* follow the Turbo-Charged Plan:

- ✔ People with diabetes (The reduced carbohydrate level may lead to dangerous drops in blood sugar.)

- ✔ Women who have had babies in the past three months

- ✔ Women who are currently breastfeeding

- ✔ People who get 90 minutes of intense exercise or more per day

The Moderation Plan

The purpose of the Moderation Plan is to promote a steady rate of weight loss to allow you to achieve significant results over time. This plan balances healthy carbohydrates, lean proteins, and belly-fighting fats to allow you to make realistic, healthy changes to your dietary habits that will allow you to feel full and satisfied while losing pounds and pounds of body fat. Most important, this plan promotes a realistic way of achieving your ideal body weight so you can maintain the results long term.

This plan is a great choice for almost everyone because it provides you with a slow, steady rate of weight loss while helping you to make small and achievable changes to your diet and lifestyle that you can stick with.

The Moderation Plan is best for

- ✔ People who want to lose weight at a steady, consistent rate
- ✔ People who participate in at least 30 minutes of moderate to high-intensity physical activity most days of the week
- ✔ People who are of moderate to tall in stature (women over 5'2", or men over 5'6")

Consult your personal physician or dietitian before making any change to your diet or lifestyle. This is especially important for those with a medical condition, such as those with diabetes. If you have inconsistent blood sugar readings (where your blood sugar crashes or spikes on a regular basis), you may be better suited for the Gradual-Change Plan.

The Gradual-Change Plan

The name really says it all with this plan. The goal is to allow you to make small, simple changes gradually over time, which will lead to big results! This plan is all about personality. Not everyone can jump right in when starting a weight loss plan and make a bunch of changes at once. Or you may try to do that and find that you burn out after a few days or weeks.

There is absolutely nothing wrong with not wanting to make significant changes all at once. There is also nothing wrong with thinking you want to make a large amount of changes at once and realizing when you get started that you're feeling overwhelmed or experiencing burnout. In the same way that no two people are the same, no two journeys to achieve your goal weight will be the same. And the Gradual-Change Plan accounts for that.

The Gradual-Change Plan allows you to make small, maintainable changes over a period of time. The result will be permanent lifestyle changes that will not only boost your health but also help you to keep away the pounds and belly fat as well.

The Gradual-Change Plan is a very effective weight loss plan, but your results will be slower on this plan than they would be on one of the others. It's all about achieving your goal — not how long it takes to get there. If the Gradual-Change Plan gets you to your goal in six months, and you can maintain your weight when you get there, that's better than losing weight in one month on a crash diet only to regain it. The Gradual-Change Plan will still allow you to blast belly fat, improve health, and achieve long-lasting results.

The Gradual-Change Plan is best for:

- ✔ People who have less than 10 pounds to lose, but who want to shrink their waistlines

- ✔ People who have burned out when following a diet in the past

- ✔ Chronic yo-yo dieters who are looking to make gradual changes they can stick with

- ✔ Very athletic or physically active individuals who have high energy demands

- ✔ People who are already at their ideal body weight or very close to it, but are still looking to improve their health and further flatten their bellies

- ✔ Women who have given birth less than three months ago

- ✔ Women who are currently breastfeeding

  If you are currently breastfeeding, don't lose more than ½ pound per week. Too-rapid weight loss can decrease your milk supply.

Always check with your physician before starting a weight loss plan if you've recently given birth or you're breastfeeding.

The Maintenance Plan

Once you've achieved your weight loss goals, you need the Maintenance Plan. This will ensure you that you're able to maintain your new body weight for the long haul. The Maintenance Plan isn't about eating perfectly every day of your life — no one can do that! It's about creating balance. There's no food you can't have, but some foods need to be consumed in moderation where others can be enjoyed more regularly. The Maintenance Plan helps you to understand this balance so that you can enjoy your new healthy body weight without living a life of deprivation. This plan shows you how to continue to make healthy choices, with occasional splurges for successful, long-term results.

The maintenance plan is most appropriate for:

- ✔ People who are at their goal weight
- ✔ People whose BMIs are within an ideal range (see Chapter 1)
- ✔ People whose waist circumferences are within the ideal range (see Chapter 1)
- ✔ People who are at a healthy body weight and whose blood pressure, cholesterol, and blood sugar are within the normal range (see Chapter 1)

The Turbo-Charged Plan

The Turbo-Charged Plan is designed to maximize weight loss by increasing your metabolism while helping you to shed excess water weight. This combination allows you to instantly slim your waistline and shed body fat more quickly than before, allowing you to achieve your goals faster than you would think possible. The Turbo-Charged plan is divided into two levels. The first two weeks of this plan are known as Level 1; here, you focus on increasing your intake of lean protein while lowering your carbohydrate intake. Then you move into Level 2, where you increase your intake of healthy carbohydrates to ensure adequate energy while you continue to lose consistent amounts of weight until you reach your long-term goal.

There are a few guidelines that are important to adhere to on the Turbo-Charged Plan:

- ✔ Level 1 lasts for only two weeks. After two weeks, you should enter Level 2. You can always move into Level 2 early, but you shouldn't extend Level 1 beyond two weeks.
- ✔ Level 2 of the Turbo-Charged Plan is designed for you to stay in until you meet your weight loss goals. If at any time you find this plan too restrictive or feel your energy levels are too low, you can move into Level 2 of the Moderation Plan, where you'll continue to experience a healthy rate of weight loss until you reach your long-term goal.
- ✔ Non-starchy vegetables are unlimited in both Level 1 and Level 2 (however, we recommend that you consume at least four servings per day).
- ✔ Starchy vegetables fall into a separate category in Level 1 only to make sure you take in an adequate amount of fiber, nutrients, and healthy

carbohydrates. In Level 2, these starchy vegetables are rolled into the starch food group and are optional to consume.

✔ Aim to choose mostly lean protein options. If you do choose a medium-fat protein or a high-fat protein, count each ounce as a serving of protein as well as a serving of fat.

✔ Drink at least 64 ounces of water daily to stay hydrated and decrease belly bloat, as well as regulate appetite.

Level 1

Level one of the Turbo-Charged Plan focuses on decreasing unhealthy sources of carbohydrates while increasing lean protein intake; however, it is not a "low-carb diet." Level 1 reduces your intake of carbohydrates from simple sugars and refined carbohydrates while still providing you with a healthy level of carbohydrates for adequate energy. A slight reduction in carbohydrates with an increase in lean protein will provide you with a slight metabolism boost, maximizing your weight loss potential. In addition, structuring your meal plan in this way allows you to shed excess water retention that can bloat your midsection, providing you with an instant slimming benefit.

Table 4-1 lists the servings you can have from each food group per day on Level 1 of the Turbo-Charged Plan. *Note:* See "What Constitutes a Serving," later in this chapter, for what constitutes a serving.

Table 4-1	Turbo-Charged Plan, Level 1						
	Vegetables	*Starchy Vegetables*	*Fruit*	*Milk/ Yogurt*	*Starch*	*Protein*	*Fat*
Men	At least 4	1	1	2	0	14 ounces	8
Women	At least 4	1	1	1	0	12 ounces	6

Level 2

After two weeks in Level 1, you enter Level 2 of the Turbo-Charged Plan. This level makes sure that you continue to consume an adequate amount of healthy carbohydrates to boost energy levels while you continue to lose weight. This level also provides you with a larger selection of food options to increase variety and prevent boredom associated with your weight loss plan. As in Level 1, non-starchy vegetables are unlimited, but you must consume at least four servings per day.

Table 4-2 lists the servings you can have from each food group per day on Level 2 of the Turbo-Charged Plan. *Note:* See "What Constitutes a Serving," later in this chapter, for what constitutes a serving.

Table 4-2	Turbo-Charged Plan, Level 2					
	Vegetables	*Fruit*	*Milk/ Yogurt*	*Starch*	*Protein*	*Fat*
Men	At least 4	2	2	4	12 ounces	7
Women	At least 4	2	2	2	10 ounces	5

The Moderation Plan

The Moderation Plan is just that, a plan that encourages you to eat in moderation, promotes incorporating the foods and nutrients that burn belly fat, and ensures that you're taking in enough calories and nutrition to not only lose weight, but also boost metabolism without feeling hungry or deprived.

There are a few guidelines you'll want to remember on the Moderation Plan:

✔ Level 1 of the Moderation Plan is designed to last for two weeks. After this time, you should move on to Level 2. You may move on to Level 2 early, but Level 1 should not be extended past two weeks.

✔ You can stay on Level 2 of the Moderation Plan until you meet your weight loss goals.

✔ Non-starchy vegetables are unlimited in both Level 1 and Level 2, but we recommend that you consume at least four servings per day.

✔ Starchy vegetables fall into a separate category in Level 1 only to make sure you take in enough fiber, nutrients, and healthy carbohydrates. In Level 2, these starchy vegetables are rolled into the starch food group and are optional.

✔ Aim to choose mostly lean protein options. If you do choose a medium-fat or high-fat protein, you must count each ounce as a serving of protein as well as a serving of fat.

✔ Drink at least 64 ounces of water daily to stay hydrated and decrease belly bloat, as well as regulate appetite.

Level 1

This level of the Moderation Plan shows you how to incorporate belly fat–burning foods while banishing the ones that store fat, all while helping to boost your metabolism with realistic changes.

Table 4-3 lists the servings you can have from each food group per day on Level 1 of the Moderation Plan. *Note:* See "What Constitutes a Serving," later in this chapter, for what constitutes a serving.

Table 4-3		Moderation Plan, Level 1					
	Vegetables	*Starchy Vegetables*	*Fruit*	*Milk/ Yogurt*	*Starch*	*Protein*	*Fat*
Men	At least 4	1	2	2	3	12 ounces	7
Women	At least 4	1	2	1	2	10 ounces	5

Level 2

This level of the Moderation Plan continues to promote a steady rate of weight loss while helping to incorporate additional variety into your meal plan. This allows you to have more flexibility when planning meals and snacks, preventing boredom or discouragement, which can cause you to get off track. Continue to make sure to choose mostly lean proteins, healthy monounsaturated fats, and whole-grain starches when meal planning to maximize your results.

Table 4-4 lists the servings you can have from each food group per day on Level 2 of the Moderation Plan. *Note:* See "What Constitutes a Serving," later in this chapter, for what constitutes a serving.

Table 4-4	Moderation Plan, Level 2					
	Vegetables	*Fruit*	*Milk/ Yogurt*	*Starch*	*Protein*	*Fat*
Men	At least 4	3	2	5	10 ounces	6
Women	At least 4	3	2	3	8 ounces	5

The Gradual-Change Plan

The goal of the Gradual-Change Plan is to show you how to improve your eating habits over time to make more belly-friendly selections to slim your waistline as well as improve your health. This plan is perfect for those who have burned out on prior weight loss attempts or feel their current dietary habits need improvement, but would like to make gradual changes over time versus jumping right in and taking on too many changes at once.

There are a few main guidelines you want to remember on the Gradual-Change Plan:

✔ Level 1 of the Gradual-Change Plan is designed to last for two weeks. After this time, you should move on to Level 2.

✔ You can stay on Level 2 of the Gradual-Change Plan until you meet your weight loss goals.

✔ If you find that your weight loss slows or stalls on the Gradual-Change Plan, you may move on to Level 2 of the Moderation Plan to continue to promote weight loss until you reach your long-term goal.

✔ Starchy vegetables fall into a separate category in Level 1 only to make sure you take in enough fiber, nutrients, and healthy carbohydrates. In Level 2, these starchy vegetables are rolled into the starch food group and are optional.

✔ Aim to choose mostly lean protein options. If you do choose a medium-fat protein or a high-fat protein, you must count each ounce as a serving of protein, as well as a serving of fat.

✔ Drink at least 64 ounces of water daily on your meal plan to stay hydrated and decrease belly bloat, as well as regulate appetite.

Level 1

The goal of Level 1 of the Gradual-Change Plan is to encourage you to begin eating more whole vegetables and fruits, which are low in calories, rich in fiber, and full of belly fat–blasting nutrients. This level starts by recommending you consume 3 servings of non-starchy vegetables per day and then gradually increases this to at least 4 servings in Level 2 to prevent you from feeling overwhelmed. Fruit intake gradually increases from Level 1 to Level 2 as well. If you want to have additional non-starchy vegetable servings in Level 1, you may do so because these aren't limited. However, you should not eat beyond the recommended fruit servings listed on your plan.

Table 4-5 lists the servings you can have from each food group per day on Level 1 of the Gradual-Change Plan. *Note:* See "What Constitutes a Serving," later in this chapter, for what constitutes a serving.

Table 4-5		Gradual-Change Plan, Level 1					
	Vegetables	*Starchy Vegetables*	*Fruit*	*Milk/ Yogurt*	*Starch*	*Protein*	*Fat*
Men	At least 3	1	3	2	4	12 ounces	6
Women	At least 3	1	2	2	4	8 ounces	5

Level 2

This level of the Gradual-Change Plan will help you to introduce additional servings of vegetables and fruits daily to help you to take in higher amounts of belly fat–fighting nutrients along with filling fiber and disease-fighting antioxidants. *Remember:* Non-starchy vegetables are always unlimited, so feel free to help yourself to more than four servings per day!

Table 4-6 lists the servings you can have from each food group per day on Level 2 of the Gradual-Change Plan. *Note:* See "What Constitutes a Serving," later in this chapter, for what constitutes a serving.

Table 4-6	Gradual-Change Plan, Level 2					
	Vegetables	**Fruit**	**Milk/Yogurt**	**Starch**	**Protein**	**Fat**
Men	At least 4	3	2	6	12 ounces	7
Women	At least 4	3	2	5	8 ounces	6

The Maintenance Plan

If you're ready for the Maintenance Plan, congratulations are in order! You've made fantastic progress to get this far and achieve your goal weight along with your overall health goals, and you should be incredibly proud of yourself! All your hard work has paid off!

Now it's time to switch gears. You're no longer trying to lose weight. Instead, you're trying to maintain your current body weight. This can feel like new territory and may be a bit confusing. How much more food should you eat? Or should you eat the same things you were eating while you were losing weight?

Weight maintenance is all about moderation. You don't need to be perfect 100 percent of the time (and you shouldn't try to be either — that's a surefire way to burn out and get off track). But you do want to focus on continuing the healthy behaviors that allowed you to achieve your goal weight. You want to avoid falling back into old habits — the ones that caused you to gain weight in the first place. On the Maintenance Plan, you make slight adjustments to your meal plan while still keeping a careful eye on portion size to prevent overdoing it.

Also, plan to weigh yourself once a week or once every other week. This way, if your weight starts to increase, you can catch it right away and correct it versus letting it get out of control. **Remember:** It's a lot easier to lose 1 or 2 pounds than it is to lose 10 or 20!

Weight maintenance can be very individualized. Use these guidelines as you follow your maintenance plan:

✔ If you find you're still losing weight, add in an additional 100 calories per day for one week and monitor your weight. Repeat this until you're maintaining your weight for at least two weeks in a row.

> ✔ If you're gaining weight while following the Maintenance Plan, cut back 100 calories per day for one week and then re-weigh yourself. Continue to cut back by 100 calories per day for a week until you can maintain your weight for two weeks in a row.

Just as a reminder, 100 calories is approximately equal to:

- ✔ 1 serving of starch
- ✔ 1 serving of fruit
- ✔ 1 serving of milk/yogurt
- ✔ 3 ounces of lean protein
- ✔ 2 servings of fat

Table 4-7 lists the servings you can have from each food group per day on the Maintenance Plan. **Note:** See "What Constitutes a Serving," later in this chapter, for what constitutes a serving.

Table 4-7	The Maintenance Plan					
	Vegetables	*Fruit*	*Milk/ Yogurt*	*Starch*	*Protein*	*Fat*
Men	At least 4	3	3	7	12 ounces	7
Women	At least 4	3	2	5	10 ounces	7

What Constitutes a Serving

In this section, we tell you the portion sizes for specific foods in each food group, to help you follow your Belly Fat Diet plan.

For belly fat–blasting meal plans, showing what a menu for a typical day may look like, check out *Belly Fat Diet For Dummies,* by Erin Palinski-Wade (Wiley).

Vegetables (non-starchy)

When it comes to non-starchy vegetables, the Belly Fat Diet plan is unlimited, but it does set a minimum number of servings that you should strive for. Here's what constitutes a serving:

- ✔ ½ cup cooked vegetable
- ✔ 1 cup raw vegetable
- ✔ 6 ounces 100 percent low-sodium vegetable juice

Non-starchy vegetables are all the vegetables *except* corn, legumes, lentils, peas, potatoes, and winter squash.

Fruit

One serving of fruit is any of the following:

- ✔ 1 medium piece of fruit (the size of a baseball)
- ✔ ½ banana
- ✔ 1 cup berries, melon, or grapes
- ✔ ½ cup canned fruit in juice
- ✔ ¼ cup no-sugar-added dried fruit
- ✔ ½ cup 100 percent fruit juice

Milk/yogurt

One serving of milk/yogurt is any of the following:

- ✔ 1 cup fat-free or 1 percent milk
- ✔ 1 cup soymilk or almond milk (with less than 10 g of sugar per cup)
- ✔ 1 cup 2 percent or whole milk (but add 1 fat serving)
- ✔ 1 cup fat-free or low-fat plain yogurt
- ✔ 1 cup fat-free or low-fat flavored yogurt (with 15 g of sugar or less per serving)
- ✔ 1 cup 2 percent or whole yogurt (but add 1 fat serving)
- ✔ ½ cup fat-free or low-fat pudding

Starches

One serving of a starch is any of the following:

✔ Whole grains:

- 1 slice 100 percent whole-grain bread
- ½ cup 100 percent whole-grain cereal
- ½ cup steel-cut oatmeal, cooked
- ½ cup whole-grain pasta, cooked
- ⅓ cup brown or wild rice, cooked
- ⅓ cup whole-grain couscous, cooked
- ½ cup quinoa, cooked
- Whole-grain tortilla, 6-inch diameter
- ½ whole-grain English muffin
- ½ whole-grain pita, 6-inch diameter
- ¼ whole-grain bagel, large deli size
- 3 tablespoons whole-grain flour

✔ Snack foods:

- 3 cups air-popped popcorn
- ¾ cup whole-grain pretzels
- 6 whole-grain crackers (totaling 1 ounce)
- 15 baked whole-grain chips
- 3 graham cracker squares
- 1 ounce dark chocolate (but add 1 fat serving)

✔ Starchy vegetables:

- ½ cup corn, cooked
- 1 medium corn on the cob
- ½ cup legumes or lentils
- ½ cup peas
- ½ cup plantains
- 3 ounces baked potato
- 3 ounces sweet potato
- 1 cup winter squash

✔ Refined grains (limit as much as possible):

- 1 slice white or Italian bread

- ⅓ cup white rice
- 2 large white rice cakes
- 1 cookie, 3-inch diameter
- ½ cup ice cream or frozen yogurt
- 3 tablespoons white flour
- 1 tablespoon sugar, syrup, jelly, or honey

Proteins

Each of the following is one serving of a *lean* protein:

✔ Fish:

- 1 ounce of any **fish** (including cod, flounder, grouper, halibut, herring, salmon, swordfish, tilapia, trout, and so on)
- ¼ cup **tuna canned in water**
- 2 **sardines canned in water**
- 1 ounce **shellfish** (clams, crab, lobster, oysters, scallops, shrimp, and so on)
- 1 ounce **imitation shellfish**

✔ Poultry:

- 1 ounce **chicken breast,** white meat, skinless
- 1 ounce **turkey breast,** white meat, skinless
- 1 ounce **Cornish hen,** skinless
- 1 ounce **ground turkey,** 100 percent breast meat
- 1 ounce **ground chicken,** 100 percent breast meat
- 1 ounce **turkey hot dog** (with 3 g of fat or less per ounce)
- 1 ounce **turkey sausage** (with 3 g of fat or less per ounce)

✔ Pork:

- 1 ounce **tenderloin**
- 1 ounce **center chop loin**
- 1 ounce **fresh ham**
- 1 ounce **boiled ham**
- 1 ounce **Canadian bacon**

✔ Beef (choose USDA Select and Choice cuts and trim all visible fat):

- 1 ounce **flank steak**
- 1 ounce **round**
- 1 ounce **tenderloin**
- 1 ounce **eye of round roast or steak**
- 1 ounce **sirloin tip side steak**
- 1 ounce **top round roast or steak**
- 1 ounce **bottom round roast or steak**
- 1 ounce **top sirloin steak**

✔ Game:

- 1 ounce **buffalo** (bison)
- 1 ounce **venison**
- 1 ounce **ostrich**
- 1 ounce **goose** (cooked without skin)

✔ Lamb:

- 1 ounce **leg of lamb**
- 1 ounce **loin chops**
- 1 ounce **loin shoulder**

✔ Cheese:

- 1 ounce fat-free or part-skim varieties with 3 g of fat or less per ounce
- ¼ cup fat-free or part skim **cottage cheese**
- ¼ cup fat-free or part-skim **ricotta cheese**
- 2 tablespoons **Parmesan cheese**

✔ Other:

- ½ cup **legumes or lentils** (but add 1 starch serving)
- 2 **egg whites**
- ¼ cup **egg substitute**
- ½ cup **tofu**
- ¼ cup **edamame**
- 1 **vegetable burger**
- 1 ounce deli meat (choose varieties with 3 g of fat or less per serving)

Each of the following is one serving of a *medium-fat* or *high-fat* protein.
Note: Add 1 fat serving per medium-fat or high-fat protein serving.

- Fish:
    - 1 ounce **fried fish**
    - 1 ounce **fried shellfish**
    - 1 ounce **sautéed fish or shellfish** in oil/butter
    - ¼ cup **tuna canned in oil**
- Poultry:
    - 1 ounce **chicken, dark meat**
    - 1 ounce **chicken, with skin**
    - 1 ounce **turkey, dark meat**
    - 1 ounce **turkey, with skin**
    - 1 ounce **fried chicken or turkey**
    - ¼ cup **ground chicken/turkey, dark meat**
- Pork:
    - 1 ounce **top loin**
    - 1 ounce **chop**
    - 1 ounce **cutlet**
    - 1 ounce **Boston butt**
    - 1 ounce **Taylor ham**
    - 1 ounce **spare ribs**
    - 1 ounce **ground pork**
    - 1 ounce **sausage, pork**
    - 3 slices **bacon**
    - 1 ounce **hot dog**
- Beef (any USDA Prime grade):
    - ¼ cup **ground beef**
    - 1 ounce **corned beef**
    - 1 ounce **filet mignon**
    - 1 ounce **Porterhouse steak**
    - 1 ounce **New York strip steak**

- 1 ounce **T-bone**
- 1 ounce **rib-eye**
- 1 ounce **prime rib**
- 1 ounce **short rib**

✔ Lamb:

- 1 ounce **rib roast**
- 1 ounce **ground lamb**

✔ Cheese:

- 1 ounce part-skim or full-fat cheese with more than 3 g of fat per ounce

✔ Other

- 1 egg
- 1 ounce deli meat with more than 3 g of fat per ounce

Each of the following is one serving of a *vegetarian* or *vegan* protein:

✔ 6 **almonds** (but add 1 fat serving)

✔ ½ cup **black beans** (but add 1 starch serving)

✔ 1 tablespoon **chia seeds** (but add 1 fat serving)

✔ ¼ cup **edamame**

✔ 1 tablespoon **flaxseeds** (but add 1 fat serving)

✔ ½ cup **lentils** (but add 1 starch serving)

✔ 2 teaspoons **peanut butter** (but add 1 fat serving)

✔ ½ cup **quinoa** (but add 1 starch serving)

✔ ½ cup **spinach** (but add 1 vegetable serving)

✔ 1 cup **plain soymilk** (but add 1 milk serving)

✔ 1 tablespoon **sunflower seeds** (but add 1 fat serving)

✔ ¼ cup **tempeh** (but add 1 fat serving)

✔ ¼ cup **tofu**

✔ 1 tablespoon **walnuts** (but add 1 fat serving)

✔ 1 slice **whole-grain bread** (but add 1 starch serving)

Fats

Each of the following is one serving of a *belly-friendly fat:*

- ✔ 1 teaspoon **oil** (canola, grape seed, olive, peanut)
- ✔ 2 teaspoons **nut butter, natural**
- ✔ 2 tablespoons **hummus**
- ✔ 2 teaspoons **tahini paste**
- ✔ ¼ **avocado**
- ✔ 8 large **olives**
- ✔ 6 **almonds**
- ✔ 6 **cashews**
- ✔ 10 **peanuts**
- ✔ 10 **pistachios**
- ✔ 4 **pecan halves**
- ✔ 4 **walnut halves** or 1 tablespoon **crushed walnuts**
- ✔ 1 tablespoon **seeds** (chia, flax, pumpkin, sesame, sunflower)
- ✔ 1 tablespoon **oil-based salad dressing** (trans fat free)
- ✔ 2 tablespoons **reduced-fat salad dressing**
- ✔ 1 teaspoon **spread** (olive or canola oil based)

Each of the following is one serving of a *less-than-belly-friendly fat:*

- ✔ 1 teaspoon **butter**
- ✔ 1 teaspoon **shortening**
- ✔ 1 teaspoon **lard**
- ✔ 2 tablespoons **creamer**
- ✔ 2 tablespoons **sour cream**
- ✔ 1 tablespoon **cream cheese**

Condiments

Although condiments aren't a food group with serving sizes on the Belly Fat Diet plan, here's how much you can have of common condiments per day:

- **All dry seasonings and spices:** Unlimited
- **Barbeque sauce:** 1 tablespoon
- **Garlic:** Unlimited
- **Horseradish:** ½ cup
- **Ketchup (no-sugar-added varieties):** 2 tablespoons
- **Lemon or lime juice:** ¼ cup
- **Mustard:** ¼ cup
- **Nonstick cooking spray:** Unlimited
- **Pickle relish:** 1 tablespoon
- **Pickles (no-sugar-added varieties):** 3
- **Salsa (fresh varieties):** Unlimited
- **Soy sauce (low-sodium varieties):** 2 teaspoons
- **Taco seasoning:** 1 tablespoon
- **Teriyaki sauce (low-sodium varieties):** 2 teaspoons
- **Vinegar:** Unlimited
- **Worcestershire sauce:** 2 tablespoons

Chapter 5

Getting Ready for Your Belly-Blasting Journey

In This Chapter

▶ Making sense of food labels

▶ Stocking your kitchen with the right kinds of foods

▶ Finding belly-friendly cooking techniques

▶ Sticking with your diet weeks and months down the road

Have you ever decided it was time to improve your eating habits; stocked up on loads of fruits, vegetables, and lean proteins; and then sabotaged your efforts by munching on the cookies and chips that were left over in the pantry? This common problem is why it's so essential to not only stock your kitchen with belly fat–blasting foods, but also rid your kitchen of belly bloaters.

We start this chapter with a guide to reading the food labels — when you know how to read labels, you can assess all the foods in your kitchen today and toss the ones that won't help you reach your goals. Then we walk you through stocking your kitchen with the *right* kinds of foods — the ones that'll help you slim your waistline for good. Even healthy vegetables can become not-so-healthy when they're cooked in loads of butter and smothered in rich sauces, so we fill you in on some healthy cooking techniques that will support — not sabotage — your belly-blasting efforts. Finally, we end this chapter with a little motivation for the long haul. Everybody starts a diet full of hope, but keeping that up for weeks or months can be difficult. With the tips in this chapter, you'll make it through the tough times and reach your goal.

Reading Food Labels

Does this sound familiar: You go to the grocery store intending to fill your cart with the healthiest foods possible. Your first stop is the bread aisle, where you become overwhelmed by all the options. You pick up loaf after loaf, scrutinizing the label and reading through the ingredients, and after more time than you have to spend, you give up and just throw the loaf you're currently holding into the cart and move along, frustrated and confused. If this situation hits home, you're not alone. Between the marketing claims, the Nutrition Facts label, the ingredients list, and the incredible selection of options, trying to make a healthy food choice can seem more complicated that a calculus exam.

But don't worry — reading food labels really isn't as complicated as it seems. When you know a few simple secrets to decoding a food label, you'll be breezing through the grocery store aisles in no time! In this section, we show you the ins and outs of the Nutrition Facts label and ingredients list, telling you what to look at and what to ignore. Most important, we explain what to buy to help you achieve your flat-belly goals!

Interpreting the Nutrition Facts label

When it comes to determining if a food is a healthy option or one to leave behind on the shelf, it all starts with looking at the Nutrition Facts label. Think of this as the window that looks deep inside the food you've selected and tells you all the *macronutrients* (carbohydrates, protein, and fat) and *micronutrients* (vitamins and minerals) it contains. The Nutrition Facts label allows you to see just how many belly-flattening nutrients the food contains, as well as nutrients that may pack on the pounds and the belly fat.

The Nutrition Facts label contains multiple parts, including the following (see Figure 5-1):

✔ **Serving size:** This part is the most important. Without the serving size, the rest of the information is meaningless because you won't have a reference point. If a food contains 200 calories, does that mean it contains 200 calories in ½ cup, in 2 cups, in a tablespoon? You won't know unless you reference the serving size. The serving size shows you the amount the manufacturer of the food used as a reference to determine all the nutrients listed on the Nutrition Facts label.

Nutrition Facts

Serving Size 2 crackers (14g)
Servings Per Container About 21

Amount Per Serving

Calories 60	Calories from Fat 15

	% Daily value*
Total Fat 1.5g	**2%**
Saturated Fat 0g	**0%**
Trans Fat 0g	
Cholesterol 0mg	**0%**
Sodium 70mg	**3%**
Total Carbohydrate 10g	**3%**
Dietary Fiber Less than 1g	**3%**
Sugars 0g	
Protein 2g	

Vitamin A 0%	•	Vitamin C 0%
Calcium 0%	•	Iron 2%

*Percent Daily Values are based on a 2,000 calorie diet. Your daily values may be higher or lower depending on your calorie needs

		Calories:	2,000	2,500
Total Fat	Less than		65g	90g
Sat Fat	Less than		20g	25g
Cholesterol	Less than		300mg	300mg
Sodium	Less than		2400mg	2400mg
Total Carbohydrate			300g	375g
Dietary Fiber			25g	30g

Figure 5-1:
The Nutrition Facts label.

The serving size is also helpful for you to reference when you come across packages that display terms such as *low calorie* or *low fat*. These foods are, indeed, low in calories or low in fat *in one serving*. But eat multiple servings, and the calories and fat multiply. If the food you've selected lists the serving size as 1 cup, but you consume 2 cups of the food, you need to double the calories and nutrients to determine how much you're truly taking in.

✔ **Calories:** Calories are the next thing you see listed on the Nutrition Facts label. They're essentially the energy the food gives you. Take in more energy (calories) than you burn, and you'll gain weight and belly fat. To shed weight and inches, you need to take in fewer calories than you burn. To put this in perspective, the belly-blasting meal plans in this book are based on 1,200 to 1,400 calories per day for women and 1,600 to 1,800 calories per day for men.

To help you stay within this range, use the following guidelines:

- When choosing a snack, keep it around 50 to 200 calories.

- When eating a meal, keep it between 200 and 400 calories.

If you follow these guidelines, you'll be able to keep your total calories per day in check.

✓ **Total fat:** Scroll down and you see that the Nutrition Facts label provides information on total fat and, directly underneath this, breaks down these fats into saturated fats and trans fats. Not all fats are bad. In fact, certain fats — such as monounsaturated fats — actually help to shed belly fat. However, saturated and trans fats are the fats that can trigger inflammation, damage your cardiovascular health, and increase belly fat. The Nutrition Facts label only has to include saturated and trans fat, but some also list monounsaturated fats and polyunsaturated fats. When looking at a food, don't focus on the total fat listed; instead, aim for foods with absolutely no trans fats and as few grams of saturated fat as possible. You'll want to try to keep your total intake of saturated fat per day to 10 g to 15 g or less.

✓ **Sodium:** Sodium is an electrolyte that is essential to your body. However, too much sodium can lead to fluid retention, which can increase blood pressure, as well as cause your stomach to look distended and bloated. To prevent excessive sodium intake, you want to aim to keep your intake to 2,000 mg per day or less.

✓ **Fiber:** Another key nutrient included on the Nutrition Facts label is fiber, which is listed under total carbohydrates. This nutrient is a potent belly fat fighter because it helps to keep you full and slows the insulin response after eating a carbohydrate-rich food. For the maximum belly-slimming benefit, you'll want to aim to consume 30 g to 35 g of soluble fiber per day.

✓ **Sugar:** Consuming a lot of dietary sugar spikes insulin levels, resulting in increased belly fat storage. However, sugar on the Nutrition Facts label includes naturally occurring sugars (such as those found in fruit) and added sugars (such as those found in candy). To differentiate between added sugar and naturally occurring sugar, check out the ingredients list, which we cover in the next section.

Knowing what to watch for in the ingredients list

So, you've picked out a food, reviewed the Nutrition Facts label, and determined the food is a great choice to help shed belly fat. Not so fast! The Nutrition Facts label doesn't tell the whole story. It does give you a view into the food and what it contains, but sometimes it can be misleading or even downright deceptive. To ensure you're making the best food choice for your health and your waistline, you have to be a bit of a detective. But luckily, the clues you need to determine if your food selection is really a belly fat fighter are right there in front of you in the ingredients list.

Be on the lookout for foods that contain belly fat–storing ingredients such as the following:

- ✔ Enriched flour

- ✔ White flour

- ✔ Any flour without the word *whole* listed in front of it (you want to look for *whole-wheat flour* as opposed to just *wheat flour*)

- ✔ High-fructose corn syrup

- ✔ Honey

- ✔ Dehydrated cane juice

- ✔ Malt syrup

- ✔ Maltodextrin

- ✔ Molasses

- ✔ Any ingredient that ends in *–ose*

- ✔ Any ingredient that starts with the words *partially hydrogenated*

Creating a Flat-Belly Kitchen

By now, you've rid your home of foods loaded with belly-bloating ingredients, such as those containing added sugars and partially hydrogenated oils, as well as foods made from refined carbohydrates. Now it's time to stock your home with belly-friendly foods that you'll love. One of the most important factors to staying on target with a weight loss plan long term is to actually enjoy the foods you're eating. If you're eating foods you don't like or feeling deprived, chances are, you aren't going to stay on track very long.

As you read through the recipes in this book, you see how many of your favorite dishes that could potentially be belly bloaters can be transformed into dishes that can actually shrink your waistline — all while maintaining their great taste and appeal. And it's not just the recipes in this book that can be transformed. If you have favorite meals and recipes that you rely on, with just a few easy tweaks, you can make almost any recipe a belly-friendly choice. But it all starts first by stocking your house with the right foods and ingredients.

Making your list

Before you head out to the grocery store, a shopping list is a must! In order to take your weight loss plan seriously and maximize your success, you have to be prepared, which is exactly what a shopping list allows you to do. Without a shopping list, you may forget to stock up on some very potent belly fat fighters, and, even worse, you may be more tempted to bring home items that can bloat your belly in a big way. A list will help you to stay organized in the store, buying just what you need and avoiding tempting options that you don't.

One great benefit of a shopping list is that it can allow you and your family to plan out your meals and snacks for the week. Not only will this strategy help you to prepare your food options in advance, but it's also a great way to create and stick to a meal-planning budget.

In order to get started with your shopping list, divide it up by food groups. This will help to prevent forgetting essential foods and also help to make sure you're purchasing a variety of items as well. When you have your list set, it's time to head to the store!

Navigating the store

You have your list in hand and you're ready to hit the grocery store. But before you head out, there are a few ways to maximize your chances at making the healthiest food choices while you shop:

- ✓ **Fill your belly before your trip.** One of the worst things you can do is walk into a grocery store hungry. Why? Think about the last time you were feeling very hungry. Did you want to eat everything in sight? Of course! And when this happens in a place filled from floor to ceiling with food options, you can bet that at least a few less-than-healthy options may sneak their way into your cart. To prevent this, grab a quick snack such as a yogurt or a handful of almonds before heading in to keep hunger and cravings at bay!

- ✓ **Become a perimeter shopper.** Think about the layout of your grocery store. Where do most of the healthy options reside? The perimeter! When you shop around the outer parts of the store, you see the produce, lean meats, low-fat dairy, and whole grains. Now, think about what's in those middle aisles. Mostly processed foods filled with refined carbohydrates, excessive sodium, and trans fats. Why tempt yourself? Start your shopping trip by exploring the perimeter of the store and fill your cart. Only venture into the middle aisles when necessary for belly-friendly condiments, spices, and frozen produce.

- **Be label savvy.** Make sure to be a savvy label reader at the store. Check the Nutrition Facts panel and ingredients list of any packaged food before adding it to your cart and ask yourself, "Is this a belly slimmer or a belly bloater?"

To stay on track with your meal plan, stock your kitchen with the best foods for fighting belly fat. Here are the most essential foods to have on hand at all times:

- **Vegetables:** Stock up on both fresh and frozen varieties. When choosing frozen options, look for varieties that include plain vegetables and not those with added seasonings and sauces. Make sure to select vegetables of all colors — stocking your kitchen with a rainbow of vegetables will help ensure that you're maximizing your nutrient intake.

Organic is always your best choice when selecting vegetables. But if cost is a factor, at least be sure to buy organic bell peppers, celery, lettuce, and spinach — these are the veggies that are most laden with pesticides when they're grown non-organically.

- **Fruit:** Just as with vegetables, stock up on both fresh and frozen varieties so you never run out of healthy fruit options. If choosing dried fruit, look at the ingredients list and avoid those containing added sugars. If you purchase canned fruit, just make sure it's canned in its own juice instead of in syrup.

Organic is always best, but if you can't afford to buy strictly organic, at least make sure to buy organic apples, cherries, grapes, nectarines, peaches, pears, and strawberries.

- **Dairy:** Dairy can be a powerful belly fat fighter, so you want to make sure you have a good supply on hand. Low-fat varieties such as skim, 1 percent, and even 2 percent milk are all better choices than whole milk, which contains a lot of saturated fat.

If you prefer non-dairy options, you can opt for almond or soy milk. Just make sure to read the ingredients list and avoid varieties in which sugar or corn syrup is among the first five ingredients listed.

When selecting yogurt, avoid varieties with large amounts of added sugar. Yogurt contains naturally occurring sugar, so you'll need to focus on the ingredients list to decipher whether sugar has been added. Avoid yogurts in which sugar or corn syrup is among the first five ingredients.

- **Starches:** Breads, pastas, cereals, and rice provide you with a great source of carbohydrates for energy. But for a flat belly, you need to make sure to choose mostly whole-grain varieties. To do so, always look at the first ingredient and make sure it lists a whole grain such as whole wheat, whole rye, or whole oats. And keep an eye out for starches that add in a large amount of sugar. Aim for varieties with less than 10 g of sugar per serving. Great options to stock up on include 100 percent whole-grain bread, steel-cut oats, whole-wheat pasta, brown rice, and quinoa.

✓ **Proteins:** Getting enough dietary protein is essential for a lean belly. However, if you choose the wrong type of protein, it can be detrimental to your belly fat–fighting efforts. Aim to stock your kitchen with mostly lean protein options such as fish, white meat poultry, and plant-based proteins legumes, edamame, and tofu. Eggs are also a terrific and versatile source of protein, so make sure to keep a carton on hand at all times. If you do stock your kitchen with beef, choose grass-fed options and leaner cuts such as flank steak to decrease the saturated fat content.

✓ **Fats:** It takes fat to fight fat — but it has to be the right type of fat: mono-unsaturated fats and omega-3 fatty acids. To get in a good source of these healthy fats daily, stock your kitchen with plant-based oils such as olive oil, flaxseed oil, and nuts and seeds such as walnuts, almonds, and even pumpkin seeds. And get adventurous! Try belly fat–fighting options you may not have had before, such as chia seeds, which are a fantastic source of omega-3 fatty acids and perfect for smoothies!

✓ **Snacks:** What type of meal plan is worth following if it doesn't include snacks and occasional treats? The Belly Fat Diet allows you to indulge in many snacks and treats that you'll love! In addition to snacking on raw vegetables and fruits, as well as nuts, seeds, and even hard-boiled eggs, you should stock up on additional healthy options, such as air-popped popcorn, dark chocolate (70 percent cacao or above), and whole-grain crackers with nut butter.

Cooking for a Flat Belly

One of the best things you can do for your waistline is to get in the habit of making your meals at home and limit eating out. Restaurant meals are often packed full of belly-bloating ingredients such as excessive calories, fat, and sodium. That doesn't mean you can *never* eat out, but the more often you prepare your meals, the better. That way, you can control exactly what goes into the meals you're eating.

Cooking doesn't have to mean spending hours upon hours slaving over a hot stove. In fact, this book is packed full of quick and easy recipes.

Making your fridge and freezer your allies in the battle of the bulge

In the battle of the bulge, sometimes what's out of sight is not always out of mind. Sure, it may seem like pushing the gallon of ice cream to the far back corner of the freeze will make it less tempting, but perhaps on a stressful day when you just want something sweet, you'll be tempted to reach way in the back and indulge. Placing healthier options in the front of your refrigerator and freezer and hiding less healthy options in the back can be a great trick to help you resist temptation, but the *best* option is to remove most of the unhealthy options from your home so there will be limited temptation, even on your most vulnerable days.

The good news, however, is that your refrigerator and freezer can actually be converted into one of the most important factors in your success. One of the biggest factors in staying on track with your Belly Fat Diet plan is making sure that you're consuming an adequate amount of fruits and vegetables daily. However, sometimes fresh produce isn't always available. Or, the produce only lasts for a few days

and you can't get to the store more often than once a week. Cue frozen options!

You may be surprised by this, but frozen vegetables and even frozen fruits are just as healthy as their fresh alternatives! These fruits and veggies are picked at the peak of ripeness, which allows them to maintain a high nutrient value. In addition, as long as you steer clear of frozen options with added sauces, frozen produce is just as low in calories and high in fiber as its fresh counterpart. And the best news is that these options last for weeks and even months. Now you have no excuses to skip your daily servings of fruits and veggies!

In addition to stocking up on produce, your fridge and freezer are great for helping you to plan ahead. You can make many of the recipes you find throughout this book in advance, portion them out into individual servings, and freeze them for healthy and quick meal options at a later date. ***Remember:*** Being prepared and planning ahead are keys to weight loss success!

If time is especially short during the week, cook some meals ahead of time on the weekend and freeze them. Then all you have to do is pop them in the microwave, and enjoy!

The tools you need

In this section, we list the most common tools you'll need for healthy cooking. Turn to Chapter 18 for a list of timesaving kitchen gadgets you may want to have on hand as well.

You don't need every piece of equipment listed in this section, but think about the meals and snacks you really love and plan to make often, and invest in the equipment that will help with those.

Blender or food processor

Recipes that contain large amounts of vegetables and fruits often call for these foods to be chopped, sliced, ground, or minced. Doing this by hand can be time-consuming. But a powerful food processor or blender can do this for you in no time! You can also use a food processor or blender to make soups, smoothies, spreads, and even homemade sauces.

Nonstick cooking pans

Monounsaturated oils such as olive oil can help to shrink belly fat while protecting your heart. However, even though these oils provide many health benefits, they're still quite rich in calories (with roughly 120 calories per tablespoon). Using too much oil can cause you to consume too many calories, slowing weight loss. To help you keep your total daily fat intake in check, use a pan that requires less oil to cook in, which is where nonstick pans come in. These pans allow you to cook your favorite foods with just a splash of oil rather than tablespoons of it!

Oil sprayer

Cooking in oil helps to prevent food from sticking together. It also allows you to give your food that nice light brown color and crispy flavor. But too much oil and added fat can be damaging to your waistline. To moderate your oil intake, instead of pouring a large amount of oil into a pan, use an oil sprayer to evenly disperse a much smaller amount of oil on the surface of your pan or even directly onto your food. Oil sprayers can come pre-filled or you can purchase a refillable sprayer that you can fill with the oil you want to use.

Slow cooker

If you want to save time with cooking, a slow cooker is your answer! It doesn't get much easier that preparing a meal in a slow cooker. You simply toss in your ingredients, set the timer on the cooker, and walk away. When you come home in the evening, your meal will be hot and ready for you to dig into. Think of a slow cooker as your own personal chef who cooks your meal while you're out running errands or going to work.

Check out Chapter 15 for delicious, belly-friendly slow-cooker meals to help you get started.

Steamer basket

Steaming is a great way to cook everything from vegetables to lean proteins such as chicken breasts. A steamer basket makes steaming easy by fitting perfectly right inside your pot. The basket works by holding food above the water's surface, which allows the steam from the water boiling below it to cook the food. Not only is steaming a quick and easy way to cook, but it also helps food retain more nutrients that many other cooking methods.

Tried-and-true techniques

You don't have to be a famous chef or a culinary school graduate to prepare a healthy and tasty meal. Just knowing a few simple tricks of the trade will have you cooking like a pro in no time. In this section, we cover some of the most common cooking techniques that you may use to prepare healthy dishes, so you can step into your kitchen confidently, knowing that cooking really can be easy!

Baking

Almost everything from poultry to beef, seafood, and bread products can be prepared by baking, which is a technique that cooks food by surrounding it with dry heat. To bake, turn on your oven and set it to the correct cooking temperature for the food you want to prepare. Allow your oven to warm to this temperature, called *preheating*, before putting food into the oven. Place your food in an oven-safe dish or pan, place the dish or pan in the fully pre-heated oven, and allow it to cook for the amount of time the recipe calls for.

Broiling

If you're looking to cook meat or fish quickly, broiling may be the best option for you. This cooking method involves placing food close to the heat element in your oven. To get started, set your oven to broil and allow it to preheat for five to seven minutes. As the oven is preheating, you can season the food you're about to broil (or you may already have it marinating). Then place your meat or fish onto a broiler pan (a shallow baking pan can work, too) and put it in the oven about 5 inches from the heat source (thicker cuts can be placed a bit farther away, but very thick cuts of meat — anything more than 2 inches thick — shouldn't be broiled). Keep an eye on your meat and around the five-minute mark, flip it (thicker cuts may need a few extra minutes to cook). Look for the meat to turn a deep, golden brown color, indicating that it's time to flip. Cook the meat on the other side for about the same amount of time until it reaches the appropriate internal temperature (see Table 5-1).

Table 5-1		Internal Cooking Temperatures for Foods	
Food	*Cut*	*Internal Temperature (°F)*	*What It Looks Like*
Beef or lamb	Roast, steak, chop (rare to medium rare)	125–135	Center very pink; exterior slightly brown
	Roast, steak, chop (medium)	140–145	Center light pink; exterior brown
	Roast, steak, chop (well done)	160 or above	Uniformly brown throughout
	Ground	160–165	Uniformly brown throughout
Poultry	Any cut	165	Juices run clear
Pork	Roast, steak, chop (medium)	140–145	Center pale pink
	Roast, steak, chop (well done)	160 or above	Uniformly brown throughout
	Ham (raw)	160	Use internal temperature to test for doneness
	Ham (precooked)	140	Use internal temperature to test for doneness
Fish	Steaks (filet or whole)	140	Flakes easily, opaque flesh
	Tuna, marlin, swordfish	125	Outer flesh firm and white, inner flesh light pink or white

Sautéing

This method involves cooking food in a skillet or sauté pan in a small amount of oil. It allows you to cook foods quickly and retain a large amount of nutrients. To get started, place a pan over medium-high heat and allow it to warm before adding oil. When the pan is hot, add a small amount of cooking oil (just enough to cover the bottom of the pan). Let the oil heat, and then add the food you want to cook. Stir the food often while cooking to prevent burning.

Steaming

Steaming is a terrific way to quickly crisp foods such as vegetables while maintaining their high nutrient content. Even better, this method of cooking doesn't require any additional fat or calories! To get started, wash and cut vegetables into equal-size pieces (to allow them to cook evenly). Fill a large pot with about 1 to 2 inches of water, and place it over a high heat until it comes to a boil. When the water is boiling, put a steamer basket into the pot and add the vegetables to the steamer basket; cover. Allow the vegetables to steam until they reach the desired level of tenderness and texture. Remove the lid carefully (watch out for steam because it can burn your hands and arms), and serve immediately.

Staying on Course

You're off to a great start! Nothing stands in your way of achieving your ultimate goals . . . except for you, of course. Keeping motivated to stay on track is the biggest reason for a failed attempt at weight loss. But if you prepare yourself for potential obstacles, you'll know just what you need to do to overcome them and prevent yourself from getting sidetracked.

When trying to lose weight and shrink your waistline, there are four major obstacles you may face:

- ✔ Cravings
- ✔ Emotional eating
- ✔ Mindless eating
- ✔ Lack of motivation

We cover all four in this section.

Managing cravings

Have you ever had a day when you woke up and you just couldn't get your mind off of a certain food? No matter what else you ate, you just didn't feel satisfied. You wanted that food and nothing else.

Cravings such as these can pop up for a number of reasons. Stress and emotions can trigger food cravings as a way to "comfort" yourself. In addition, waiting too long between meals and allowing yourself to get too hungry can bring on intense cravings. Even eating the wrong foods, such as foods that lead to spikes in insulin, can create and intensify cravings.

To help prevent cravings and manage them when they do occur, try to follow these simple rules:

- ✔ Avoid skipping meals or waiting more than four or five hours between meals and snacks to prevent excessive hunger.

- ✔ Limit your intake of simple sugars and refined carbohydrates.

- ✔ Practice the stress management techniques outlined in Chapter 2 to reduce stress-related eating.

- ✔ Drink plenty of water to reduce hunger and avoid cravings that stem from mild dehydration.

- ✔ Get seven to eight hours of sleep each night. Too little sleep can lower your resistance and energy levels, making you more susceptible to cravings.

Coping with emotional eating

Emotional eating can be a tricky cycle to break. Most people, at least sometimes, eat for reasons other than just true hunger. Perhaps you eat for comfort when you're feeling down or have the urge to "crunch" on food when feeling stressed. Whatever the emotion that's driving you to eat, it's important to become aware of your emotional eating patterns so you can work on correcting them. If you don't manage it, emotional eating can lead to weight gain, not to mention a less-than-healthy relationship with food.

To help your recognize the emotions that are driving you to eat, ask yourself the following:

- ✔ Are there times throughout the day I eat for reasons other than hunger? If so, when does this typically occur?

- ✔ When I eat for reasons other than hunger, what emotions am I experiencing at that time?

- ✔ Do I feel guilty after eating when I'm not truly hungry? If so, does this guilt drive me to eat more?

- ✔ When I am emotional, is my first thought or action to reach for food?

Recognizing the time of day that you tend to eat for emotional reasons and why it occurs is the first step in overcoming this dangerous habit. When you're aware of the emotions that trigger you to eat, you can brainstorm ways to handle these emotions that don't involve food. For instance, if you tend to eat when you're bored at night, plan an activity, such as exercising, in the evening to keep you busy while avoiding the pantry. If you reach for food to comfort you when you're feeling down, try journaling about your emotions or calling a good friend to boost your mood and keep your mind off food.

Use the following activity to help you combat emotional eating: Write down all the reasons throughout a typical day that you eat that are unrelated to hunger. Then write down the behaviors that tend to keep you from emotionally eating in your daily life. What healthy behaviors (that is, ones that don't involve eating) can you engage in to help you manage your emotions? For instance, does exercising to fast music help you burn off stress or does taking a bubble bath help you to wind down? Write down any behaviors *other than eating* that help you manage your emotions. Then, when you're experiencing an emotion that may drive you to eat, refer to this list and perform an activity that helps you manage the emotion without food.

Identifying mindless eating

Mindless eating is the behavior of eating food without really paying attention to it. If you've ever sat down with a plate of food or a bag of chips only to minutes later wonder where the food went, you've eaten mindlessly. This behavior can lead to excessive food intake, causing both weight gain and an increase in belly fat. To prevent mindless eating, you have to identify the situations when it's most likely to occur:

- ✔ Eating while distracted (such as eating in front of the TV or computer)
- ✔ Skipping meals throughout the day
- ✔ Eating because something looks good rather than because you're truly hungry
- ✔ Grazing or picking at food throughout the day rather than sitting for meals
- ✔ Eating rapidly

To overcome mindless eating, you need to focus on becoming a mindful eater. This is where you focus on why you're eating and how you're eating your food rather than just what foods you're actually eating. Mindful eating allows you to listen to your body and eat just enough to be satisfied without being overly full. To become more mindful when eating, practice the following strategies:

- ✔ Remove distractions such as TV and computers from mealtime.
- ✔ Focus on involving all your senses as you eat. Think about what the food tastes like, smells like, feels like, and so on.
- ✔ Chew each bite at least ten times to help you slow your speed of eating.
- ✔ Listen to your body. Eat slowly so you can recognize when you start to feel satisfied, and then stop eating. Eating too quickly or being distracted when eating causes you to miss this signal, which can lead to overeating.

Eating out

You may feel as though making the commitment to lose weight and achieve a flat belly means that you have to give up on eating out. Although eating away from home *can* increase temptation and present you with oversized meals packed full of belly bloaters, you don't have to give up on eating out entirely to lose weight and keep it off. Eating at home and preparing your own foods is always the best choice, but eating out still has a place in your meal plan.

Follow these simple tips to help you stay on track with your Belly Fat Diet plan the next time you do eat out:

✔ **Don't go to a restaurant hungry.** If you sit down at a restaurant and feel so hungry that your stomach is growling, you'll have trouble making a healthy choice. Being too hungry also leads to your eating your meal too quickly, and thanks to oversized restaurant portions, this can lead to quickly consuming more calories than you should. Instead, have a light snack, such as a piece of fruit or a low-fat string cheese, before going out to eat to help you eat slower and make a healthier choice.

✔ **Be choosy.** Look for words such as *broiled, grilled,* or *steamed* in your meal description, and avoid *fried, crispy,* or *sautéed* foods (which are typically prepared in much greater amounts of oil in a restaurant than if you were to sauté them yourself at home). Don't be afraid to make special requests or

substitutions. For instance, always ask for salad dressing on the side. If a meal comes with a fried side, such as french fries, ask for it to be subbed out with a baked potato or even better, steamed vegetables, instead.

✔ **Try sharing.** Portions in most restaurants are much larger than the portion you should be eating. If you're distracted with good conversation at a meal, you may find yourself eating more than necessary. To prevent this, order one entree and share it with a friend.

✔ **Avoid excessive alcohol.** Alcohol is allowed on your Belly Fat Diet plan; however, excessive amounts can actually increase appetite and lower your willpower and resistance. To prevent this, limit yourself to one alcoholic beverage and save it for the end of the meal instead of the beginning to prevent overeating.

✔ **Keep an eye on your speed.** In restaurants, paying more attention to the distractions around you instead of the food itself is easy. But these distractions can lead to mindless eating. To prevent this, focus on slowly chewing each bite at least ten times. Keep in mind that it takes 20 minutes to recognize your stomach is full. By eating slowly, you give yourself a chance to recognize your body's cues of satiety before you overeat.

Staying motivated

Weight loss is a journey — it takes time to achieve your long-term goals. During this journey, you need to stay motivated or you may find yourself struggling with boredom, which can lead to cravings and the desire to get off track.

So, how can you motivate yourself to help you stay on course until you achieve your ultimate goal? Here are a few suggestions:

✔ **Focus on making lifestyle changes.** You are *not* on a diet. Slip-ups are allowed and even encouraged from time to time. You don't need to be perfect. If you get off track, just get yourself back on track at the next meal or snack. *Remember:* You don't have to be perfect to achieve your goals.

✔ **Prevent boredom.** If you eat the same meals and same snacks day after day, it gets old. And if you get sick of the foods you're eating, you stop enjoying them. This is a recipe for food cravings — especially for less-than-healthy choices. To prevent this, mix up your meal plan! Try a new recipe from this book. Give your favorite meal or dessert a Belly Fat Diet makeover, and enjoy it on occasion.

✔ **Change up your tried-and-true meals and snacks.** Just by adding a dash of flavor or a change in texture, you can satisfy your taste buds and significantly decrease boredom with your eating plan. Try using seasonings and spices you may not always use, such as cinnamon on your fruit or cereal and garlic or hot peppers on your chicken. To vary texture, change your standard snack of yogurt topped with fruit for a blended smoothie instead. Or switch from the standard dry morning cereal to a cooked option, such as oatmeal or quinoa.

Part II
Belly-Blasting Main Courses

The Leanest Protein Choices		
Protein Source (3 ounces)	*Calories*	*Total Fat (g)*
Turkey breast, boneless, skinless	115	0.6
Cod	89	0.7
Tuna, light, canned in water	99	0.7
Halibut	94	1.4
Pork tenderloin	122	3.0
Chicken breast, boneless, skinless	140	3.0
Beef, eye round roast and steak	133	4.0
Beef, top round roast	169	4.3
Beef, top sirloin steak	151	5.0
Beef, ground, 93% lean	154	6.8

Find out more about the top belly fat–fighting foods in an article at www.dummies.com/extras/flatbellycookbook.

In this part . . .

- ✔ Find the best way to shed belly fat with breakfast, lunch, and dinner.
- ✔ Learn the secrets to lunch-box success.
- ✔ Discover healthy ways to prepare poultry, meat, and seafood.
- ✔ Find delicious comfort foods that burn belly fat.

Chapter 6

Breakfast

The key to feeling your best and finding the healthy weight that is right for you is to eat regularly throughout the day. Feeding your body well begins at breakfast. For sustainable energy, make sure to include a variety of food groups at each meal — fruits, vegetables, proteins, whole grains, and dairy. This way of eating not only helps to boost your metabolism, but also helps control appetite and cravings. When you get too hungry, warding off the chocolate chip cookies or second helpings is almost impossible. Eating more than your body needs at one sitting is the biggest culprit of weight gain and the accumulation of belly fat. That's why breakfast is so critical to your success with your Belly Fat Diet plan. If you skip breakfast, you're setting yourself up for fatigue, cravings, and overeating later on in the day.

We know breakfast can be hard to fit in. Maybe you aren't a morning person and you like to hit the snooze button a few times, or maybe you just don't feel hungry in the morning. But we're willing to bet if your stomach isn't growling when you wake up, it's because you've trained it to respond that way, or because you overate the night before and you still feel bloated and full. Start incorporating breakfast in your diet to get started on the right track and a healthy pattern of eating. In this chapter, we offer some quick and delicious breakfast recipes that you can make in a hurry (or the night before) to start your day off right.

Breakfast truly is the most important meal of the day and a must if you want to successfully shed belly fat once and for all. This chapter proves that there are no excuses for not eating a healthy breakfast every day. Besides, when you taste these recipes and feel how your body responds, you'll be looking forward to breakfast so much, you won't *want* to skip it!

Got Dairy?

One easy food group to get in at breakfast is dairy. Not only is dairy an excellent source of bone-building calcium and protein to keep you satisfied, but it may actually help to promote weight loss because of a fatty acid called *conjugated linoleic acid* (CLA), which is found mainly in dairy and beef and has recently been gaining attention for its potential aid in weight loss.

Choosing the right type of dairy is important. Your best bet when looking in the dairy section is to opt for low-fat dairy milk, yogurt, and cheese. You don't need anything higher in fat than 1 percent milk. Over time, high levels of saturated fat in the diet can clog arteries and trigger an increase in inflammation. (The only exception to this 1 percent rule: children under the age of 2, who need that extra fat.)

Lactose intolerant?

If you can't tolerate dairy, no problem! A variety of healthy options can stand in for cow milk. Soymilk is most comparable in nutrition to cow milk, but you can try other options as well. Unsweetened versions are the healthiest options, but if you prefer a little sweeter taste, choose a brand with less than 10 g of sugar per cup.

Here are some options to consider if you prefer not to drink cow milk:

✔ **Soymilk:** Soymilk is made from the whole soybean, a plant protein that is naturally low in saturated fat and has zero cholesterol. Soy is a complete protein, meaning it has all nine of the essential amino acids in the right quantities, like animal proteins do. Soymilk is very similar in nutrition to low-fat cow milk because it contains calcium, vitamin D, and protein. You can swap soymilk for milk in creamy soups and mashed potatoes; it also tastes delicious in baked goods.

✔ **Almond milk:** Unsweetened almond milk has a nutty taste, a light feel, and very few calories — usually 25 percent less calories than skim milk. Almond milk is made from — you guessed it! — almonds. It's high in calcium and low in fat, yet contains an insignificant amount of protein. To slash calories but not flavor, stir almond milk into your latte or smoothie.

✔ **Coconut milk:** Coconut milk is made from the white pulp of the coconut and is mixed with water, vitamins, and minerals. Coconut milk is a smoothie and mixer sensation! It's also yummy in puddings, oatmeal, baked desserts, and Asian-inspired meals like coconut curry noodle bowls or coconut rice.

✔ **Lactose-free milk:** *Lactose-free* doesn't mean *dairy-free*. In fact, many people who can't tolerate lactose (the sugar found in milk) can still drink cow milk. Lactose-free milk is milk without the sugar lactose, but it still contains all the key nutrients found in cow milk, like calcium, protein, vitamin D, and potassium, to name just a few.

Greek Yogurt Banana Pancakes

Prep time: 5 min • **Cook time:** 15 min • **Yield:** 12 pancakes

Ingredients	Directions
1 cup spelt flour	*1* In a large bowl, whisk the flour, baking soda, baking powder, and cinnamon. Set aside.
¼ teaspoon baking soda	
1 teaspoon baking powder	
¼ teaspoon cinnamon	*2* In a small bowl, mash the banana and stir in the Greek yogurt. Set aside.
1 over-ripe banana	
1 cup nonfat plain Greek yogurt	*3* In a medium bowl, whisk the eggs. Add the banana and Greek yogurt mixture to the eggs, and stir until combined. Add the almond milk and stir until incorporated.
2 eggs	
¾ cup vanilla almond milk	
¼ cup walnuts, chopped	*4* Pour the liquids into the bowl with the flour, and gently fold until just incorporated, taking care not to overmix.
½ cup fresh blueberries	
½ teaspoon butter	*5* Stir in the walnuts and blueberries.
	6 Heat a nonstick skillet or electric skillet over medium-low heat, and coat the skillet with the butter. ***Note:*** Only coat the skillet with butter for the first batch.
	7 Pour ¼ cup of the pancake batter the skillet and heat until bubbly and golden brown, about 2 to 2½ minutes.
	8 Flip the pancake with a flat-sided spatula and cook an additional 30 seconds to 1 minute.

Per pancake: *Calories 76 (From Fat 19); Fat 2g (Saturated 0g); Cholesterol 0mg; Sodium 74mg; Carbohydrate 12g (Dietary Fiber 2g); Protein 3g.*

Tip: You'll know that your pancake is ready to flip when you see little bubbles on the surface.

Tip: Make extra pancakes on the weekend, and freeze the leftovers! They reheat quickly in the microwave, and you'll have a homemade, no-fuss breakfast in a flash.

Note: Spelt flour is a whole grain, giving you whole-food nutrition, as well as more fiber, vitamins, and minerals. Spelt flour is ideal for baking because it has a soft texture and a nutty flavor.

Warm Cinnamon Quinoa Cereal

Prep time: 2 min • **Cook time:** 16 min • **Yield:** 4 servings

Ingredients	*Directions*
1 cup water	*1* In a small saucepan, bring the water, soymilk, quinoa, and banana to a boil. Reduce the heat to low, cover, and simmer until the liquid is almost absorbed, about 14 minutes.
1 cup low-fat plain soymilk	
1 cup quinoa, pre-rinsed	
1 banana, mashed	
¼ teaspoon ground cinnamon, plus more for topping	*2* Stir in the cinnamon, and continue to cook uncovered until all the liquid is absorbed, about 2 minutes.
1 cup fresh blueberries, rinsed and drained, for topping	*3* Serve with a sprinkle of cinnamon and top each serving with ¼ cup blueberries and 2 tablespoons walnuts.
½ cup walnut halves, for topping	

Per serving: Calories 319 (From Fat 118); Fat 13g (Saturated 1g); Cholesterol 0mg; Sodium 33mg; Carbohydrate 43g (Dietary Fiber 6g); Protein 10g.

Vary It! No quinoa in the pantry? Use old-fashioned oats, and this recipe will revolutionize your typical bowl of oatmeal.

What is quinoa?

Quinoa (*keen*-wah) is an ancient grain (technically, a seed) found in South America. It dates back over 5,000 years to the Inca Empire. The Incas considered quinoa sacred and called it the "mother grain." Although this ancient grain has been around for millennia, it has recently become more popular in our culture. From a nutrition standpoint, quinoa is a superfood because it has a host of nutritional perks packed into one tiny seed:

✔ It's a complete protein, providing all the essential amino acids in a balanced form.

✔ It has more protein than any other whole grain.

✔ It has good-quality fiber. Fiber is filling, keeping you fuller longer, so you eat less. It can also help to reduce cholesterol, stabilize blood sugar, and promote digestive health.

✔ It's a good source of iron, which can be troublesome to get for pre-menopausal women or for those following a vegetarian diet.

✔ It's gluten-free, which is great news for anyone who has celiac disease or sensitivity to gluten.

Probably the best reason to eat quinoa is that it has a wonderful, light-tasting flavor and is truly effortless to prepare. Try it out in any recipe in which rice or couscous would be used.

Veggies for Breakfast!

Getting enough vegetables throughout the day isn't always easy. In fact, most people aren't even coming close to their daily goal, which is at least 3 cups of vegetables. (Only 6 percent of people are hitting that target!) Poor consumption of vegetables may lead to increased risk of heart disease, high blood pressure, and cancer, as well as weight gain and increased belly fat.

Start getting your veggies first thing in the morning, with breakfast. Aim for 1 cup of vegetables at the start of your day to help you reach your nutrition goals.

All vegetables are packed with fiber, which lowers bad cholesterol, stabilizes blood sugar, and aids in digestion. But not all vegetables are created equal as far as nutrients go. Phytonutrients are plant compounds found in the many colors of vegetables, and they've been shown to be essential in keeping the body in tip-top shape. Phytonutrients work synergistically with the whole plant to prevent disease, so you can't just take a phytonutrient supplement.

Instead of eating the same produce all the time, aim to diversify your veggie palate to get the most nutrient benefits. One way to do that is to try to eat a variety of different-colored veggies. Table 6-1 gets you started.

If you're looking for even more ideas for ways to incorporate veggies into your breakfast, beyond the recipes in this chapter, try sautéing them and combining with eggs for breakfast. Some great options for sautéing include broccoli, mushrooms, onions, peppers, kale, and Swiss chard. You can also opt for a breakfast salad, loaded with veggies. Not sure about salad for breakfast? Try the Blueberry Breakfast Salad recipe, later in this chapter!

Other great ways to get more vegetables are juices and smoothies. Reach for 100 percent vegetable juice or make your own. You can juice beets, carrots, celery, lemon, lime, and more! And pack smoothies with beets or greens and your favorite fruits. Use light-colored fruits like bananas, green grapes, kiwi, peaches, and pineapples to make your smoothie pop with color when you add the beets or greens.

Check out *Juicing & Smoothies For Dummies,* by Pat Crocker (Wiley), for lots of great tips and recipes.

Table 6-1	Examples of Vegetables by Color			
Red	**Yellow/ Orange**	**Green**	**White**	**Blue/Purple**
Beets	Acorn squash	Artichokes	Cauliflower	Black olives
Red onions	Butternut squash	Arugula	Garlic	Blue or purple potatoes
Radicchio	Carrots	Asparagus	Ginger	Eggplant
Radishes	Orange bell peppers	Broccoli	Jicama	Purple cabbage
Red bell peppers	Pattypan squash	Brussels sprouts	Kohlrabi	Purple carrots
Red potatoes	Pumpkins	Cucumbers	Leeks	Purple endive
Rhubarb	Rutabagas	Endive	Mushrooms	
Tomatoes	Spaghetti squash	Green beans	Onions	
	Sweet corn	Green bell peppers	Parsnips	
	Sweet potatoes	Green onions	Potatoes	
	Yellow beets	Kale	Shallots	
	Yellow bell peppers	Lettuce	Turnips	
	Yellow crookneck squash	Peas	White corn	
	Yellow potatoes	Spinach		
	Yellow tomatoes	Zucchini		

Swiss Chard and Mushroom Frittata

Prep time: 10 min • **Cook time:** 35 min • **Yield:** 6 servings

Ingredients	*Directions*
½ teaspoon plus 1 tablespoon olive oil	*1* Preheat the oven to 400 degrees.
1 cup chopped leeks, well rinsed	*2* In a 12-inch ovenproof, nonstick skillet, heat ½ teaspoon of olive oil over medium-high heat. Sauté the leeks, mushrooms, and peppers until softened, about 8 minutes.
1 cup thinly sliced mushrooms	
1 cup diced red bell peppers	
1 cup chopped Swiss chard, leaves only	*3* Add the Swiss chard, mint, and salt, and cook for 2 more minutes. Turn off the heat.
1 tablespoon chopped fresh mint	*4* In a large bowl, whisk the eggs. Add the milk, and whisk until combined. Combine the cooked vegetables in the bowl with the eggs.
⅛ teaspoon kosher salt	
10 eggs	*5* In a clean 12-inch ovenproof, nonstick skillet, heat 1 tablespoon of olive oil over medium heat and add the frittata mixture.
½ cup nonfat milk	
¼ cup reduced-fat feta cheese	*6* Sprinkle the cheese on top of the frittata.
	7 Cook the frittata on the stovetop for 10 minutes, occasionally releasing the eggs on the side of the pan to allow the uncooked mixture to move to the bottom of the pan.
	8 When the frittata is halfway set, place the pan in the oven for 15 minutes or until the frittata is browned, bubbly, and cooked through.
	9 Serve warm.

Per serving: Calories 94 (From Fat 39); Fat 4g (Saturated 1g); Cholesterol 6mg; Sodium 213mg; Carbohydrate 6g (Dietary Fiber 1g); Protein 9g.

Tip: This recipe is delicious reheated, so you can make it in advance on the weekend and enjoy a quick breakfast on a busy weekday morning. Store it in a resealable plastic bag or airtight container in the refrigerator for up to 3 days.

Breakfast Burrito Bowl

Prep time: 5 min • **Cook time:** 25 min • **Yield:** 4 servings

Ingredients	Directions
1½ tablespoons canola oil	**1** In a 12-inch nonstick skillet, heat 1 tablespoon of the oil over medium heat until hot.
2 cups shredded refrigerated hash browns, no salt added	**2** Add the hash browns to the skillet and spread evenly on the pan, pressing down gently with a spatula to flatten.
1 red bell pepper, stemmed, seeded, and diced	**3** Cook 6 to 7 minutes, or until golden brown on the bottom.
1 yellow onion, diced	
1 cup reduced-sodium canned black beans	**4** Flip the hash browns over and cook an additional 6 to 7 minutes, until browned and crispy. Remove the hash browns from the skillet.
4 eggs	
1 cup shredded Monterey Jack cheese	**5** In the skillet, heat the remaining ½ tablespoon of oil over medium heat. Add the pepper and onion, and sauté until tender.
¼ cup fresh salsa	
1 lime, segmented (optional)	**6** Add the black beans, and cook until warmed. Remove the vegetable mixture from the pan, and set aside.
	7 In a small bowl, whisk the eggs and pour into the skillet. Cook until fully scrambled.
	8 To serve, layer the hash browns, vegetables, eggs, cheese, and salsa. Serve with a squeeze of lime juice if desired.

Per serving: Calories 342 (From Fat 134); Fat 15g (Saturated 6g); Cholesterol 25mg; Sodium 357mg; Carbohydrate 39g (Dietary Fiber 7g); Protein 17g.

Blueberry Breakfast Salad

Prep time: 30 min • **Yield:** 4 servings

Ingredients	*Directions*
Blueberry Vinaigrette (see the following recipe)	*1* Toss the salad greens with ¾ cup of the Blueberry Vinaigrette.
1 pound mixed torn salad greens	*2* Divide the dressed greens among 4 large plates.
2 cups orange sections or canned mandarin oranges, drained	*3* Arrange ½ cup of the orange sections and ½ cup of the blueberries on top of each salad.
2 cups fresh blueberries	*4* Sprinkle each salad with ¼ cup granola.
1 cup granola	*5* Drizzle the remaining dressing on top.
	6 Serve immediately.

Blueberry Vinaigrette

½ **cup olive oil**	*1* In a food processor, combine all the ingredients. Process until the mixture is smooth, and chill at least 30 minutes to blend the flavors.
½ **cup frozen unsweetened blueberries, thawed**	
½ **tablespoon Dijon mustard**	
1 tablespoon brown sugar	
1 teaspoon minced shallot	
¼ **teaspoon kosher salt**	
¼ **teaspoon ground white pepper**	
¼ **teaspoon paprika**	

Per serving: Calories 507 (From Fat 316); Fat 35g (Saturated 5g); Cholesterol 0mg; Sodium 208mg; Carbohydrate 45g (Dietary Fiber 9g); Protein 8g.

Note: This recipe is reproduced from www.blueberrycouncil.org. Reproduced with the permission of the U.S. Highbush Blueberry Council.

Breakfast on the Go

Research shows that those who eat breakfast consume fewer calories throughout the day than people who skip breakfast. In addition, your metabolic rate decreases when you skip breakfast. Breakfast is meant to *break* the *fast* from your slumber and kick your metabolism into gear, allowing you to be more effective and productive in your daily activities and with following your Belly Fat Diet plan.

Despite your best intentions, sometimes you just don't have enough time to sit down and eat breakfast. Mornings are so rushed, what with taking care of the kids, walking the dog, packing lunches, working out, getting dressed for the day, and so on. But we have good news! You can still enjoy a healthy breakfast despite a hectic morning routine. You just have to plan ahead for a breakfast on the run. Having a well-stocked pantry and fridge is essential for breakfast success.

In addition to the recipes in this section, here are some on-the-go breakfast ideas:

- Toasted whole-grain waffle or English muffin with nut butter
- Low-fat Greek yogurt with berries
- Fresh fruit and a hard-boiled egg
- Oatmeal, nuts, and fruit
- Whole-grain cereal and string cheese
- Breakfast burrito
- Peanut butter and jelly sandwich
- String cheese, an apple, and 100 percent vegetable juice

Microwave Egg Sandwich

Prep time: 2 min • **Cook time:** 1 min • **Yield:** 1 sandwich

Ingredients	*Directions*
One 100 percent whole-wheat English muffin	*1* Slice the English muffin in half and toast.
1 egg	*2* Coat a microwave-safe coffee mug with cooking spray and crack the egg into the mug.
2 tablespoons reduced-fat shredded cheddar cheese	*3* With a fork, whisk the egg and sprinkle with cheese.
1 teaspoon strawberry preserves	*4* Cover the coffee mug with a paper towel and place in the microwave for 60 seconds, or until cooked through.
1 teaspoon whipped butter spread	*5* Smear the butter and jelly on the muffin, and sandwich the egg between both sides of the English muffin.

Per serving: *Calories 238 (From Fat 47); Fat 5g (Saturated 3g); Cholesterol 11mg; Sodium 503mg; Carbohydrate 36g (Dietary Fiber 4g); Protein 14g.*

Tip: Wrap the sandwich in foil and take it with you in the car.

Vary It! Swap your English muffin for a 100 percent whole-grain bagel thin for an easy twist on this breakfast favorite.

Vary It! Add chopped spinach to the egg mixture to get your veggie servings at breakfast.

Cheesy Jalapeño Egg White Poppers

Prep time: 5 min • **Cook time:** 35 min • **Yield:** 24 poppers

Ingredients	Directions
1 teaspoon olive oil	**1** Preheat the oven to 350 degrees.
½ red bell pepper, diced	**2** In a medium skillet, heat the olive oil over medium heat.
½ small red onion, diced	
1 cup spinach, chopped	**3** Sauté the bell pepper and onion until softened. Add the spinach, salt, and pepper, and cook until wilted. Stir in the cilantro.
⅛ teaspoon kosher salt	
A pinch of pepper	
2 tablespoons chopped cilantro	**4** Remove from the heat and stir in the cheddar cheese.
3 ounces jalapeño cheddar cheese, very small dice	**5** Liberally coat a 24-count nonstick mini muffin pan with cooking spray.
1½ cups 100 percent egg whites	**6** Evenly distribute the vegetable mixture into the muffin cups.
	7 Pour the egg whites into each muffin cup until filled to the edge.
	8 Bake 20 to 25 minutes, until puffed and the eggs are fully set.

Per serving: Calories 25 (From Fat 13); Fat 1g (Saturated 1g); Cholesterol 4mg; Sodium 64mg; Carbohydrate 1g (Dietary Fiber 0g); Protein 3g.

Vary It! Not a jalapeño fan? No worries. Simply sub in your favorite cheese instead.

Tip: Make a batch of these poppers, and you can enjoy them all week. Just store in the refrigerator in a resealable plastic bag for up to 3 days.

Lemon Berry Muffins

Prep time: 15 min • **Cook time:** 18 min • **Yield:** 12 muffins

Ingredients	*Directions*
2 cups spelt flour	*1* Preheat the oven to 400 degrees.
½ cup sugar	
1 teaspoon baking powder	*2* In a large bowl, whisk the flour, sugar, baking powder, baking soda, salt, and cinnamon. Set aside.
½ teaspoon baking soda	
½ teaspoon kosher salt	*3* In a separate bowl, whisk the egg. Then whisk in the almond milk, oil, lemon zest, and 1 tablespoon of the lemon juice. Set aside.
¼ teaspoon cinnamon	
1 egg	
1¼ cups unsweetened vanilla almond milk	*4* In another bowl, place the berries. Add 2 tablespoons of the flour mixture to the bowl, and toss to coat the berries.
¼ cup canola oil	
1 tablespoon packed lemon zest	*5* Add the liquid mixture to the dry ingredients, and gently mix until just incorporated, being sure not to overmix. Toss in the berries coated in flour, and mix just until combined.
3 tablespoons lemon juice	
1 cup frozen mixed berries (blueberries and raspberries only)	*6* Coat a 12-count nonstick muffin pan with cooking spray, or line with muffin papers.
	7 Spoon the batter evenly into the muffin cups and bake for 18 minutes, or until a toothpick inserted in the middle is clean. Allow the muffins to cool in the pan on a wire rack for 5 minutes.
	8 Remove the muffins from the pan and place them individually on a wire rack.
	9 Using a pastry brush, spread the remaining lemon juice evenly on top of the muffins.

Per serving: Calories 151 (From Fat 49); Fat 5g (Saturated 0g); Cholesterol 0mg; Sodium 210mg; Carbohydrate 23g (Dietary Fiber 3g); Protein 3g.

Note: Spelt flour is a whole grain, giving you whole-food nutrition, as well as more fiber, vitamins, and minerals. Spelt flour is ideal for baking because it has a soft texture and a nutty flavor.

Sunrise Protein Shake

Prep time: 2 min • **Cook time:** 1 min • **Yield:** 2 servings

Ingredients	Directions
1 frozen banana 1 cup frozen unsweetened strawberries 2 tablespoons unsweetened whey protein powder	*1* Break up the banana into chunks, and place it in a blender along with the strawberries and protein powder.
1 cup almond milk ½ cup 100 percent orange juice	*2* Add the milk and orange juice to the blender and blend until smooth and creamy. *3* Serve with a straw.

Per serving: Calories 195 (From Fat 29); Fat 3g (Saturated 1g); Cholesterol 30mg; Sodium 129mg; Carbohydrate 34g (Dietary Fiber 5g); Protein 11g.

Tip: Whey protein powder is an excellent addition to smoothies. It provides balanced nutrition instead of using only fruit. It also lends a creamier, fluffier texture to smoothies. This protein shake can be enjoyed as an energy-packed breakfast on the go.

Note: Frozen fruit is key to smoothie success. When you use frozen fruit, you don't need to add ice, which only waters down the flavor of the drink. Frozen fruit locks in the natural sweetness, too, so you won't need added or artificial sweeteners.

Mango-Pineapple Overnight Oatmeal

Prep time: 5 min • **Cook time:** 2 min • **Yield:** 2 servings

Ingredients	Directions
½ cup old-fashioned oats	**1** In a bowl, mix the oats, chia seeds, coconut water, and water. Cover, place the bowl in the refrigerator, and let sit overnight.
1 tablespoon chia seeds	
1 cup ZICO Pure Premium Coconut Water	
1 cup water	**2** In the morning, microwave the mixture for 1½ minutes or until the desired temperature is reached.
1 cup mango, cubed	
1 tablespoon shredded coconut	**3** Top with mango and shredded coconut. Serve warm.

Per serving: Calories 199 (From Fat 41); Fat 5g (Saturated 1g); Cholesterol 0mg; Sodium 32mg; Carbohydrate 38g (Dietary Fiber 6g); Protein 4g.

Note: If you prefer, you can serve this chilled instead of heating it in the microwave.

Chapter 7

Brown-Bag Lunches

In This Chapter

▶ Sidestepping lunchbox pitfalls

▶ Making healthy sandwiches and wraps

▶ Packing a belly-friendly salad

▶ Stepping outside the box

We've all been there: running out the door without breakfast, only to realize you don't a have a lunch in hand either. You may be thinking to yourself, "I'll just have to grab lunch out" or even "I guess I'll skip lunch today."

When people think about what they need to do to eat healthy, they often assume they have to resort to eating salads all day. Although salads make up an important part of a healthy diet (and you'll find lots of yummy salad recipes in this chapter), eating healthy is about more than noshing on lettuce. In fact, if you look up the nutrition information for salads at many restaurants, salads may be among the most unhealthful items on the menu, often because they're loaded down with high-fat cheeses, meats, and creamy dressings.

Eating healthy begins at home. At home, you're in the driver's seat. You can pick the foods that promote health and well-being. When you're dining out, knowing if you're being served a lean cut of meat or reduced-fat cheese is often difficult. You don't know how much salt the chef used or if she was heavy-handed with the oil or butter when sautéing. Eating out every now and then is okay, and you have to do your best to eat nutritionally when you do. But with so many unknowns on the menu, dining out should be the exception rather than the rule.

So, that means that packing a lunch is key for maintaining a healthy weight and achieving your health goals! Here's the good news: You don't have to spend countless hours in the kitchen to eat healthy on the run. In this chapter, we give you simple and quick recipes for a brown-bag lunch. With the recipes in this chapter, you can't say you didn't have enough time to pack a lunch at home.

Avoiding Common Lunchbox Mistakes

Packing a successful lunch takes practice, planning, and patience, especially if you're the packer for a picky eater. Often, people get stuck in the routine of eating the same foods over and over again. Avoid the following common lunchbox mistakes and become a smarter brown bagger:

- ✔ **Not getting enough protein:** Protein has staying power because it takes longer to digest and keeps you satisfied longer. Squeeze in protein in the form of beans, yogurt, cottage cheese, string cheese, deli meats, tofu, leftover meats, veggie burgers, and rotisserie chicken.

- ✔ **Not planning for snacks:** Snacks are meant to bridge the gap between meals, but if you don't pack them, you'll get too hungry and you may overeat later in the day or be tempted by less-than-healthy snacks from the vending machine.

- ✔ **Relying on potato chips:** Many people like their crunch midday, but it doesn't have to be in the form of greasy potato chips. Choose a new crunchy treat like nuts, whole-grain cereals, kale chips, roasted chickpeas, popcorn, baked corn chips, whole-grain crackers, or crispy fruits and vegetables.

- ✔ **Waiting until the last minute to think about lunch:** We all want to think we can pull something together at the last minute, but the reality is we can't. Pack your lunch the night before, especially if you're not a morning person. This way, you won't fall into the trap of not having enough time.

- ✔ **Not keeping your pantry and fridge stocked with healthy foods:** This pitfall is easy to avoid if you shop wisely. Keep simple ingredients on hand so you never run out. And make a list of the meals you'll make for the week ahead and check to be sure you have all the ingredients before you head to the grocery store.

- ✔ **Not making enough for leftovers:** If you're cooking dinner, double the recipe so that you have leftovers. Leftovers are the easiest lunch — no prep required. You can easily freeze individual portions for later, too. Think casseroles, soups, spaghetti and meatballs, pasta salad, or sides like roasted veggies.

- ✔ **Not having the right gear:** You need plenty of reusable containers of all shapes and sizes. Prep fruit salads and sides at the beginning of the week and place them in individual containers or resealable plastic bags so you can just grab a bag and toss it in your lunchbox. When making salads, place the dressing in a separate small container to keep the greens from getting soggy.

- ✔ **Not packing enough produce:** Produce is key, so don't skimp! Fill up on the good stuff by packing a salad and choosing fruit for snacks.

That's a Wrap! Sandwiches and Wraps

When you're brown-bagging it day after day, the typical sandwich can get boring. Plus, it may be loaded with belly-busting condiments and spreads. But not to worry — in this section, we reinvent the sandwich and wrap to get you excited about packing your lunch again!

Sandwiches and wraps are quick and easy, and they travel well, which makes them ideal for brown-bag lunches. Here are some tips for building a better sandwich:

✔ **Choose a healthy bread.** Opt for breads made from 100 percent whole grains like wheat, rye, pumpernickel, spelt, sprouted grains, and nuts and seeds. These types of bread are packed with fiber, vitamins, and minerals, and they don't have the refined carbs you find in white bread and other breads that aren't whole grain.

✔ **Focus on lean proteins.** Look for low-sodium deli meats, rotisserie chicken breast, tofu, beans, eggs, veggie patties, and nut butters.

✔ **Don't pass up cheese.** Adding cheese to your sandwich ups the calcium and gets you closer to your daily quota. Just keep portions in check, and choose real, part-skim cheeses for less fat and calories.

✔ **Hold the mayo.** Instead of dousing your sandwich with unhealthy fats and excessive calories, give yourself more nutrients with hummus, vegetable oil–based salad dressings, balsamic vinegar, pesto, avocado, Greek yogurt, and spicy mustard.

✔ **Top it off with vegetables and herbs.** Layer on the tomatoes, onions, peppers, sprouts, lettuce, mushrooms, cucumber, and eggplant. When it comes to veggie toppings, the more the better! Also, try fresh herbs like basil, mint, or cilantro to give your sandwich more flavor and antioxidants.

Black Bean Veggie Wrap

Prep time: 10 min • **Yield:** 4 servings

Ingredients	*Directions*
One 14.5-ounce can reduced-sodium black beans	**1** Rinse and drain the beans and place them in a food processor. Add the salsa to the food processor and process until smooth.
3 tablespoons fresh salsa, medium heat	
Four 10-inch whole-wheat tortillas	**2** Heat the tortillas in the microwave for 15 to 20 seconds until they're soft.
2 cups baby spinach	
1 tomato, diced	**3** Spread ¼ of the black bean dip on one tortilla. Layer the tortilla with ½ cup of the spinach, ¼ of the tomato, ¼ cup of the carrots, ¼ of the red pepper, and ¼ of the avocado slices.
1 cup matchstick carrots	
½ red bell pepper, sliced	
1 avocado, sliced	**4** Fold the sides of the tortilla in 1 inch. Then roll together to form a wrap.
	5 Repeat Steps 3 and 4 with the remaining tortillas.

Per serving: Calories 370 (From Fat 80); Fat 9g (Saturated 1g); Cholesterol 0mg; Sodium 630mg; Carbohydrate 66g (Dietary Fiber 15g); Protein 14g.

Note: Black beans are so good for you because they're rich in filling fiber and protein. They're also an economical protein source, and they make a great lunch protein because of their simplicity and portability.

Protein on the go

Adding the right proteins to your diet is necessary to build lean muscle mass and may help trim your waistline. Proteins don't have to be high maintenance — you may be surprised to learn that many of them travel well and don't need heating! Try these combinations for a protein-rich twist on the traditional sandwich.

✔ Low-sodium deli turkey, thinly sliced green apple, low-fat cheddar cheese, honey mustard, and whole-grain bread

✔ Peanut butter, sliced strawberries, sliced almonds, and whole-grain bread

✔ Rotisserie chicken, roasted vegetables, hummus, feta crumbles, and whole-grain pita

✔ Hardboiled eggs, carrot sticks, whole-grain pita, fresh pineapple, and almonds

Egg Salad Sandwiches

Prep time: 10 min • **Cook time:** 15 min • **Yield:** 4 servings

Ingredients	Directions
6 eggs	**1** In a medium pot, place the eggs and fill with water. Bring the water to a boil over high heat.
⅓ cup Greek yogurt	
½ teaspoon lemon juice	**2** Continue boiling for 5 minutes.
Pinch of pepper	
¼ cup green onion, thinly sliced	**3** Turn off the heat and cover, allowing the eggs to rest for 5 minutes.
1 celery stalk, thinly sliced	**4** Pour off the water, and cover the eggs with ice for 5 minutes.
1 tablespoon fresh dill, chopped	
8 large lettuce leaves	**5** Peel the eggs and place them in a medium bowl.
8 slices whole-wheat bread	**6** Smash the eggs with a fork and stir in the yogurt until a chunky paste is formed.
	7 Mix in the lemon juice and pepper to taste.
	8 Stir in the onion, celery, and dill until incorporated.
	9 Toast the bread, and serve the egg salad on the 2 slices of bread with 2 leaves of lettuce each.

Per serving: Calories 262 (From Fat 85); Fat 9g (Saturated 3g); Cholesterol 317mg; Sodium 388mg; Carbohydrate 25g (Dietary Fiber 4g); Protein 19g.

Vary It! Try serving egg salad over a bowl of lettuce greens.

Tip: This sandwich pairs well with fresh grapes or cherries as a side.

DIY Lunchables

Prep time: 5 min • **Yield:** 4 servings

Ingredients	Directions
4 ounces sliced low-fat Swiss cheese	***1*** Place one slice of cheese on a flat surface and stack a slice of turkey on top of the cheese. Roll the two up together to form a pinwheel, with the cheese on the outside. Repeat this step with all the remaining slices of cheese and turkey to form additional pinwheels.
8 ounces sliced low-sodium deli turkey	
1 cup cherries	
2 cups blueberries	***2*** In a medium bowl, combine the cherries, blueberries, and grapes and gently toss.
2 cups grapes	
1 cup baby spinach	***3*** Using a bento box or individual containers, evenly arrange the turkey and cheese roll-ups, the baby spinach, the pitas, the fruit mixture, and the dark chocolate.
Eight mini (2-inch diameter) whole-wheat pitas	
Four ½-ounce squares dark chocolate, 70 percent to 85 percent cacao	

Per serving: Calories 363 (From Fat 83); Fat 9g (Saturated 5g); Cholesterol 35mg; Sodium 671mg; Carbohydrate 48g (Dietary Fiber 7g); Protein 26g.

Vary It! Toss some roasted tofu or edamame into the mix for protein.

Tip: Always keep low-sodium deli meat and your favorite reduced-fat cheeses in the fridge for easy lunches.

More DIY lunchable ideas

Give lunch a wakeup call with a lunchable. You may be thinking, "Lunchables are for kids." Not anymore! We love lunchables for adults because they offer portion control and variety, both helping to prevent overeating. Instead of relying on store-bought versions that are processed and filled with chemically based ingredients, do it yourself! Pack a bento box using fresh ingredients for a well-balanced, adult-approved lunch that your body will thank you for.

Here are some ideas to get you started:

- Roll slices of lean deli meat and cheese in a Boston lettuce cup.

- Use flat sandwich rounds with marinara, sliced bell peppers, and mozzarella cheese for mini pizzas.

- Snack on fruit skewers, nuts and dried fruit, vegetables and hummus, and applesauce.

Sidling Up to a Salad

Salads make a yummy brown-bag lunch! It's not surprising that eating healthy includes salads, right? In fact, some research suggests that eating a salad before your meal can reduce caloric intake by 12 percent. A reason for this could be that the fiber in the salad can really fill you up, and it takes longer to eat a salad, giving you time to recognize that you're full.

But don't rush off to build your salad, before you consider the toppings. High-calorie toppings like the following will make a salad belly busting in no time, so use them in moderation:

Avocado	Croutons	Mayonnaise	Olives
Bacon	Dried fruit	Meats (fried or breaded)	Peas
Cheese	Guacamole	Nuts	Seeds
Corn	Hummus	Oil	Sour cream
Creamy dressings			

On the other hand, feel free to go crazy with the following toppings:

Apples	Broccoli	Grapes	Pears
Balsamic vinegar	Carrots	Lemon juice	Raspberries
Beets	Cauliflower	Lime juice	Sugar snap peas
Bell peppers	Fresh herbs	Mandarin oranges (fresh or canned in juice, not syrup)	Water chestnuts
Blueberries			

To keep your salad fresh until lunch, follow these suggestions:

- When packing a salad, keep the dressing separate, and mix just before eating.

- If items need to be warmed (for example, leftover chicken), store them in a separate container, so you can heat them up before you add them to your salad.

- Pack lettuce and veggies in a single-serving container. You can do this the night before to save time.

- Be sure to refrigerate your salad until you're ready to eat it.

Mediterranean Pasta Salad

Prep time: 20 min • **Cook time:** 12 min • **Yield:** 8 servings

Ingredients	Directions
13 ounces 100 percent whole-grain penne pasta	**1** Cook the pasta to al dente according to package directions. Drain and rinse with cold water to cool.
½ English cucumber, diced	
1 cup grape tomatoes, halved lengthwise	**2** In a large bowl, place the cucumber, tomatoes, onion, edamame, and watercress and mix together.
½ red onion, diced	
2 cups shelled edamame	**3** In a food processor, mince the garlic. Add the artichokes and basil and process until blended.
1 cup watercress, stems removed and roughly chopped	
3 large cloves garlic	**4** In a liquid measuring cup, pour the lemon juice and olive oil.
½ cup frozen artichoke hearts, defrosted	**5** Stream the olive oil mixture into the food processor while it's running and process until it's incorporated.
¼ cup fresh basil	
1 lemon, juiced	**6** Pour the cold pasta into the large bowl with the vegetables, but don't mix.
¼ cup olive oil	
½ cup reduced-fat feta cheese	**7** Drizzle the artichoke dressing on top of the pasta and mix with the pasta first. Then toss the vegetables on the bottom into the dressed pasta.
Pinch of pepper	
	8 Top the pasta with the feta cheese and pepper and gently stir. Refrigerate until ready to eat.

Per serving: Calories 380 (From Fat 145); Fat 16g (Saturated 4g); Cholesterol 15mg; Sodium 444mg; Carbohydrate 43g (Dietary Fiber 4g); Protein 22g.

Vary It! Add ½ cup chopped black olives to this pasta for more olive flavor!

Note: Edamame is an immature green soybean that provides an excellent fiber and protein punch.

Fiesta Chicken Salad

Prep time: 5 min • **Yield:** 1 serving

Ingredients	*Directions*
2 cups mixed salad greens	*1* In a to-go container, layer the salad greens, brown rice, chicken, beans, and bell peppers.
⅓ cup precooked brown rice	
¼ cup shredded rotisserie chicken	*2* Top with the salsa, avocado, and yogurt.
¼ cup canned reduced-sodium black beans, rinsed and drained	*3* Squeeze lime juice on top of the salad before eating.
¼ cup diced red bell pepper	
2 tablespoons salsa	
¼ avocado, diced (see Figure 7-1)	
1 tablespoon nonfat Greek yogurt	
1 lime wedge	

Per serving: Calories 308 (From Fat 91); Fat 10g (Saturated 2g); Cholesterol 26mg; Sodium 357mg; Carbohydrate 39g (Dietary Fiber 11g); Protein 20g.

Tip: Purchase precooked rotisserie chicken, and shred the meat off the bone for easy grab-'n'-go.

Tip: After topping with the dressing, place a lid on the container and give it a shake to help coat all the ingredients.

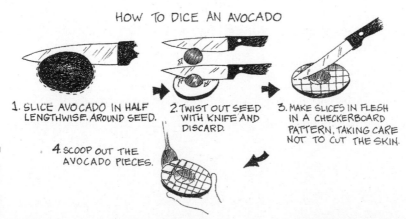

HOW TO DICE AN AVOCADO

1. SLICE AVOCADO IN HALF LENGTHWISE. AROUND SEED.

2. TWIST OUT SEED WITH KNIFE AND DISCARD.

3. MAKE SLICES IN FLESH IN A CHECKERBOARD PATTERN, TAKING CARE NOT TO CUT THE SKIN.

4. SCOOP OUT THE AVOCADO PIECES.

Figure 7-1: Dicing an avocado.

Illustration by Elizabeth Kurtzman

BLT Salad

Prep time: 15 min • **Yield:** 4 servings

Ingredients

1 tablespoon nonfat plain Greek yogurt

1 tablespoon honey

1 lime, juiced

1/16 teaspoon paprika

1/4 cup extra-virgin olive oil

8 cups romaine lettuce

8 ounces deli turkey, sliced and diced

1 cup cherry tomatoes, diced

1/2 red onion, thinly sliced

1 avocado, diced (refer to Figure 7-1)

8 strips Canadian bacon, cooked and crumbled

Directions

1 To prepare the dressing, pour the yogurt, honey, lime, paprika, and olive oil into a large bowl, and whisk ingredients together until smooth.

2 Pour the dressing into small to-go containers.

3 Assemble the salad into containers by placing the lettuce on the bottom, and topping with turkey, tomatoes, onions, avocado, and bacon.

Per serving: Calories 396 (From Fat 235); Fat 26g (Saturated 5g); Cholesterol 52mg; Sodium 991mg; Carbohydrate 16g (Dietary Fiber 6g); Protein 27g.

Note: Wait to mix the dressing with the salad until you're ready to eat it, or the lettuce will get soggy.

Tip: Need it faster? Use a store-bought dressing like balsamic vinaigrette, and prep this salad in less than 5 minutes!

Going green with salads

Salads should never be boring! Get creative by using a variety of greens to enhance flavor and nutrition. After all, not all greens are created equal! Here are our suggestions:

✔ **Baby spinach:** The sweet flavor of baby spinach makes a refreshing salad filled with iron and vitamin A.

✔ **Arugula:** Peppery in flavor, arugula is loaded with vitamins A and C.

✔ **Dandelion greens:** These edible weeds are fiber filled and packed with antioxidants. Mix into salads for a slightly bitter and tangy flavor.

✔ **Kale:** All varieties of kale are antioxidant rich. Plus, kale is one of the best sources of vitamin A around.

✔ **Beet greens:** Supplement your salad with these calcium-rich greens for a spicy flavor boost.

Getting Creative with Lunch

You probably wouldn't send your kids off to school with just a measly sandwich for lunch — they need fruits, veggies, milk, and snacks, right? Well, you do, too! So, sometimes you need to think outside the sandwich box, so to speak, and get creative with foods that you love in order to make lunch interesting again.

If you want to feel better, you need to keep your energy levels high during the day by eating mini meals or snacks about every three to four hours. So, planning ahead when you pack your lunch is key! Here are our favorite sides and snacks that make lunch more creative:

✔ Roasted anything (for example, cauliflower, sweet potato, tofu, broccoli, green beans, beets, chickpeas, or kale chips)

✔ Low-fat string cheese or cheese cubes

✔ Popcorn (as long as it's not loaded with butter and salt)

✔ Side salad with tomato, cucumber, and shredded carrots

✔ Hummus and veggies like red bell pepper, carrots, grape tomatoes, sugar snap peas, and broccoli

✔ Baked corn chips and salsa

- Baked sweet potato or regular potato
- Greek yogurt
- Edamame
- Whole-wheat crackers (like low-sodium Triscuits)
- Whole fruit and nut bars
- Cottage cheese with berries
- Homemade trail mix
- Dried fruit
- Unsweetened applesauce
- Unsalted nuts
- Whole-grain cereal
- Fruit like apple, banana, cherries, clementine, grapes, peach, pear, plum, or fresh fruit salad
- Healthy homemade whole-grain muffin (check out the Lemon Berry Muffin recipe in Chapter 6)
- Spaghetti squash

We think you'll find the meals in this section to be out of the box. Plus, they get you munching on extra doses of veggies!

Fruity Ham Skewers with Pumpkin Dip

Prep time: 10 min • **Yield:** 4 servings

Ingredients	Directions
12 ounces low-sodium ham, cubed	*1* On skewers, arrange the ham, pineapple, bananas, strawberries, and mango.
1 cup pineapple, cubed	
2 bananas, large dice	*2* In a small bowl, mix together the yogurt, pumpkin, pumpkin pie spice, and maple syrup until combined.
1 cup strawberries, tops removed	
1 cup mango, large dice	*3* Serve the skewers with a side of pumpkin dip.
½ cup nonfat plain Greek yogurt	
½ cup 100 percent pure pumpkin puree	
1 teaspoon pumpkin pie spice	
1 teaspoon maple syrup	

Per serving: Calories 285 (From Fat 64); Fat 7g (Saturated 2g); Cholesterol 48mg; Sodium 915mg; Carbohydrate 34g (Dietary Fiber 4g); Protein 24g.

Vary It! Mix it up with your favorite fruits and meats! You could even try swapping the ham for tofu.

Tip: Squeeze lemon juice on the freshly cut fruits to keep them from browning before lunchtime.

Mad about mangos

The vibrant yellow color of mango screams nutrient rich! Just typing the word *mango* has our mouths watering. Its juicy goodness is addicting. Plus, one mango is filled with almost a day's worth of vitamin C! Mangos are a great source of fiber, so they fill you up without weighing you down.

Their versatility makes mangos the perfect accompaniment for your lunch. Here are some ideas:

- Add chopped mango to Greek yogurt.
- Place sliced mango in a separate container (to prevent soggy greens), and when you're ready to eat, add them to your salad for added flavor and antioxidants.
- Make a salsa using mango, tomatoes, red onion, cilantro, and lime juice for a tasty snack, or use as a topping for reheated chicken or seafood.

Roasted Tofu and Eggplant Medley

Prep time: 10 min • **Cook time:** 35 min • **Yield:** 4 servings

Ingredients	*Directions*
1 small Japanese eggplant	**1** Preheat the oven to 450 degrees, and line a rimmed baking dish with parchment paper.
12 ounces super-firm sprouted tofu, well drained	
2 tablespoons low-sodium soy sauce	**2** Cut the eggplant and tofu into uniform bite-size dice.
¼ teaspoon cinnamon	**3** In a medium bowl, marinate the tofu in the soy sauce, cinnamon, and coriander.
⅛ teaspoon coriander	
2 cups baby spinach, chopped	**4** Bake the tofu and eggplant for 25 minutes. Turn off the oven, and allow to rest in the oven for an additional 10 minutes to continue dehydrating.
¼ cup fresh basil, chopped	
½ cup reduced-fat feta cheese	
	5 In a large bowl, combine the eggplant, tofu, spinach, basil, and feta cheese.

Per serving: Calories 148 (From Fat 66); Fat 7g (Saturated 2g); Cholesterol 8mg; Sodium 498mg; Carbohydrate 11g (Dietary Fiber 5g); Protein 14g.

Note: Tofu is a vegetarian protein that is simple to incorporate into lunches. It doesn't have much flavor on its own; instead, it takes on the flavors you add to it.

Vary It! Turn up the heat by sprinkling cayenne pepper into the marinade!

Tip: When purchasing eggplant, make sure it's heavy for its size and free of blemishes.

Tofu verses sprouted tofu: What's the difference?

Tofu is a soy-based product with high nutritional value. Vegetarians and non-vegetarians benefit from tofu as an alternative to meat by searing, sautéing, grilling, and roasting without adding cholesterol or saturated fat.

So, what's the difference between tofu and sprouted tofu? Tofu is made from whole soybeans and is lower in calories and fat, but also lower in protein. Sprouted tofu is made from sprouted soybeans, which tend to be more nutritious and easier to digest; it also contains more calcium, iron, and protein than regular tofu does.

Creamy Lentil Soup

Prep time: 15 min • **Cook time:** 40 min • **Yield:** 4 servings

Ingredients	Directions
1 teaspoon olive oil	**1** In a large soup pot, heat the olive oil over medium-high heat.
2 cups chopped celery	
2 cups chopped onion	**2** Cook the celery, onion, and carrots until softened, about 8 minutes.
2 cups matchstick carrots	
4 cloves garlic, chopped	**3** Stir in the garlic and cook an additional 2 minutes, until fragrant.
1 teaspoon coriander	
1½ teaspoons cumin	**4** Add the coriander, cumin, lentils, tomatoes, and vegetable broth.
1 cup lentils	
One 14.5-ounce can no-salt-added diced tomatoes	**5** Bring the soup to a boil; reduce the heat to medium, and cover.
4 cups reduced-sodium vegetable broth	**6** Cook for 30 minutes or until the lentils are tender.
½ cup skim milk	**7** Pour the soup into a blender, or use an immersion blender. Add the milk and blend until smooth and creamy.

Per serving: Calories 304 (From Fat 19); Fat 2g (Saturated 0g); Cholesterol 0mg; Sodium 251mg; Carbohydrate 53g (Dietary Fiber 19g); Protein 16g.

Note: Lentils are so tasty and filling! They're an excellent source of fiber and protein.

Tip: This meal is packed with protein, complex carbohydrates, and vegetables. Eat it alongside a small apple, a fruit salad, or even half of a turkey sandwich for delicious dunking!

Curried Couscous

Prep time: 10 min • **Cook time:** 10 min • **Yield:** 4 servings

Ingredients	*Directions*
1½ cups low-sodium chicken broth	*1* In a medium pot, place the chicken broth and curry powder and bring to a boil. Stir in the couscous; cover. Remove from the heat and let stand for 5 minutes.
2 tablespoons curry powder	
1⅓ cups whole-wheat couscous, dry	*2* Pour the couscous in a large bowl. Stir in the curry powder until blended.
½ cup parsley, chopped	
½ cup Honeycrisp apple, diced	*3* Add the parsley, apple, raisins, bell pepper, and orange juice. Stir until all the ingredients are incorporated.
½ cup raisins	
½ cup red bell pepper, diced	
3 tablespoons 100 percent orange juice	

Per serving: Calories 381 (From Fat 27); Fat 3g (Saturated 0g); Cholesterol 0mg; Sodium 31mg; Carbohydrate 83g (Dietary Fiber 8g); Protein 14g.

Vary It! For more protein, stir chickpeas or shredded rotisserie chicken breast (see the nearby sidebar) into the couscous.

Tip: Serve this grain salad over a bed of spinach for extra veggies. Complement this dish with a yummy side like low-fat Greek yogurt and berries.

Rotisserie chicken: A quick and easy protein boost

Precooked rotisserie chicken from the deli is inexpensive and convenient. The carving process may seem overwhelming, but it's easy when done correctly. Prepare the night before and add meat to quesadillas, wraps, pastas, salads, and soups for a healthy lunch in minutes.

Follow these steps for carving:

1. **Place the chicken, breast side up, on a cutting board.**

2. **Pull the drumstick away from the chicken while cutting through the connective tissue.**

3. **Pull the wing tip away from the breast; cut where the two join.**

4. **Remove the breast; slice, chop, dice, or shred the meat.**

Remember: Don't toss the carcass! Save the bones to make homemade chicken stock.

Chapter 8

Poultry, Meat, and Seafood

In This Chapter

▶ Cooking a healthy meal based around poultry

▶ Making meat a part of your Belly Fat Diet plan

▶ Shaking things up with tasty seafood dishes

*P*rotein is essential to the body for a host of reasons. Scientifically, proteins are the building blocks of every cell in the body. They help to maintain lean body mass and build and repair tissues and cells. Some proteins even work as antibodies to fight off infection and build the immune system.

Protein plays a key role in fighting belly fat, too. It contributes to feeling full when you eat a meal. Because your body needs more time to digest proteins, they stick around for longer, so you're less likely to find yourself needing to snack an hour later.

One of the exciting benefits of eating protein is that it can actually help you burn more calories! This metabolism booster is called the *thermic effect* of food — it's the amount of energy the body needs to burn in order to break down, digest, and metabolize a food. Protein contains a higher thermic effect than carbs and fats, which allows your body to burn more calories during digestion.

As you embark on your belly fat reduction plan and begin to lose weight, you need to preserve muscle mass. If you lose muscle mass, your metabolism will slow down, contributing to a weight gain or plateau (where the scale seems stuck on one number). Strength training is essential to maintaining muscle mass, but the foods you eat can play a role in preserving muscle tissue as well. Protein contains a branched-chain amino acid called leucine, which helps to protect against muscle loss and may actually help you build muscle.

The more muscle you have, the more metabolically active you are, so you burn more calories throughout the day.

Keep your portions in check with protein foods. Because they're filling, you'll be less likely to overindulge in too many carbs or fats. By making your plate one-quarter lean proteins, you keep your plate balanced with adequate whole grains, fruits, vegetables, and healthy fats.

Taking in too much or too little protein can sabotage your weight loss efforts and health. Everyone needs a different amount each day depending on your goals, fitness level, age, and gender. Refer to Chapter 4 to see how much you need.

In this chapter, we provide recipes for protein dishes, including poultry, meat, and seafood. With the wide variety of recipes in this chapter, you have no excuse for not getting enough protein every day!

Birds of a Feather: Poultry

When you decided to shed some belly fat, you may have thought you'd need to eliminate all the red meat in your diet and eat more poultry. Although poultry can be a very smart protein choice, to save on fat and calories you need to make sure you're making the right poultry selections. We often hear our clients boasting about using ground turkey in place of beef in their recipes. But ground turkey or chicken can be higher in fat that you would imagine because it often contains the dark meat and skin, too. For a low-fat poultry choice, choose ground turkey or chicken breast.

Fried chicken may be a popular comfort food, but it's high in fat and not recommended on the Belly Fat Diet plan. Not only should you choose lean poultry, but you should keep your proteins lean by using a low-fat cooking method. Although fat carries lots of flavor, chicken and turkey breast doesn't have to be dry and flavorless. To keep the flavor and moisture locked into your poultry, cook the chicken breast with skin on and then remove it after cooking. If making burgers with ground turkey, add moisture with onions and peppers, and spice it up with dried seasonings. Marinate whole chicken breast pieces in a low-fat sauce made with an acidic ingredient, like lemon or orange juice, to tenderize the meat and add moisture.

In this section, we show you how to prepare lean poultry in a belly-friendly way, without sacrificing flavor and taste.

Baked Chicken Parmesan

Prep time: 10 min • **Cook time:** 20 min • **Yield:** 4 servings

Ingredients	*Directions*
¾ **cup panko breadcrumbs, plain**	*1* Preheat the oven to 400 degrees, and coat a large baking dish with cooking spray.
¼ **teaspoon red pepper flakes**	*2* In a medium bowl, mix the breadcrumbs, red pepper flakes, basil, garlic powder, garlic, and oregano. Set aside.
¼ **teaspoon basil**	
¾ **teaspoon garlic powder**	
¾ **teaspoon oregano**	*3* In another medium bowl, place the flour. Set aside.
¼ **cup whole-wheat flour**	
1 egg	*4* In another medium bowl, whisk the egg.
Two 8-ounce boneless, skinless chicken breasts	*5* Cut each chicken breast in half on the bias, to reduce the thickness. Blot dry with paper towels.
2 cups marinara sauce	*6* Dip the chicken breasts into the flour, then into the egg, and finally into the breadcrumbs, shaking off the excess with each coating.
1 cup mozzarella cheese	
¼ **cup freshly grated Parmesan cheese, for garnish**	
¼ **cup parsley chopped, for garnish**	*7* Place the breaded chicken in a baking dish and coat each piece of chicken with cooking spray. Bake for 20 minutes.
	8 Top each piece of chicken with marinara sauce and mozzarella.
	9 Garnish with Parmesan and parsley, if desired.

Per serving: *Calories 465 (From Fat 136); Fat 15g (Saturated 6g); Cholesterol 96mg; Sodium 1,066mg; Carbohydrate 40g (Dietary Fiber 5g); Protein 42g.*

Tip: Shaking off the excess flour in Step 6 prevents it from burning in the pan and helps to save on calories.

Tip: Butterflying a chicken breast (or cutting it in half on the bias) helps with even and faster cooking, keeps the chicken moist and juicy, and keeps portions in check!

Grilled Chicken Salad with Fresh Blueberries, Pecans, and Honey-Poppy Vinaigrette

Prep time: 2 min • **Cook time:** 12 min • **Yield:** 8 servings

Ingredients	Directions
Honey-Poppy Vinaigrette (see the following recipe)	**1** Heat the grill or grill pan to medium-high.
16 ounces boneless, skinless chicken breasts	**2** Sprinkle the chicken with the garlic, salt, and pepper.
1 clove garlic, minced	**3** Place the chicken on the grill, and grill until the internal temperature of the chicken (as measured with a meat thermometer) reaches 165 degrees, about 8 minutes per side. Set aside to cool.
¼ teaspoon salt	
¼ teaspoon pepper	
1 cup pecans	**4** Heat the oven to 375 degrees. On a cookie sheet, spread the pecans. Bake until fragrant, 5 to 7 minutes.
6 ounces arugula	
6 ounces spinach	**5** With two forks, shred the chicken.
2 cups fresh blueberries	
½ cup crumbled blue cheese or feta cheese	**6** In a large salad bowl, toss the arugula and spinach with ½ of the vinaigrette.
	7 Top with the chicken, blueberries, cheese, and pecans, and toss gently.

Honey-Poppy Vinaigrette

½ cup balsamic vinegar

½ cup white balsamic vinegar

¼ cup honey

2 tablespoons Dijon mustard

¼ teaspoon salt

¼ teaspoon pepper

½ cup extra-virgin olive oil

2 tablespoons poppy seeds

1 In a medium bowl, whisk the balsamic vinegar, white balsamic vinegar, honey, mustard, salt, and pepper.

2 Continue whisking while gradually adding the olive oil. Stir in the poppy seeds. Set aside.

Per serving: Calories 307 (From Fat 187); Fat 21g (Saturated 4g); Cholesterol 43mg; Sodium 343mg; Carbohydrate 16g (Dietary Fiber 3g); Protein 17g.

Note: This recipe is reproduced from www.blueberrycouncil.org. Reproduced with the permission of Sodexo, Garden Cafe, Chicago Botanic Garden.

Measuring up

If you're eating out, knowing how much protein is on your plate can be tough. Use your hand as a guide to estimate portion size for proteins.

The palm and thickness of a woman's hand is a good estimate for a 3-ounce serving.

Chipotle Lime Avocado Chicken Salad

Prep time: 20 min • **Cook time:** 20–25 min • **Yield:** 4 servings

Ingredients	Directions
1 pound boneless, skinless chicken breasts Pinch of kosher salt 2 pinches of pepper 1 Haas (California) avocado ⅛ teaspoon garlic powder 1 tablespoon fresh cilantro, roughly chopped 1 tablespoon green onions, chopped 3 tablespoons nonfat plain Greek yogurt 1 teaspoon chipotle hot sauce 1 lime, juiced ⅔ cup corn, canned and drained 4 cups Bibb lettuce, for serving	**1** Remove any visible fat from the chicken breasts, rinse, and pat dry. Season the chicken with the salt and 1 pinch of the pepper. **2** Heat the grill or grill pan to medium heat. Place the chicken on the grill and cook for about 10 minutes on one side; flip, continuing to grill until cooked through, about 12 to 14 minutes for medium-size chicken breasts. **3** In a medium bowl, mash the avocado. Stir in the garlic powder, cilantro, green onions, yogurt, hot sauce, lime juice, and the remaining pinch of pepper. **4** When the chicken is cooked through and the juices run clear, transfer it to a cutting board and let it rest for 5 minutes. Dice the chicken into bite-size pieces and add to the avocado mixture. Add the corn and mix until incorporated. Serve the chicken salad over Bibb lettuce leaves.

Per serving: Calories 226 (From Fat 78); Fat 9g (Saturated 1g); Cholesterol 73mg; Sodium 306mg; Carbohydrate 11g (Dietary Fiber 4g); Protein 27g.

Vary It! Like it hot? Take it up a notch with a few drops of Sriracha hot sauce!

Note: Using Greek yogurt instead of mayonnaise slashes the fat compared to traditional chicken salad.

Aloha Turkey Burgers with Creamy Mango Sauce

Prep time: 10 min • **Cook time:** 15 min • **Yield:** 4 servings

Ingredients	Directions
Creamy Mango Sauce (see the following recipe)	**1** In a large bowl, mix together the shallot, turkey, lime juice, paprika, soy sauce, and coconut. Form 4 burger patties.
½ shallot, minced	
1 pound ground turkey breast	**2** Grill the burgers for 7 to 8 minutes on each side, until cooked through. Two minutes before the burgers are done, top each burger with cheese.
½ lime, juiced	
¼ teaspoon paprika	
1 tablespoon soy sauce	**3** Serve each burger on a whole-grain bun and drizzle with Creamy Mango Sauce.
1 tablespoon coconut, shredded	
4 slices Monterey Jack cheese	
4 whole-grain burger buns	

Creamy Mango Sauce

2 cloves garlic	Chop the garlic in a food processor. Add the cilantro and process until chopped. Blend in the yogurt, hot sauce, and lime juice.
⅓ cup cilantro	
6 ounces mango Greek yogurt	
⅛ teaspoon Sriracha hot sauce	
½ lime, juiced	

Per serving: Calories 395 (From Fat 109); Fat 12g (Saturated 6g); Cholesterol 95mg; Sodium 670mg; Carbohydrate 30g (Dietary Fiber 3g); Protein 44g.

Note: Make sure you purchase "ground turkey breast," not "ground turkey," for a lean protein option.

Buffalo Chicken Sliders with Blue Cheese Dip

Prep time: 10 min • **Cook time:** 12 min • **Yield:** 4 servings

Ingredients	Directions
Blue Cheese Dip (see the following recipe)	**1** In a large bowl, mix the chicken and Buffalo-wings seasoning. Gently fold in the onion, spinach, and Buffalo-wings sauce, and mix until incorporated.
16 ounces ground chicken breast	
½ teaspoon Buffalo-wings seasoning mix	**2** Form 8 uniform patties with ¾-inch thickness, and grill over medium-high heat with lid closed until cooked through, about 4 minutes on each side.
¼ cup minced red onion	
1 cup packed spinach, thinly chopped	**3** Place each slider on a whole-wheat bun, and top with Blue Cheese Dip and lettuce.
1 tablespoon Buffalo-wings sauce	
8 whole-grain slider buns	
8 pieces Bibb lettuce	

Blue Cheese Dip

⅓ cup nonfat plain Greek yogurt	In a medium bowl, mix all ingredients until blended.
¼ cup crumbled blue cheese	
1 tablespoon lemon juice	
½ teaspoon minced garlic	

Per serving: Calories 369 (From Fat 75); Fat 8g (Saturated 2g); Cholesterol 76mg; Sodium 580mg; Carbohydrate 38g (Dietary Fiber 2g); Protein 39g.

Note: Serve sliders with celery and carrot sticks to get all the traditional flavors of Buffalo chicken wings. It's a great way to get more veggies, too!

Meat: It's What's for Dinner

Meats like beef and pork have gotten a bad rep. The fats they contain typically come in the form of unhealthy, saturated fats, which can lead to increased inflammation in the body and may cause you to put on more belly fat.

But here's the good news: Not all meats are created equal! They can differ in fat and calorie content. What you want to do is look for lean meats, which typically have 3 g of fat or less per ounce. Here are meats that fall into that category:

- Lean ham
- Canadian bacon
- Pork tenderloin
- Beef tenderloin
- Flank steak
- 95 percent lean ground beef
- Eye-of-round roast beef
- Top sirloin beef
- Wild game
- Lamb chops
- Some deli meats

But lean meats are expensive!

Bologna! (And no, bologna is not lean.) Don't fall into the trap of thinking that every healthy food is more expensive. Yes, you'll find a higher price tag on lean meats, but have you considered shrinkage? Shrinkage is caused by moisture loss, so the more fatty the meat is, the higher rate of shrinkage you see. Lean meats barely shrink, because they're low in fat. Not only are lean meats better for your health, but you're getting a better value and more bang for your buck, and you'll see less shrinkage.

Wild Rice Dried Blueberry Stuffed Pork Tenderloin

Prep time: 2½ hr • **Cook time:** 35 min • **Yield:** 4 servings

Ingredients	Directions
Wild Rice Dried Blueberry Stuffing (see the following recipe)	**1** Clean off any silver skin from the pork tenderloins, and slit the pork lengthwise. Slit each side again so you're opening the tenderloins like a book.
16 ounces pork tenderloin	
½ tablespoon fresh oregano	**2** Season the pork with the oregano, mustard, salt, and pepper. Stuff the pork gently with the Wild Rice Dried Blueberry Stuffing, and tie as you would a roast. Season again and set aside in the refrigerator to marinate for 2 hours.
½ tablespoon Dijon mustard	
½ teaspoon kosher salt	
¼ teaspoon pepper	
2 tablespoons olive oil	**3** Preheat the oven to 400 degrees. In a large sauté pan, add the olive oil and heat on medium-high. Add the pork to the pan and sear the pork on all sides to create a nice color. Remove the pork from the pan with tongs and place it on a rack on a sheet pan.
2 cups watercress, stems removed	
1 cup endive, shredded	
½ cup Fuji apple, cored and cut into thin, long strips	**4** Bake for 10 minutes, or until the internal temperature of the fork (as measured with a meat thermometer) reaches 140 to 160 degrees. Remove from the oven and let rest in a warm area for at least 8 minutes before slicing.
	5 Slice the pork and serve.

Wild Rice Dried Blueberry Stuffing

1½ tablespoons olive oil

1½ tablespoons shallots

¼ cup onions, diced

¼ cup celery, small dice

½ tablespoon garlic, minced

1 small bay leaf

½ teaspoon thyme leaves

¼ cup white wine

½ cup wild rice, cooked

½ cup dried blueberries

¼ cup Granny Smith apple, grated

½ tablespoon tarragon, minced

1 In a large sauté pan, heat the olive oil. Add the shallots, onion, celery, garlic, bay leaf, and thyme, and cook until soft over medium-low heat, about 15 minutes. You want a deep caramelization of the vegetables.

2 Add the white wine, turning up the heat to medium and cooking until the pan is near dry and the wine has almost completely cooked off.

3 In a large bowl, combine the wild rice, blueberries, apple, and tarragon. Remove the pan from the heat and pour the contents of the pan into the large bowl. Stir well. Chill and set aside. Remove the bay leaf before stuffing.

Per serving: Calories 462 (From Fat 137); Fat 15g (Saturated 3g); Cholesterol 74mg; Sodium 444mg; Carbohydrate 49g (Dietary Fiber 13g); Protein 31g.

Note: This recipe is reproduced from www.blueberrycouncil.org. Reproduced with the permission of the U.S. Highbush Blueberry Council.

Mongolian Pork and Vegetables

Prep time: 15–30 min • **Cook time:** 10 min • **Yield:** 4 servings

Ingredients	Directions
16 ounces boneless pork loin fillets	**1** Slice the pork into ¼-inch-thick bite-size pieces. In a large bowl or resealable plastic bag, marinate the pork for 15 to 30 minutes in the ginger, garlic, chili, lime juice, brown sugar, soy sauce, and water.
1 tablespoon freshly grated ginger	
4 cloves garlic, minced	**2** In a large skillet or wok, heat the sesame oil over medium-high heat.
½ Serrano chili, thinly sliced	
1 lime, juiced	**3** Add the pork and the marinade to the heated pan and cook for 2 minutes.
1 teaspoon brown sugar	
⅓ cup low-sodium soy sauce	
¼ cup water	**4** Add the pepper, carrots, and broccoli, and continue to cook until the vegetables are slightly tender but still crispy, about 6 to 8 minutes.
2 tablespoons sesame oil	
1 red bell pepper, thinly sliced	
1 cup matchstick carrots	**5** Stir in the green onions, and remove the pan from the heat.
2 cups broccoli florets	
3 green onions, chopped	

Per serving: Calories 337 (From Fat 132); Fat 15g (Saturated 4g); Cholesterol 62mg; Sodium 733mg; Carbohydrate 23g (Dietary Fiber 4g); Protein 30g.

Tip: Serve the pork with brown rice or in lettuce cups.

Jamaican Jerk Beef and Shrimp Shish Kebabs

Prep time: 15–30 min • **Cook time:** 8–10 min • **Yield:** 6 servings

Ingredients	Directions
16 ounces top sirloin steak, cubed 1-inch thick	*1* In a large bowl or resealable plastic bag, marinate the steak and shrimp in the lemon juice, jerk seasonings, and orange juice for 15 to 30 minutes.
8 ounces jumbo shrimp, deveined, peeled, and tails removed (see Figure 8-1)	
1 lemon, juiced	*2* On wooden skewers, line the steak and pineapple together and the shrimp separately.
1 tablespoon jerk seasonings	
1 tablespoon 100 percent orange juice	*3* Grill the steak and pineapple on high heat for 7 to 10 minutes; grill the shrimp for 2 minutes, until cooked through.
2 cups diced pineapple	

Per serving: Calories 233 (From Fat 94); Fat 10g (Saturated 4g); Cholesterol 93mg; Sodium 96mg; Carbohydrate 11g (Dietary Fiber 1g); Protein 24g.

Tip: Serve these delicious shish kebabs with Ginger Coconut Rice (see Chapter 11).

CLEANING AND DEVEINING SHRIMP

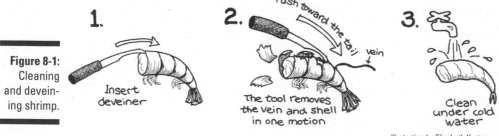

Figure 8-1: Cleaning and deveining shrimp.

1. Insert deveiner

2. Push toward the tail — vein — The tool removes the vein and shell in one motion

3. Clean under cold water

Illustration by Elizabeth Kurtzman

Steak Fajitas with Chimichurri

Prep time: 10 min • **Cook time:** 8 min • **Yield:** 6 servings

Ingredients	*Directions*
Chimichurri	*1* In a cast-iron skillet, cook the sirloin over medium-high heat for about 2 minutes on each side. Remove from the pan and allow to rest on a cutting board.
1 teaspoon canola oil	
1 Vidalia onion, thinly sliced	
1 yellow bell pepper, thinly sliced	*2* Heat the canola oil in the pan and sauté the onion and pepper until softened.
One 16-ounce top sirloin steak	*3* Warm the tortillas in the microwave for 10 seconds.
Six 6-inch whole-grain tortillas	*4* Serve the tortillas warm with the onions, peppers, and steak, and top with Chimichurri.

Chimichurri

3 cloves garlic	In a food processor, pulse the garlic. Add the cilantro, parsley, red pepper flakes, salt, lime juice, olive oil, water, and vinegar, and pulse until combined.
½ cup cilantro	
½ cup parsley	
¼ teaspoon red pepper flakes	
⅛ teaspoon kosher salt	
1 lime, juiced	
2 tablespoons extra-virgin olive oil	
1 tablespoon water	
½ teaspoon white wine vinegar	

Per serving: *Calories 310 (From Fat 149); Fat 17g (Saturated 5g); Cholesterol 39mg; Sodium 227mg; Carbohydrate 22g (Dietary Fiber 3g); Protein 19g.*

Tip: Make the Chimichurri first; then cook the steak.

Vary It! Switch up this recipe by using corn tortillas instead of whole grain, or toss in chicken in place of the beef.

What is chimichurri?

Chimichurri is an Argentinean sauce that can be used as a marinade or sauce for grilled meats. It's similar to pesto but with a more liquid consistency. Chimichurri is often zesty or spicy and made from parsley, garlic, olive oil, and vinegar. It's easy to personalize this sauce to your liking by adding your favorite herbs and spices as we did in this recipe. This sauce would also be scrumptious in pasta or with baked fish or chicken.

Pumpkin Bolognese

Prep time: 10 min • **Cook time:** 15–20 min • **Yield:** 6 servings

Ingredients	*Directions*
1 tablespoon olive oil	*1* In a Dutch oven or large pot, heat the olive oil over medium-high heat. Sauté the onion, garlic, mushrooms, carrots, and celery until tender.
1 large Vidalia onion, diced	
3 cloves garlic, minced	
1 cup diced mushrooms	*2* Add the ground beef, and cook until no longer pink.
1 cup matchstick carrots	
2 stalks celery with leaves, thinly sliced	*3* Stir in the cinnamon, oregano, and thyme until combined.
16 ounces 95 percent lean ground sirloin beef	
¼ teaspoon cinnamon	*4* Mix in the vinegar, pumpkin, and crushed tomatoes, and bring to a boil. Then reduce to a simmer until ready to eat.
¼ teaspoon oregano	
3 sprigs thyme, de-stemmed	
2 tablespoons balsamic vinegar	
1 cup canned pumpkin	
28 ounces canned crushed tomatoes	

Per serving: Calories 241 (From Fat 96); Fat 11g (Saturated 3g); Cholesterol 45mg; Sodium 510mg; Carbohydrate 21g (Dietary Fiber 5g); Protein 17g.

Tip: Serve Pumpkin Bolognese sauce over a bed of whole-grain pasta or spaghetti squash.

Tip: This dish makes a yummy make-ahead meal for your hectic workweek. Whip up a batch of this sauce on the weekend, and serve it as an easy weeknight or to-go lunch.

The power of pumpkin

You'd never guess that this dish is filled with pumpkin — pumpkin is rather flavorless but adds lots of body to dishes. Pumpkin adds more than texture, though. It's actually low in calories and an excellent source of vitamin A, which promotes good vision and healthy skin. It may also help to protect skin from sun damage and promote brain health. One cup of cooked, mashed pumpkin contains nearly 250 percent of your recommended dietary allowance for vitamin A, all for only 49 calories!

Seafood: Plenty More Fish in the Sea

You really can't go wrong in the nutrition department when you're eating seafood — it's all good for you. Fatty fishes (such as salmon and tuna) contain essential omega-3 fatty acids, and non-fatty fishes are a lean protein choice. (For more on omega-3s, see the nearby sidebar.)

Depending on where you live, you may be able to find local fishes at the grocery store or fish market, which have the best flavor when they're fresh-caught. Freshness is the most important element when selecting seafood, so take note of the following markers of freshness:

- Fish should not *smell* fishy. In fact, fresh fish should smell mild, like saltwater, or odorless.

- The flesh should be firm and elastic, without milky moisture.

- The skin should be moist and bright with no trace of slime.

- Whole fish should have clear, bright eyes with deep red gills.

Here are some more tips for fish buying:

- Fish should have a dense texture. Avoid purchasing fish with gaps in the flesh.

- Only purchase pre-cut fillets if they're displayed on a bed of ice.

- Don't let seafood sit in your shopping cart for too long. To ensure freshness, ask for it to be packed on ice.

- Don't be afraid to ask questions. Your fishmonger should be able to show you the freshest catches and tell you where the fish was caught.

- Frozen fish should always be vacuum-packed for freshness.

- For the best flavor, eat fish within one to two days of purchase.

Eco-friendly fishes

With the emerging emphasis on going green, environmentally friendly fishes has become a popular demand. Many activists are concerned about overfishing and the destruction to the marine ecosystem. Fish from sustainable fisheries are evaluated and labeled by a third party so that consumers can make an informed choice. Some of the best choices for sustainable fish are: Alaskan Pacific halibut, albacore tuna, farmed U.S. barramundi, farmed U.S. catfish, farmed U.S. tilapia, U.S. yellowfin tuna, wild Alaskan Pacific long-line cod, wild Alaskan salmon, wild Atlantic haddock, and wild Atlantic mahi-mahi.

Omega-3 fatty acids

Omega-3s have been shown to lower risk of heart attacks and strokes by reducing inflammation. They can also aid in reducing stress hormones in the body. Too much stress in your life is often linked to a higher percentage of belly fat because of the release of the stress hormones cortisol and adrenaline.

Two specific omega-3 fatty acids — docosahexaenoic acid (DHA) and eicosapentaenoic acid (EPA) — are found primarily in fish and are essential to optimal health. The brain is made up of DHA, and EPA is essential to building every structural cell in the body.

The catch (pun intended) is that you have to eat foods with omega-3 fatty acids to meet your daily goals. The body doesn't make them on its own, and it relies on your getting them from your diet. The good news is, you don't have to bust your budget when selecting high-quality fishes, because many of the top omega-3 sources (such as anchovies, sardines, and canned tuna) are super-economical and convenient!

Here's a list of the combined EPA and DHA content of some common seafood:

Fish	Amount	Combined EPA and DHA Content
Atlantic salmon, farmed	3 ounces cooked	1,835 mg
Tuna, fresh, Bluefin	3 ounces cooked	1,414 mg
Anchovies	2 ounces canned	1,386 mg
Alaskan sockeye salmon	3 ounces cooked	1,210 mg
Atlantic mackerel	3 ounces cooked	1,209 mg
Coho, salmon, wild	3 ounces cooked	1,087 mg
Sardines	3 ounces canned	835 mg
Albacore tuna	3 ounces canned	808 mg
Halibut	3 ounces cooked	569 mg
Crab	3 ounces cooked	335 mg
Flounder	3 ounces cooked	255 mg
Clams	3 ounces cooked	241 mg
Light tuna	3 ounces canned	230 mg

Roasted Shrimp Salad with Honey-Mustard Dressing

Prep time: 10 min • **Cook time:** 10 min • **Yield:** 4 servings

Ingredients	Directions
Honey-Mustard Dressing (see the following recipe)	*1* Preheat the oven to 400 degrees.
16 ounces large shrimp, peeled, deveined, and tails removed (refer to Figure 8-1)	*2* Line a baking sheet with parchment paper, and arrange the shrimp and corn on the baking sheet.
1 cup sweet yellow corn, frozen and defrosted	*3* Season the shrimp with salt and pepper, and bake 8 to 10 minutes, until the shrimp are pink.
⅛ teaspoon kosher salt	
Pinch of pepper	*4* To serve, in a bowl, layer the lettuce, tomatoes, onions, avocado, corn, and shrimp. Drizzle with the Honey-Mustard Dressing.
8 cups chopped romaine lettuce	
2 Roma tomatoes, diced	
½ red onion, diced	
1 avocado, diced (refer to Figure 7-1)	

Honey-Mustard Dressing

¼ cup nonfat plain Greek yogurt	In a bowl, combine all the ingredients.
1 tablespoon honey	
2 tablespoons coarse ground mustard	

Per serving: Calories 262 (From Fat 73); Fat 8g (Saturated 1g); Cholesterol 172mg; Sodium 366mg; Carbohydrate 22g (Dietary Fiber 6g); Protein 28g.

Tip: Avocados are high in monounsaturated fats, which help to fight belly fat!

Vary It! Go vegetarian by roasting tofu instead of shrimp! It gets nice and crispy, and tastes great in this salad.

Pan-Seared Citrus Scallops

Prep time: 15 min • **Cook time:** 15–20 min • **Yield:** 4 servings

Ingredients	Directions
½ **small shallot**	*1* In a food processor or blender, mix the shallot, cilantro, lime zest and juice, orange juice, hot sauce, and salt.
¼ **cup cilantro**	
1 **lime, zested and juiced**	*2* In a small bowl or resealable plastic bag, marinate the sea scallops in the citrus mixture for 10 to 15 minutes. Pat the scallops dry.
2 **tablespoons 100 percent orange juice**	
1 **teaspoon Sriracha hot sauce**	*3* In a nonstick skillet, heat the oil over high heat.
⅛ **teaspoon kosher salt**	
16 **ounces large sea scallops, dry packed and cleaned**	*4* Place the scallops flat side down in the hot pan, making sure not to overcrowd the pan.
1 **teaspoon canola oil**	
	5 When the scallops have cooked about 2 to 3 minutes and have formed a nice crust underneath, flip them. Cook an additional 1 to 1½ minutes and remove from the pan.

Per serving: Calories 120 (From Fat 18); Fat 2g (Saturated 0g); Cholesterol 37mg; Sodium 215mg; Carbohydrate 5g (Dietary Fiber 0g); Protein 19g.

Tip: To form a nice crust on the scallops, be sure not to move them until they're ready to flip.

Tip: Serve these citrus scallops with steamed sugar snap peas and carrots and a small side of brown rice.

Buying and cleaning fresh scallops

The two types of scallops that you'll likely find in your grocery store are sea and bay. Bay scallops are small and delicate, yet easily overcooked. Sea scallops are larger, making them great for grilling and pan-searing; their larger size makes them less likely to be overcooked and tough to chew.

Choose scallops that have been dry packed and are chemical free, which means they've been shipped fresh over ice instead of submerged in water and laced with preservatives. Preservatives often cause the scallops to retain too much moisture, making them difficult to pan-sear.

When you purchase scallops, they're usually shucked from the shell, but commonly part of the muscle is attached. This muscle is used for protection and helps to keep the shell clamped. This muscle is strong and hard to chew, so you'll want to remove the muscle by gently plucking it off the scallop. Don't worry if you don't find muscles on all your scallops — some may have already been removed.

Sweet Tuna Salad

Prep time: 10 min • **Yield:** 4 servings

Ingredients	Directions
12 ounces canned albacore tuna, packed in water and drained	**1** In a large bowl, mix the tuna, yogurt, lemon zest, pepper, and cinnamon together just until combined.
6 ounces nonfat lemon Greek yogurt	**2** Gently toss the celery, bell pepper, walnuts, and raisins with the tuna mixture.
½ lemon, zest only	
Pinch of pepper	**3** Fold in the blueberries, taking care not to crush them.
¹⁄₁₆ teaspoon cinnamon	**4** Serve in lettuce cups.
1 stalk celery, thinly sliced with leaves	
½ red bell pepper, diced	
½ cup walnuts, chopped	
⅓ cup raisins	
1 cup fresh blueberries	
4 Bibb lettuce leaves	

Per serving: Calories 296 (From Fat 111); Fat 12g (Saturated 2g); Cholesterol 36mg; Sodium 363mg; Carbohydrate 20g (Dietary Fiber 3g); Protein 28g.

Tip: Albacore tuna is higher in omega-3 fatty acids than other types of tuna and is an excellent source of selenium, which is needed for proper thyroid and immune function. A 3-ounce serving of albacore tuna contains 808 mg of omega-3s, compared to 239 mg in chunk light tuna.

Warning: Pregnant women and women who could potentially become pregnant should substitute chunk light tuna for albacore because it's lowest in mercury.

Poached Thai Coconut Fish

Prep time: 10 min • **Cook time:** 40 min • **Yield:** 3 servings

Ingredients	*Directions*
One 11.2-ounce container ZICO Pure Premium Coconut Water Tetra Pak	*1* Heat 9.2 ounces of the coconut water in a large pot to 160 degrees.
½ cup dry, unsweetened shredded coconut	*2* In the meantime, in a hot wok, toast the coconut over medium heat. Remove it from the pan when it begins to brown. Set aside half the coconut.
1 lime, zested and juiced	
1 kaffir lime leaf	
1 clove garlic, minced	*3* Add to the wok with the coconut the lime zest, lime juice, lime leaf, garlic, ginger, honey, chili, fish sauce, lemongrass, curry powder, and coconut milk. Stir to combine.
2 teaspoons ginger	
½ teaspoon honey	
1 Thai bird chili (or spicy fresh red chili), diced	
1 tablespoon fish sauce	*4* Allow the sauce to simmer on very low heat for 10 to 15 minutes.
1 stalk fresh lemongrass, bruised (see Tip)	
1 teaspoon curry powder	*5* When the coconut water has come to temperature, drop in the vegetable bouillon and allow to dissolve.
2 ounces coconut milk (canned)	
1 cube vegetable bouillon	
Three 3-ounce filets white-flesh fish (tilapia, mahi-mahi, or trout)	
1 lime, for garnish	
Salt, to taste	
Fish sauce, to taste	

6 Slide the fish into the pot of coconut water and allow it to poach for 5 minutes. Remove from the heat and transfer to a warm plate.

7 If the sauce is too thick, spoon the remaining poaching liquid and coconut water into the sauce until the desired consistency is achieved. Taste for seasoning, and add salt and fish sauce as needed.

8 Remove the lemongrass and kaffir lime leaf, spoon the sauce over the fish, and garnish with lime wedges and the remaining toasted coconut.

Per serving: Calories 457 (From Fat 226); Fat 25g (Saturated 17g); Cholesterol 198mg; Sodium 674mg; Carbohydrate 16g (Dietary Fiber 4g); Protein 42g.

Tip: You can find kaffir lime leaf in Asian grocery stores.

Tip: To bruise the lemongrass, simply whack it firmly with the blunt edge of a knife.

Tip: Serve over brown rice or steamed vegetables for a healthy meal.

Note: This recipe is reproduced from www.zico.com. Reproduced with the permission of ZICO Pure Premium Coconut Water.

One fish, two fish, red fish, blue fish

Eating fish is highly recommended and essential for a healthy and balanced diet, but it's important not to go overboard. Nearly all fish contain contaminants like methlymercury. In large amounts, mercury can be toxic and cause nerve damage, vision problems, and poor concentration. Because fish is the primary source of omega-3 fats, it's best to eat fish but limit consumption to a 3-ounce portion of fish two to three times per week. Fish with the highest mercury content are shark, swordfish, king mackerel, tilefish, and albacore tuna. If you're pregnant or breastfeeding, be sure to choose fish low in mercury.

Grilled Salmon Flatbreads

Prep time: 5 min • **Cook time:** 10 min • **Yield:** 4 servings

Ingredients	*Directions*
1 teaspoon coriander	**1** In a small bowl, stir together the coriander, cumin, fennel seed, cardamom, mustard seed, salt, and pepper to form a spice blend.
1 teaspoon cumin	
1 teaspoon fennel seed	
1 teaspoon cardamom	
1 teaspoon mustard seed	**2** Heat an oiled grill or grill pan to medium-high, and sprinkle 4 teaspoons of the spice blend and the garlic on both sides of the salmon. Grill just until opaque in the center, about 4 minutes on each side. With two forks, flake the salmon.
½ teaspoon salt	
¼ teaspoon pepper	
1 garlic clove, minced	
Two 8-ounce skinless salmon filets	
Four 4-inch whole-wheat pita breads	**3** Grill the pita until toasted, about 30 seconds per side. Place on 4 plates.
1 cup fresh blueberries	**4** In a medium bowl, toss the blueberries, avocado, cilantro, onion, jalapeño, lime zest, and 1 teaspoon of the remaining spice blend with the lime juice and oil.
½ avocado, diced (refer to Figure 7-1)	
⅓ cup chopped cilantro	
¼ cup diced red onion	**5** Top the pitas with the watercress, salmon, and blueberry salsa, dividing evenly.
1 tablespoon minced jalapeño	
1 teaspoon lime zest	
3 tablespoons lime juice	
2 tablespoons olive oil	
1 bunch watercress, trimmed (about 2 cups)	

Per serving: Calories 370 (From Fat 157); Fat 17g (Saturated 3g); Cholesterol 51mg; Sodium 504mg; Carbohydrate 26g (Dietary Fiber 5g); Protein 29g.

Note: This recipe is reproduced from www.blueberrycouncil.org. Reproduced with the permission of Sodexo, Garden Cafe, Chicago Botanic Garden.

What organic really means

Organic is a buzzword that you see all the time in the media and at the supermarket. Organic foods can cost twice as much as non-organic foods, so most people pause and evaluate whether organic is worth the money. In general, health professionals don't agree as to whether organic is better for your health. But here's what *organic* means:

- ✔ Organic meat, poultry, dairy, and eggs have to come from animals that were not given any growth hormones or antibiotics.

- ✔ Certified organic farms must maintain U.S. Department of Agriculture (USDA) inspections to ensure standards are being met.

- ✔ Food additives, fortifying agents, and processing aids are restricted to an approved list of allowed substances.

- ✔ Organic foods do not contain artificial sweeteners, preservatives, artificial flavors, artificial colors, or monosodium glutamate (MSG).

Remember: Just because something is labeled *organic* doesn't mean that food safety is guaranteed. Organic foods can be tainted with *E. coli* or salmonella just as much as non-organic foods, so be sure to follow basic safety precautions when handling raw meat.

Chapter 9

Comfort Foods

In This Chapter

▶ Paying attention when you're using food for comfort

▶ Making comfort foods flat-belly friendly

Although the main purpose of food is to provide our bodies with the nutrients they need to power through the day, for most people, food isn't just about physical sustenance — it's also about emotional sustenance. And that's where the term *comfort food* comes from. Food can provide comfort. If your mother's meatloaf reminds you of her warm home, and you're feeling lonely in a new city, eating meatloaf may bring back that feeling of home.

We absolutely believe that the foods you eat should be scrumptious and that you should truly enjoy them. But at the same time, don't lose sight of the fact that food is fuel — its primary purpose is to nourish your body. If you're using food primarily to soothe difficult emotions, like depression, boredom, stress, nervousness, loneliness, frustration, or guilt, that can be a problem not only for your waistline, but for your emotional health as well.

In this chapter, we walk you through the importance of becoming a mindful eater — making sure you're aware of the foods you're eating, and why you're eating them — so that you don't end up relying on food to cope. Then we provide belly-friendly recipes for comfort foods so that you have options that won't leave you feeling bloated and guilty for blowing your "diet."

Becoming a Mindful Eater

Being a mindful eater is all about being aware of what you're eating and why you're eating it. If you're using food to cope with emotions, odds are, you aren't doing so consciously. You aren't thinking, "Work is stressing me out, and I'm craving ice cream. I bet I'm craving ice cream because I have to maintain control at work, and I feel like rebelling when it comes to my eating." Instead, you're mindlessly reaching for that pint of ice cream from Vermont and eating it in front of the TV, reaching the bottom of the container before you even realize it.

If you see a connection between emotional ups and downs and your eating, or if you're prone to periods of bingeing, talking with a licensed therapist can help. Finding more productive ways to cope with your emotions (other than by stuffing yourself with food) is key.

Knowing when to eat and how much is a vital skill to learn when finding your healthy weight. The focus isn't so much on *what* you're eating but *how* and *why* you're eating. It allows you to recognize early signs of hunger and act on them instead of waiting until you're starving, which often leads to eating too much. Here are some tips to getting connected to your body's hunger and fullness:

- **Recognize the signs of physical hunger.** If your stomach is growling, your attention is waning, you have a headache, or you feel lightheaded, you may be physically hungry. If you want to eat, but you aren't physically hungry, try to get to the bottom of what you're feeling. Are you stressed, lonely, bored? Once you identify what's making you want to eat, address that problem with a solution that'll actually work (without making you feel lousy). For example, if you're stressed, try writing in a journal about how you feel, going for a walk with your dog, or calling a friend to talk about it. If you're lonely, find someone to go to a movie with or if you're short on friends, volunteer your time to a cause you believe in. There's nothing like giving back to others to make yourself feel good.

- **Know your number.** On a scale of 1 to 10 (with 1 being ravenous and 10 being so full that you're nauseated), how hungry are you? Ask yourself this question before you start eating, during your meal, and after you finish to connect with your hunger and fullness. Knowing your number can help you regulate your eating pattern. People who let themselves get overly hungry often end up on the other side of the scale, overstuffed, in a matter of minutes.

- **Eat sitting down, at a table.** No noshing in front of the TV or standing up in the kitchen. If you're going to eat, put your food on a plate and sit at a table.

- **Slow down.** Speed-eating makes it difficult to connect with hunger and fullness. It can take 20 minutes before your stomach tells your brain that it's satisfied and you should stop eating.

- **Eat light and eat often.** Space out your smaller meals with snacks. This way of eating keeps your blood sugar stable.

✓ **Get rid of distractions.** Get away from the TV, computer, phone, books, magazines, and video games, and don't eat while driving. These activities often lead to eating on auto-pilot. Don't do anything else while you eat. Just enjoy your food and pay attention to how your body feels.

✓ **Savor it!** Food appeals to all your senses. How does it taste, smell, and feel in your mouth or hands? Is it bursting with color? What does it look like? Does it appeal to your eyes? Does it make a noise, crunch in your mouth, or sizzle on the plate? Savoring food instead of just shoveling it in greatly increases meal satisfaction. When you savor food, you can often fill up on less.

✓ **Don't forget to hydrate.** Sometimes people reach for more food when they're really just thirsty. Drink enough fluids throughout the day, as well as at meals. Water will help to fill you up and keep you from eating more food than your body needs.

Making Comfort Foods Belly Friendly

Comfort foods are often laden with calories and fat. But it's not too hard to give old recipes a face-lift. With a few simple tweaks, you can lighten up even the most indulgent recipes without sacrificing flavor. What more could you ask for? (Just don't tell Grandma!) Here are some of our favorite belly-friendly tricks:

✓ **Avocado:** Avocado is creamy and naturally high in monounsaturated fat, which is an excellent belly-fat fighter! It tastes yummy in place of mayonnaise, oil, or cream in recipes.

✓ **Bananas:** If you want a creamy, thick texture, add mashed bananas. They taste excellent in smoothies and baked goods, and can often substitute for butter and oil in recipes.

✓ **Cauliflower:** Cauliflower is a sneaky healthy food that is easy to disguise for cream. We show you how in our Chicken Alfredo Pizza and Shepherd's Pie with Cauliflower Mash recipes, and it can even be used as a side, like in our Cauliflower Bites (see Chapter 11).

✓ **Cinnamon:** A little sprinkle of cinnamon can fool your brain into thinking you're eating something loaded with sugar. Instead of loading your oatmeal down with brown sugar, use cinnamon. Plus, cinnamon may make fat cells more responsive to insulin, helping to better regulate blood sugar levels!

- ✔ **Low-fat cottage cheese:** Cottage cheese is oh-so-yummy, and it's good for you, too! High in protein and low in fat, it adds an excellent creamy texture to many dishes like pasta and pizza. Substitute cottage cheese for ricotta to slash unhealthful saturated fats.

- ✔ **Herbs:** Adding herbs to a recipe is the best way to get better flavor without overdoing it on the salt. Herbs are also high in antioxidants that are beneficial to your overall health.

  When a recipe says "season to taste," it doesn't mean you should season until you taste the salt. *Season to taste* means salt enough to bring out the flavors of the recipe, but it shouldn't taste salty.

- ✔ **Olive oil:** It's an easy substitute for butter. Plus, it's packed with heart-healthy and belly-flattening monounsaturated fats, unlike butter, which is loaded with unhealthy saturated fats. If you like a lighter flavor, use canola oil, which is also a rich source of monounsaturated fats, including omega-3s.

- ✔ **Whole-wheat flour:** Adding nutrient-dense whole-wheat flours to your recipes instantly ups the nutrition. You can add it to virtually anything that calls for all-purpose flour. Our top whole-grain flours to bake with are spelt flour and whole-wheat pastry flour; they have a lighter texture and can typically replace all white flour called for in a recipe. Get creative with your grains and try new ones like amaranth, almond, flax, quinoa, teff, and so on. There are so many wonderful whole-grain flours at the supermarket!

- ✔ **Nonfat plain Greek yogurt:** It tastes excellent in place of sour cream on tacos or chili — you won't know the difference! We always keep nonfat Greek yogurt on hand and frequently add it to baked goods in place of butter, or to tuna salad instead of mayo.

In this section, we provide loads of recipes for comfort foods that are sure to satisfy you, without leaving you feeling bloated or stuffed.

Sloppy Joes

Prep time: 5 min • **Cook time:** 15 min • **Yield:** 6 servings

Ingredients	Directions
1 teaspoon canola oil	**1** In a large sauté pan, heat the oil over medium-high heat. Add the onions, celery, carrots, and bell pepper, and sauté until translucent.
1 yellow onion, diced	
1 celery stalk with leaves, thinly chopped	
½ cup matchstick carrots, chopped	**2** Add the garlic and sauté until fragrant, about 30 seconds.
1 green bell pepper, seeded and diced	**3** Remove the veggies from the pan and set aside in a bowl.
1 tablespoon minced garlic	
1 pound 96 percent lean ground beef	**4** In the same pan over medium-high heat, add the ground beef, Worcestershire sauce, molasses, and cayenne pepper and cook until the meat is browned.
1 tablespoon Worcestershire sauce	
1 tablespoon blackstrap molasses	**5** Stir in the tomato sauce and cooked vegetables.
⅛ teaspoon cayenne pepper	
¾ cup tomato sauce	**6** Serve on whole-grain buns with lettuce.
6 whole-wheat burger buns	
6 large Bibb lettuce leaves	

Per serving: Calories 274 (From Fat 61); Fat 7g (Saturated 2g); Cholesterol 47mg; Sodium 466mg; Carbohydrate 34g (Dietary Fiber 5g); Protein 21g.

Vary It! You can use ground turkey breast instead of beef, or make it vegetarian with ground tempeh.

Tip: This meal is excellent for a busy weeknight and tastes great reheated, too!

Santa Fe Chili

Prep time: 5 min • **Cook time:** 15 min • **Yield:** 8 servings

Ingredients	*Directions*
1 teaspoon olive oil	*1* In a large soup pot, heat the olive oil over medium-high heat.
1 sweet onion, peeled and diced	
1 green bell pepper, seeded and diced	*2* Sauté the onions, peppers, and garlic for about 5 minutes.
1 clove garlic, minced	*3* Add the ground turkey and cook until it's no longer pink, about 6 minutes.
1 pound extra-lean ground turkey breast	
3 tablespoons chili powder	*4* Stir in the chili powder, cumin, and oregano.
1 teaspoon cumin	
½ teaspoon oregano	*5* Add the remaining ingredients to the pot, and increase the heat to bring to a boil.
One 28-ounce can low-sodium canned diced tomatoes	
16 ounces tomato sauce	*6* Remove from the heat and serve with your favorite toppings.
One 15.5-ounce can no-salt-added yellow corn, drained	

Per serving: Calories 157 (From Fat 19); Fat 2g (Saturated 0g); Cholesterol 33mg; Sodium 373mg; Carbohydrate 22g (Dietary Fiber 4g); Protein 17g.

Tip: This chili is so hearty and warm, and it's delicious on a cold day.

Tip: Keep this recipe on hand for an easy and healthy weeknight meal in minutes. It freezes well, too, so you can easily enjoy it later.

Note: Toppings can add up fast, so go light to keep calories and fat in check. Nonfat Greek yogurt tastes great in place of sour cream. Also, try adding avocado and chives.

Grownup Grilled Cheese

Prep time: 10 min • **Cook time:** 20 min • **Yield:** 2 sandwiches

Ingredients	Directions
1 teaspoon canola oil	**1** In a medium pan, heat the canola oil over medium heat.
1 medium yellow onion, peeled and sliced	
Small pinch of kosher salt	**2** Sauté the onion with the salt and balsamic vinegar until softened and caramelized, about 10 to 12 minutes.
1 teaspoon balsamic vinegar	
4 ounces low-sodium deli turkey	**3** Build a sandwich by layering the caramelized onions, turkey, apple slices, kale leaves, and cheese onto the bread.
½ small Gala apple, thinly sliced	
1 cup kale leaves, shredded and cooked	**4** Coat a nonstick grill pan or skillet with cooking spray and heat to medium.
½ cup shredded reduced-fat Gruyère or Swiss cheese	**5** Place the sandwiches on the heated pan and gently press down with the back of a flattened spatula.
4 slices seedy whole-wheat bread	
	6 Allow to cook for 3 to 5 minutes on each side or until golden brown and the cheese melts.

Per serving: Calories 355 (From Fat 62); Fat 7g (Saturated 2g); Cholesterol 34mg; Sodium 688mg; Carbohydrate 48g (Dietary Fiber 7g); Protein 27g.

Vary It! Mix it up with baby spinach instead of kale, and use your favorite reduced-fat cheese!

Tip: Grilled cheese and tomato soup make the perfect comforting pair, and it's an easy way to get more veggies in your meal. Just make sure the tomato soup isn't filled with cream!

Shepherd's Pie with Cauliflower Mash

Prep time: 20 min • **Cook time:** 40 min • **Yield:** 8 servings

Ingredients	*Directions*
1 teaspoon olive oil 1 yellow onion, peeled and chopped	*1* In a large pot, heat the olive oil over medium-high heat, and sauté the onions, peppers, and garlic just until softened.
1 medium green bell pepper, seeded and chopped 1 tablespoon minced garlic	*2* Add the ground beef, chili powder, oregano, and vinegar and cook until browned.
1 pound 96 percent lean ground sirloin 1 teaspoon chili powder	*3* After the meat is browned, add the flour and cook until it's golden and starting to stick, about 2 minutes.
½ teaspoon oregano 1 tablespoon balsamic vinegar	*4* Pour in the beef broth to deglaze the pan and stir in the corn, carrots, green beans, and peas.
3 tablespoons 100 percent whole-grain flour	*5* Cover with a lid and cook, stirring occasionally, until the veggies are soft and the sauce has thickened.
14 ounces beef broth ½ cup yellow corn, frozen and defrosted	*6* Meanwhile, cook the cauliflower in the microwave for 3 to 4 minutes until softened, and then pat the cauliflower dry with paper towels.
½ cup carrots, diced ½ cup green beans, chopped ½ cup peas	*7* With an immersion blender or regular blender, blend the cauliflower, yogurt, and skim milk until creamy. Season with garlic powder, salt, pepper, and chives.
16 ounces frozen cauliflower, defrosted ¼ cup Greek yogurt	*8* Preheat the oven to 450 degrees and spray a large casserole dish with cooking spray. Spread the meat mixture into the bottom of the pan.
2 tablespoons skim milk ¼ teaspoon garlic powder	*9* Top the meat mixture with cauliflower mash and bake in the oven for 15 minutes, until the top of the cauliflower is beginning to brown.
¼ teaspoon kosher salt ¼ teaspoon pepper ¼ cup chopped chives	

Per serving: Calories 158 (From Fat 36); Fat 4g (Saturated 1g); Cholesterol 35mg; Sodium 315mg; Carbohydrate 15g (Dietary Fiber 3g); Protein 17g.

Creamy Avocado Quesadillas

Prep time: 10 min • **Cook time:** 15 min • **Yield:** 4 servings

Ingredients	*Directions*
1 teaspoon olive oil	*1* In a nonstick skillet, preferably heavy cast iron, heat the olive oil over medium heat.
½ green bell pepper, diced	
½ small red onion, diced	*2* Sauté the peppers, onions, carrots, and mushrooms until tender; season with salt and paprika.
¼ cup shredded carrots	
½ cup sliced baby bella mushrooms	*3* Add the garbanzo beans and cook until warmed; then remove the vegetables from the skillet and set aside.
⅟₁₆ teaspoon kosher salt	
⅛ teaspoon paprika	*4* Place a tortilla in the skillet, and flip after 1 minute.
1 cup reduced-sodium canned garbanzo beans, rinsed and drained	*5* Sprinkle ¼ cup of the cheese and ¼ of the avocado onto the tortilla. When the cheese begins to melt, top with ¼ of the vegetable mixture and fold the tortilla in half, pressing down with a spatula to secure together.
1 cup reduced-fat jalapeño cheddar cheese, shredded	
1 avocado, diced (refer to Figure 7-1)	*6* Heat 1 to 2 more minutes, flipping if necessary, until the tortilla is crispy and evenly browned.
Four 8-inch whole-wheat tortillas	*7* Remove from the heat, slice into three even triangles, and serve warm.
	8 Repeat Steps 4 through 7 for the remaining tortillas.

Per serving: Calories 289 (From Fat 108); Fat 12g (Saturated 3g); Cholesterol 6mg; Sodium 414mg; Carbohydrate 34g (Dietary Fiber 9g); Protein 15g.

Note: If you want to dip these tortillas, don't reach for the sour cream. Instead, use nonfat plain Greek yogurt for less fat and a great taste!

Orange Peel Chicken and Vegetables

Prep time: 10 min • **Cook time:** 15 min • **Yield:** 4 servings

Ingredients	Directions
1 pound chicken breast, cubed	**1** Marinate the chicken breast in ½ the orange juice and zest, and 1 tablespoon of the soy sauce for 10 to 15 minutes.
1 large orange, zest and juice	
3 tablespoons soy sauce	**2** Heat a wok or large skillet over high heat. Once it's hot, add 1 teaspoon of the sesame oil and swirl to coat the bottom of the pan.
2 teaspoons sesame oil	
3 tablespoons garlic, minced	**3** Add the chicken and marinade to the pan, cooking until no longer pink and cooked through, about 6 minutes. Remove the chicken from the wok and set aside.
1 teaspoon fresh ginger, minced	
1 red bell pepper, seeded and thinly sliced	**4** Reduce the heat to medium-high and add the remaining teaspoon of sesame oil to the pan. Sauté the garlic and ginger until fragrant.
½ cup matchstick carrots	**5** Add the pepper, carrots, the remaining 2 tablespoons of soy sauce, and the vinegar to the wok and cook just until the vegetables are tender.
1 tablespoon rice vinegar	
3 cups broccoli florets	**6** Stir in the broccoli florets and cook until bright green and gently steamed.
	7 Remove the vegetables from the wok and combine with the chicken mixture. Serve immediately.

Per serving: Calories 220 (From Fat 51); Fat 6g (Saturated 1g); Cholesterol 73mg; Sodium 922mg; Carbohydrate 14g (Dietary Fiber 3g); Protein 29g.

Tip: Prep all the ingredients before you begin to cook to ensure that the vegetables and chicken are properly cooked.

Note: Serve the chicken and vegetables over brown rice or Ginger Coconut Rice (see Chapter 11).

Fish Taco Quinoa Bowl

Prep time: 5 min • **Cook time:** 35 min • **Yield:** 4 servings

Ingredients	*Directions*
16 ounces haddock filets	*1* Preheat the oven to 450 degrees, and spray a large glass baking dish with cooking spray.
2 tablespoons taco seasoning	
1 lime, circularly sliced	
2 teaspoons olive oil	*2* Place the haddock filets in the baking dish, and sprinkle with taco seasonings. Place the lime wedges on top of the filets and drizzle 1 teaspoon of the olive oil over the filets.
1 red bell pepper, seeded and diced	
1 onion, peeled and diced	*3* Bake for 10 to 12 minutes, or until the filets begin to flake with a fork.
1 tablespoon minced garlic	
One 15-ounce can low-sodium black beans, rinsed and drained	*4* Meanwhile, in a nonstick skillet, heat the remaining teaspoon of olive oil over medium heat. Sauté the pepper, onion, and garlic until softened.
One 15.5-ounce can no-salt-added yellow corn, rinsed and drained	*5* Stir in the black beans and corn and cook until heated through.
4 cups romaine lettuce, shredded	
2 cups quinoa, cooked	*6* In 4 serving bowls, layer the lettuce, quinoa, vegetables, tomatoes, and haddock filets. Top with your favorite toppings.
2 Roma tomatoes, diced	

Per serving: Calories 422 (From Fat 53); Fat 6g (Saturated 1g); Cholesterol 65mg; Sodium 712mg; Carbohydrate 61g (Dietary Fiber 10g); Protein 34g.

Tip For toppings, try salsa, cilantro, avocado, and Greek yogurt.

Vary It! Easily incorporate a different protein into this dish. It's yummy with chicken, ground beef, and even tofu!

Chicken Alfredo Pizza

Prep time: 15 min • **Cook time:** 30 min • **Yield:** 8 slices

Ingredients for Pizza	*Directions*
1 cup Alfredo Sauce (see the following recipe)	**1** Heat a grill or grill pan over medium-high heat. Season the chicken breast with salt, pepper, and Italian seasoning.
8 ounces chicken breast, butterflied	**2** Grill the chicken for 2 to 3 minutes per side or until cooked through. Allow to rest for 10 minutes, and thinly slice the chicken into strips.
1/16 teaspoon salt	
1/16 teaspoon pepper	**3** Preheat the oven to 425 degrees.
1/2 teaspoon dried Italian seasoning	**4** Dust the pizza dough, rolling pin, and countertop with whole-grain flour to keep the dough from sticking. Roll out the dough into a thin circular pizza pie. Place on a baking stone or pizza sheet.
16 ounces whole-grain pizza dough, room temperature	
1 cup shredded 2 percent mozzarella cheese	**5** Spread the Alfredo Sauce evenly on the pizza. Top with spinach, chicken, and mozzarella cheese.
1 cup baby spinach	
	6 Bake the pizza for 18 minutes or until the crust begins to turn golden brown and the cheese is melted. Slice the pie into 8 even triangles.

Alfredo Sauce

16 ounces cauliflower, frozen **1 teaspoon olive oil** **2 teaspoons garlic, minced** **⅓ cup nonfat Greek yogurt** **¾ cup nonfat milk** **¼ teaspoon kosher salt** **⅛ teaspoon pepper**	**1** In a large microwave-safe bowl, heat the cauliflower for 8 minutes or until softened. **2** In a small nonstick skillet, heat the olive oil over medium heat. Add the garlic and sauté just until fragrant, taking care not to burn it. **3** In a blender, puree the cauliflower, oil, garlic, yogurt, milk, salt, and pepper until smooth and creamy.

Per serving: Calories 236 (From Fat 63); Fat 7g (Saturated 3g); Cholesterol 26mg; Sodium 458mg; Carbohydrate 29g (Dietary Fiber 6g); Protein 17g.

Tip: For workable dough, allow to come to room temperature, about 1 to 2 hours if stored in the refrigerator.

Note: Store the remaining Alfredo Sauce in an air-tight container or freeze it for later use.

Broccoli and Chicken Mac 'n' Cheese

Prep time: 15 min • **Cook time:** 15 min • **Yield:** 4 servings

Ingredients	Directions
8 ounces 100 percent whole-grain pasta shells	*1* Preheat the oven to 450 degrees. In a large pot, boil the water and add the pasta shells, cooking to al dente, or still slightly chewy.
1 teaspoon olive oil	
1 tablespoon minced garlic	*2* In a large skillet, heat the olive oil over medium heat. Sauté the garlic and red pepper flakes until fragrant. Add the broccoli and spinach, cooking just until bright green and tender. Remove from the pan.
⅛ teaspoon red pepper flakes	
2 cups broccoli florets, bite size	
2 cups baby spinach	*3* In a food processor, puree the beans, milk, and cheese together until creamy. Set aside.
One 15.5-ounce can reduced-sodium cannellini beans, rinsed and partially drained	
1 cup skim milk	*4* In a large bowl, combine the pasta, chicken breast, and cheese mixture. Gently stir in the vegetables.
1 cup shredded cheddar cheese	
2 cups shredded rotisserie chicken breast	*5* Spray a square glass 9-x-9-inch baking dish with cooking spray. Pour the macaroni and cheese into the baking dish, and cook for 10 minutes, until bubbly and heated through.
¼ cup sundried tomatoes	

Per serving: Calories 547 (From Fat 129); Fat 14g (Saturated 7g); Cholesterol 90mg; Sodium 463mg; Carbohydrate 63g (Dietary Fiber 5g); Protein 46g.

Note: Beans are high in fiber and protein. Cannellini beans contain one of the highest levels of resistant starch, which controls hunger swings and resists digestion. Your body has to work hard to digest it, burning more calories and helping in weight loss.

Eggplant Lasagne Pie

Prep time: 15 min • **Cook time:** 35 min • **Yield:** 4 servings

Ingredients	*Directions*
1 teaspoon olive oil	*1* Preheat the oven to 400 degrees.
1 medium yellow onion, peeled and diced	*2* In a cast-iron skillet, heat the oil over medium heat. Sauté the onions and mushrooms until softened.
8 baby bella mushrooms, sliced	
One 14.5-ounce can no-salt-added diced tomatoes, drained	*3* Add the tomatoes, garlic, red pepper flakes, fennel seeds, and salt, cooking until the garlic is fragrant. Remove from the heat.
1 teaspoon minced garlic	
⅛ teaspoon crushed red pepper flakes	*4* In a medium bowl, whisk the egg, and stir in ½ cup of the mozzarella and the milk until combined.
⅛ teaspoon fennel seeds	
¹⁄₁₆ teaspoon kosher salt	*5* Coat a round 9-inch pie dish with cooking spray.
1 egg	*6* Spread the tomato sauce on the bottom of the pan.
1 cup mozzarella	
¼ cup skim milk	*7* Place the lasagna noodles in an evenly layer on top of the sauce, breaking the noodles to fit the shape of the dish and avoiding overlapping the noodles.
¼ cup tomato sauce	
8 ounces no-cook lasagna noodles	*8* Spread ⅓ of the mozzarella mixture on top of the noodles.
1 small eggplant, thinly sliced rounds and blanched	*9* Layer the eggplant and then the tomato and onion mixture. Repeat to form a lasagne-style pie.
¼ cup Parmigiano-Reggiano cheese, shredded	*10* Top the pie with the remaining mozzarella and the Parmigiano-Reggiano cheese.
	11 Bake for 30 minutes. Allow to cool 10 minutes before serving.

Per serving: Calories 412 (From Fat 68); Fat 8g (Saturated 3g); Cholesterol 62mg; Sodium 657mg; Carbohydrate 69g (Dietary Fiber 10g); Protein 19g.

Tip: Up the protein in this meal, by mixing in sliced chicken or cottage cheese, or serve with a side salad topped with grilled chicken or fish.

Managing cravings

Some foods can bring on the cravings. Have you ever had a piece of candy and then suddenly wanted to keep eating more? We all have favorite foods. Some people love sweet treats or salty foods; others crave a combination of the two. But cravings aren't necessarily about the foods you're eating, but the context of how you're eating those foods.

If you were to eat candy, your blood sugar and insulin would spike and drop quickly because sugar is digested rapidly. It may taste yummy, but this type of energy is not sustaining or filling. It just gives you a sugar rush and then leaves you. To have sustained energy, you need to incorporate more food groups, specifically protein, healthy fats, and fiber-filling carbohydrates. This meal mix is sustainable, even if you were to on occasion have a few jellybeans at your meal.

Here are some tips for managing cravings:

✔ **Aim for protein, fiber, and healthy fats.** These three ingredients delay digestion, providing sustained energy. Instead of eating a piece of toast for breakfast, add an egg and avocado slices with a side of raspberries for longer-lasting energy.

✔ **Eat light and eat often.** Keep from giving into cravings by being properly nourished. When you go too long without eating, you may be more tempted to reach for that chocolate bowl.

✔ **Snacks shouldn't fill you up.** Snacks are just meant to bridge that gap to keep you from getting too hungry, not to fill you up. Snacking also helps with managing cravings.

✔ **Set limits.** A snack or dessert should not be laden with calories if you're trying to get in shape. If you're craving an additional scoop of ice cream, is there an emotional reason for this craving? If it's physical hunger, don't reach for dessert; instead, have something more substantial and nutritious.

✔ **Nothing is off limits.** If you label a food "good" or "bad," it can take control of you. Instead, allow yourself to eat any food — just moderate how much you have of it. Portions matter.

Part III
Belly-Burning Starters, Sides, Desserts, and More

Find out how to have your cake and eat it too in a free article at www.dummies.com/extras/flatbellycookbook.

In this part . . .

- ✔ Cool down and warm up with satisfying and refreshing recipes for soups and salads.

- ✔ Discover the difference between starchy and non-starchy sides, and find the best sides for shedding belly fat.

- ✔ Make scrumptious smoothies and drinks that are balanced with nutrition to not only hydrate you but also satisfy your sweet tooth.

- ✔ Discover how to enjoy desserts and snacks on your Belly Fat Diet plan.

Chapter 10

Soups and Salads

In This Chapter

▶ Warming your heart with belly-trimming soups

▶ Making like a rabbit and munching on salads to stay trim

Recipes in This Chapter

▶ Chilled Spring Green Soup

▶ Asian Chicken Noodle Soup

▶ White Bean Chili

▶ Lemon Orzo Soup with Pesto

↻ Spicy Coconut Soup

↻ Baby Beet and Orange Salad with Pomegranate Dressing

↻ Mushroom Flatbread and Arugula Salad

▶ Shrimp and Blue Salad with Sherry-Thyme Dressing

↻ Kale Caesar Salad

▶ Blueberry, Watermelon, and Walnut Salad with Chicken

Soups and salads make the ultimate pair — hot and cold, sweet and tangy, spicy and cooling. This lighthearted duo screams "health" (when done right, of course). It makes a filling and fabulous meal, too. Many restaurants are noticing the popularity of soups and salads and are putting them front and center on the menu. Even fast-food chains are offering unique salads and soups to please their health-conscious clientele.

We love soups and salads because they're all about the good stuff: vegetables! Filling up on the fibrous vegetables and lean proteins that you find in soups and salads can prevent you from overdoing it in on higher-calorie foods.

Another reason to love this pair: They transport well! Packing a soup or salad to go for lunch is effortless. Plus, they can taste scrumptious and so fresh eaten as leftovers, which means less time spent in the kitchen.

Soups and salads are often pretty simple and easy for even the novice chef to prepare. With the recipes in this chapter, you'll quickly find yourself creating healthy soups and salads in the comfort of your own kitchen!

Soup R' Crackers: Making Soups from Scratch

Soups make the simplest one-pot meal and have unlimited versatility! With the hustle and bustle of everyday life, finding the time for nutritious and complete meals can be difficult. But not to worry — soup is a throw-every-thing-in-one-pot kind of meal that's easy to assemble any day of the week.

You can find a soup for every culture, every flavor, and every occasion. Historically, soups have been the starter or first course before a main meal, but they can also be the foundation for lunch or dinner on their own — just pair your favorite soup with whole grains and a protein source, and you're good to go! (Try the Lemon Chicken Orzo Soup recipe in this section, if you're not sure where to start.) Pair a soup with a salad or sandwich for a light lunch, or try a heartier recipe (such as White Bean Chili or Asian Chicken Noodle Soup) for a filling, nutritionally balanced meal.

If done right, soups make an excellent low-calorie way to get the vitamins, minerals, and nutrients you need, all while burning belly fat. Cooking soups in one pot conserves more nutrition — even if some nutrients escape the veggies during the cooking process, they don't get too far because you'll be eating the broth, too!

Here are some tips for making your soup a belly blaster:

- **Base it on vegetables.** Vegetable soups are supreme because of the high-quality nutrients and low calorie count. For these reasons, they're great when you're trying to lose belly fat — and they still leave you feeling satisfied!

- **Go easy on the toppings.** You may be tempted to add cheese, crackers, and a dollop of sour cream to soup. But flavorful soups won't leave you craving added toppings. If you still can't imagine soup without something on top, opt for lighter toppings, like fresh herbs, lemon juice, lime juice, Sriracha hot sauce, Greek yogurt, green onions, or jalapeños.

- **Go fresh and go home.** Homemade soup is where it's at! Canned varieties can be jam-packed with sodium and fat, to preserve the product's shelf life and add flavor. Plus, they often tend to be lower in vegetables, protein, and nutrients. Dried soups like packaged ramen noodles are also a no-no. You may have lived off them back in college, but these prepackaged soups are laced with nearly an entire *day's* worth of sodium, leaving your belly bloated.

✔ **Stick with low-calorie broth-based soups (as opposed to high-calorie cream-based soups).** Broth-based soups tend to have a higher water content, keeping you hydrated, which is key for a flat belly. If you're craving cream, slash the fat with cauliflower, smashed beans, milk, or Greek yogurt, instead of using butter, heavy cream, cream cheese, or sour cream. (Check out the Chilled Spring Green Soup and White Bean Chili recipes later in this section for examples of this approach.)

✔ **Make soups ahead of time.** The recipes in this chapter are perfect for making in advance or in bulk. Refrigerate them for leftovers or freeze them for a rainy day when you don't feel like cooking.

The great thing about soups is you can vary them to suit your individual taste. Here are some belly-slimming ingredients you can add to soup for added bulk, texture, and flavor, without the added fat:

✔ **Cauliflower:** One cup of raw cauliflower has almost a full day's worth of vitamin C, a key player in warding off sickness. Mix pureed cauliflower into your soup to give it a creamy texture without all the calories.

✔ **Spinach:** Spinach is a great source of iron, which aids in transporting oxygen throughout the body, so you can push it through a tough workout.

✔ **Kale:** Kale is super-rich in vitamin K, which helps to reduce cancer risks. Plus, the added fiber boost from this vegetable can help you lose belly fat.

✔ **Spaghetti squash:** Spaghetti squash can stand in for regular pasta! It's a low-calorie and low-carb swap that's loaded with nutrition, too.

✔ **Zucchini:** Shred it into your soup or keep it chunky. Zucchini adds a nice body and is mild, so it takes on the flavors of the other ingredients in soup.

✔ **Lentils:** Lentils are a great vegetarian source of protein that can help you reduce your intake of the less-than-belly-friendly saturated fat.

✔ **Whole-grain orzo and quinoa:** Whole grains help to boost fiber and keep you full. Plus, quinoa is a complete protein source!

✔ **Nonfat Greek yogurt:** Get the cream without the fat by adding Greek yogurt to soups.

✔ **Tofu:** Tofu is great for creamy soups.

✔ **Cannellini beans:** Smashed cannellini beans give a thick and creamy texture to soups. Plus, they add protein.

✔ **Ginger:** Ginger helps to slim the midsection by fighting inflammation.

Chilled Spring Green Soup

Prep time: 5 min • **Cook time:** 15 min • **Yield:** 6 servings

Ingredients	Directions
1 teaspoon olive oil	**1** In a large soup pot, heat the olive oil over medium-high heat.
½ large onion, diced	
2 stalks celery, diced	**2** Sauté the onion, celery, and garlic for about 2 minutes.
2 cloves garlic, minced	
7.5 ounces frozen asparagus spears	**3** Add the asparagus and cauliflower to the pot, and sauté until softened.
3 cups frozen cauliflower florets	
1 teaspoon fresh rosemary, chopped	**4** Add the rosemary, salt, peas, spinach, and broth. Cover and bring to a boil.
¼ teaspoon salt	
1 cup frozen peas	**5** Remove from the heat and puree with an immersion blender or pour soup contents into a regular blender and puree until smooth.
10 ounces frozen spinach	
4 cups reduced-sodium chicken broth	
2 ounces garlic and herbed goat cheese	**6** Stir in the goat cheese and yogurt, and allow them to melt into the soup.
¼ cup plain nonfat Greek yogurt	**7** Chill and serve.

Per serving: Calories 131 (From Fat 44); Fat 5g (Saturated 2g); Cholesterol 7mg; Sodium 254mg; Carbohydrate 13g (Dietary Fiber 4g); Protein 11g.

Vary It! This soup also tastes great warm, so feel free not to chill it if you prefer a warm soup.

Tip: You can serve this soup topped with crumbled goat cheese and sprigs of rosemary for garnish, if you like.

Blueberry Breakfast Salad (Chapter 6), Sunrise Protein Shake (Chapter 6), and Microwave Egg Sandwich (Chapter 6)

Peanut Butter and Banana Honey Sticks (Chapter 16) and Baked Egg-in-a-Hole (Chapter 16)

DIY Lunchables (Chapter 7), Egg Salad Sandwiches (Chapter 7), and Cinnamon Applesauce (Chapter 15)

Orange Peel Chicken and Vegetables (Chapter 9) and Mongolian Pork and Vegetables (Chapter 8)

Tropicolada (Chapter 13), Curried Couscous (Chapter 7), and Jamaican Jerk Beef and Shrimp Shish Kebabs (Chapter 8)

White Bean and Tomato Pesto Pizza (Chapter 14), Smoked Chickpeas (Chapter 12), and Buffalo Chicken Sliders with Blue Cheese Dip (Chapter 8)

Shrimp and Blue Salad with Sherry-Thyme Dressing (Chapter 10), Blueberry Party Mix (Chapter 12), and Fiesta Chicken Salad (Chapter 7)

Asian Chicken Noodle Soup

Prep time: 10 min • **Cook time:** 20 min • **Yield:** 6 servings

Ingredients	*Directions*
1 small spaghetti squash (or 2 cups cooked)	*1* Spear the spaghetti squash with a knife several times on each side. Cook in the microwave on high for about 4 minutes, or until tender and easily sliced with a knife.
1 teaspoon olive oil	
1 yellow onion, diced	
3 cloves garlic, minced	*2* Cut the squash in half. Remove the seeds, and gently scrape the edges with a fork until all the "spaghetti" is removed. Set aside.
½ pound shredded white meat chicken	
¾ cup carrot sticks	*3* In a large soup pot, heat the olive oil over medium heat for about 2 minutes, until hot.
1 cup shiitake mushrooms, sliced	
1 cup chopped fresh kale	*4* Add the onion and garlic to the pot and sauté.
1 teaspoon fresh ginger, minced	*5* Stir in the carrots, mushrooms, kale, ginger, and soy sauce.
3 tablespoons low-sodium soy sauce	
¼ teaspoon Chinese five spice powder	*6* Mix in the Chinese five spice, bean sprouts, spaghetti squash, broth, and Sriracha.
1 cup bean sprouts	*7* Stir in the shredded chicken. Cover and bring the contents to a boil.
4 cups reduced-sodium chicken broth	
⅛ teaspoon Sriracha hot sauce	*8* Remove from the heat and serve.

Per serving: Calories 130 (From Fat 28); Fat 3g (Saturated 1g); Cholesterol 24mg; Sodium 387mg; Carbohydrate 14g (Dietary Fiber 2g); Protein 14g.

Note: This soup is ideal on a cold winter's night or to soothe cold symptoms.

Tip: Using spaghetti squash in place of traditional egg noodles significantly reduces the calories and carbohydrates and provides an array of nutrients you don't want to miss out on, like fiber, vitamin C, and potassium.

White Bean Chili

Prep time: 5 min • **Cook time:** 10 min • **Yield:** 6 servings

Ingredients	Directions
1 teaspoon canola oil	*1* In a Dutch oven or a medium soup pot, heat the canola oil over medium-high heat. Add the onions, garlic, and red pepper to the pot and sauté until softened, about 6 minutes.
1 yellow onion, diced	
2 cloves garlic, minced	
1 red pepper, diced	
One 15-ounce can no-salt-added cannellini beans, rinsed and drained	*2* In a small bowl, smash half the cannellini beans and half the garbanzo beans with a fork.
One 15.5-ounce can reduced-sodium garbanzo beans, rinsed and drained	*3* Add the corn, beans (both the smashed and the whole ones), chilies, chili powder, and cumin to the Dutch oven or pot, and stir until combined.
One 15.25-ounce can no-salt-added whole-kernel corn, rinsed and drained	*4* Add the chicken broth and bring to a boil.
One 4-ounce can green chilies	*5* Remove from the heat and serve.
3 teaspoons chili powder	
2 teaspoons cumin	
3 cups low-sodium chicken broth	

Per serving: Calories 214 (From Fat 14); Fat 2g (Saturated 0g); Cholesterol 0mg; Sodium 508mg; Carbohydrate 41g (Dietary Fiber 9g); Protein 11g.

Note: This is the perfect make-ahead soup. Whip up a batch of soup on the weekend, and eat it all week. Don't forget to freeze the leftovers!

Tip: Dinner in a flash? The ingredients in this recipe are pantry staples. Keep your pantry stocked so you can whip up a healthy dinner in 15 minutes!

Tip: If you like, top with chopped cilantro, lime juice, and a dollop of nonfat plain Greek yogurt.

Lemon Orzo Soup with Pesto

Prep time: 10 min • **Cook time:** 25 min • **Yield:** 8 servings

Ingredients	Directions
1 teaspoon olive oil	**1** In a Dutch oven or large soup pot, heat the olive oil over medium-high heat. Add the onion, celery, carrots, and salt, and sauté until softened, about 8 minutes.
1 white onion, chopped	
3 celery stalks, chopped	
1 cup baby carrots, chopped	
⅛ teaspoon kosher salt	**2** Tie the thyme springs together with kitchen string, and toss in the pot.
1 bunch fresh thyme	
12 ounces whole chicken breast	**3** Add the chicken breast and broth and bring to a boil. Partially cover the pot and continue to cook for 10 minutes, or until the chicken is cooked through. Remove the chicken from the pot and set aside.
6 cups low-sodium chicken broth	
1 cup whole-wheat orzo	**4** Add the orzo to the Dutch oven or pot, and continue to boil until the orzo is cooked al dente, about 5 minutes.
1 lemon, halved, with one half sliced into 8 rounds, for topping	
2 cups spinach, chopped	**5** Shred the chicken, and squeeze with the juice of one-half of the lemon.
8 teaspoons jarred pesto, for topping	
	6 Stir the shredded chicken and spinach into the soup. Remove the thyme springs.
	7 To serve, top each bowl of soup with a lemon slice and 1 teaspoon of the pesto.

Per serving: Calories 169 (From Fat 40); Fat 4g (Saturated 1g); Cholesterol 28mg; Sodium 685mg; Carbohydrate 18g (Dietary Fiber 3g); Protein 15g.

Vary it! Create a new flavor combo by making a homemade pesto with mint or rosemary: In a food processor or blender, puree 3 cloves garlic with ⅓ cup walnuts or pine nuts, and then blend in 2 cups of your favorite fresh herbs. Slowly add in ½ cup olive oil, and process until smooth. Transfer the pesto to a bowl and stir in ½ cup shredded Parmesan cheese, and season with salt and pepper. Voilà!

Spicy Coconut Soup

Prep time: 10 min • **Cook time:** 20 min • **Yield:** 2 servings

Ingredients	*Directions*
1 tablespoon coconut oil	*1* In a large saucepan, add the coconut oil and garlic over medium heat. Add the tomato, onion, pepper, and coconut, and cook until tender, about 5 minutes.
1 tablespoon minced garlic	
1 medium tomato, diced	
1 medium onion, chopped	*2* Transfer the vegetables into a food processor, along with the coconut water, cayenne pepper, curry powder, ginger powder, salt, and pepper, and blend until smooth.
1 yellow bell pepper, sliced	
2 tablespoons shredded coconut	
1½ cups ZICO Natural Pure Premium Coconut Water	*3* Pour the mixture from the food processor back into the saucepan over low heat. Bring the mixture to a slight simmer. Remove from the heat and serve warm. Garnish with lemon zest, if desired.
¼ to 1 teaspoon cayenne pepper, to taste	
1 teaspoon curry powder	
1 tablespoon ginger powder	
Salt, to taste	
Pepper, to taste	
1 tablespoon lemon zest, for garnish	

Per serving: Calories 266 (From Fat 106); Fat 12g (Saturated 10g); Cholesterol 0mg; Sodium 92mg; Carbohydrate 40g (Dietary Fiber 7g); Protein 4g.

Note: Balance this spicy soup with protein by adding your favorite seafood. Shrimp or scallops would be delicious.

Tip: Feeling fancy? Garnish this dish with sliced green onions and grated lime zest.

Going Green with Salads

We're willing to bet this won't shock you: Americans don't eat enough fruits and vegetables. Eating salads is an easy way to meet your daily quota. A big bowl of greens can provide up to two to three servings of vegetables and one serving of fruit, depending on how you build it.

One of our favorite ways to eat salads is to make them an entree by adding protein and a carbohydrate (like fruit, peas, corn, sweet potatoes, or quinoa). A light salad can provide diversity and take the edge off your hunger so you don't end up overeating during a main course.

When you include a variety of colors in your salad, you're getting an assortment of vitamins and minerals, all of which are important. Antioxidants (like vitamins A, C, D, E, and selenium) can keep you healthy by assisting your immune system in fighting illness and infection and helping you recover from injuries.

A variety of salad ingredients — like fruits, vegetables, nuts, and seeds — are excellent sources of fiber. The average American doesn't get enough fiber, and salads are delicious ways to boost your fiber intake. Dietary fiber can help to reduce cholesterol and blood sugar, and helps to fight heart disease. Fiber also plays a role in the movement of foods through the digestive tract and can prevent constipation. Enough said.

Fruits and vegetables are satisfying and naturally low in calories and fat. Filling up on the good stuff like salads can help you shed unwanted belly fat.

You have all kinds of leeway when it comes to building your own salad. The recipes in this section are great places to start, but don't let yourself be limited by recipes — feel free to toss in any fruits and vegetables you have in the kitchen that sound appealing to you!

Baby Beet and Orange Salad with Pomegranate Dressing

Prep time: 15 min • **Cook time:** 25 min • **Yield:** 4 servings

Ingredients	Directions
Pomegranate Dressing (see the following recipe)	*1* Preheat the oven to 450 degrees. Line a baking sheet with parchment paper.
3 medium beets, peeled and cubed	
⅛ teaspoon kosher salt	*2* In a large bowl, mix the beets with the salt, pepper, and olive oil, and roast in the oven for 25 minutes. While the beets are roasting, make the dressing (see the following recipe).
Pinch of pepper	
1 tablespoon olive oil	
8 cups baby greens spring mix	*3* After the beets are done roasting, remove them from the oven and place them in a large bowl. Pour the dressing into the bowl with the beets and mix to coat well.
1 cup blackberries	
2 navel oranges, sectioned	*4* Divide the spring mix among four plates.
½ cup pistachios, chopped, for topping	
½ cup blue cheese, for topping	*5* Top each salad evenly with blackberries, orange sections, and beets. Sprinkle the pistachios and blue cheese on top.

Pomegranate Dressing

¼ cup cucumber, cubed with peel

¼ cup parsley

1 tablespoon red wine vinegar

¼ cup pomegranate juice

¼ cup extra-virgin olive oil

1 tablespoon agave nectar

1 teaspoon Dijon mustard

¼ teaspoon kosher salt

3 tablespoons plain nonfat Greek yogurt

1 teaspoon orange zest

In a food processor or blender, add all the ingredients and blend until smooth. Set aside.

Per serving: Calories 433 (From Fat 269); Fat 30g (Saturated 6g); Cholesterol 13mg; Sodium 507mg; Carbohydrate 35g (Dietary Fiber 10g); Protein 12g.

Note: Beets have a vibrant color, which can stain easily. Keep them clear of light-colored countertops, sinks, and clothes. Wear an apron and, if you can, take them outdoors to cut them.

Mushroom Flatbread and Arugula Salad

Prep time: 20 min • **Cook time:** 40 min • **Yield:** 2 servings

Ingredients	Directions
1 cup whole mushrooms	**1** Preheat the oven to 375 degrees.
1 clove garlic, minced	
1 tablespoon olive oil	**2** In a food processor, blend the mushrooms, garlic, olive oil, lemon, and salt until slightly chunky.
½ lemon, juiced	
⅛ teaspoon kosher salt	**3** Place the flatbreads on a cookie sheet, spread the mixture on the flatbreads, and top with the figs. Bake for 12 minutes.
Two 8-inch whole-wheat flatbreads	
5 dried figs, sliced	**4** While the flatbreads are baking, in a large bowl, combine the lemon zest, lemon juice, cheese, and pepper. Toss with the arugula.
Zest and the juice of ½ lemon	
2 tablespoons grated Parmigiano-Reggiano cheese	**5** When the flatbreads are done, remove them from the oven and top with the arugula mixture. Drizzle with balsamic vinegar, and serve.
Pepper, to taste	
2 cups arugula	
2 tablespoons thick balsamic vinegar, drizzled for topping (see Tip)	

Per serving: Calories 265 (From Fat 105); Fat 12g (Saturated 2g); Cholesterol 4mg; Sodium 431mg; Carbohydrate 37g (Dietary Fiber 11g); Protein 13g.

Tip: You can buy thick balsamic vinegar in some specialty food shops or use an aged balsamic vinegar that is thicker and already good for drizzling. Or, to make 2 tablespoons of your own thick balsamic vinegar, just pour ½ cup balsamic vinegar into a small pan over medium-high heat. Bring the vinegar to a boil and reduce to a simmer, stirring occasionally until you reduce the liquid to a thick yet still drizzly consistency.

Shrimp and Blue Salad with Sherry-Thyme Dressing

Prep time: 5 min • **Cook time:** 10 min • **Yield:** 4 servings

Ingredients	Directions
Sherry-Thyme Dressing (see the following recipe)	**1** Preheat the oven to 400 degrees. Line a baking sheet with parchment paper, and roast the shrimp for 5 minutes, flipping halfway through, until they're pink. Set aside.
16 ounces frozen raw large shrimp, peeled, deveined, and defrosted (refer to Figure 8-1)	
½ cup slivered almonds	**2** Toast the almonds in a dry skillet over medium heat. Cook just until fragrant, and remove from the pan.
4 cups baby spinach	
2 cups arugula	**3** In a large bowl, mix the spinach and arugula with the dressing, gently coating all the leaves.
1 Granny Smith apple, diced	
½ red onion, sliced	**4** Divide the greens among 4 individual bowls. Top with the shrimp, apple, onion, almonds, cherries, and blue cheese.
½ cup dried tart cherries	
½ cup blue cheese	

Sherry-Thyme Dressing

½ large shallot	In a blender or food processor, combine all ingredients and process until blended.
5 sprigs thyme, stems removed	
Pinch of kosher salt	
2 tablespoons sherry vinegar	
2 tablespoons olive oil	

Per serving: Calories 415 (From Fat 207); Fat 23g (Saturated 5g); Cholesterol 185mg; Sodium 561mg; Carbohydrate 21g (Dietary Fiber 5g); Protein 32g.

Vary It! We love the blue cheese in this recipe because it provides a nice pungent contrast with the dressing and tart cherries, but if you prefer another cheese, by all means toss in your favorite instead!

Kale Caesar Salad

Prep time: 10 min • **Cook time:** 15 min • **Yield:** 4 servings

Ingredients	*Directions*
1 cup diced day-old whole-grain baguette	*1* Preheat the oven to 400 degrees. Line a baking sheet with parchment paper, and evenly space the baguette pieces on the sheet.
1 tablespoon lemon zest	
½ teaspoon crushed red pepper flakes	*2* Mist the baguette pieces with cooking spray or olive oil, and sprinkle with red pepper flakes and lemon zest. Bake for 15 minutes.
½ tablespoon lemon zest	
1 clove garlic	*3* In a food processor or blender, mince the garlic. Add the tofu, olive oil, lemon juice, and salt, and process until smooth.
¼ cup silken tofu, patted dry	
2 tablespoons olive oil	
4 tablespoons lemon juice	*4* In a large bowl, massage the dressing into the kale leaves to soften up the kale. Stir in baguette pieces and garnish with cheese.
⅛ teaspoon kosher salt	
6 cups chopped dinosaur kale leaves	
½ cup Parmesano-Reggiano cheese, for garnish	

Per serving: Calories 317 (From Fat 111); Fat 12g (Saturated 3g); Cholesterol 11mg; Sodium 617mg; Carbohydrate 40g (Dietary Fiber 3g); Protein 15g.

Tip: Turn this salad into a comforting entree by topping it with warm grilled chicken.

Blueberry, Watermelon, and Walnut Salad with Chicken

Prep time: 10 min • **Cook time:** 8 min • **Yield:** 6 servings

Ingredients	Directions
1 cup California walnuts, chopped, unsalted	**1** Preheat the oven to 350 degrees. On a baking sheet, spread the walnuts in one layer. Bake until toasted and aromatic, about 8 minutes. Remove them from the baking sheet and place them in a separate bowl to allow to cool.
¼ cup lime juice	
¼ cup olive oil	
2 tablespoons honey	**2** To prepare the vinaigrette, in a small bowl, whisk together the lime juice, olive oil, honey, salt, and pepper. Set aside.
¼ teaspoon sea salt	
¼ teaspoon pepper	
2 cups seedless watermelon, cubed	**3** In a medium bowl, combine the watermelon, blueberries, walnuts, and bell pepper. Add half the vinaigrette, and toss to coat.
1 cup fresh blueberries	
1 yellow bell pepper, cut in bite-size pieces	**4** In a large bowl, toss the greens with the remaining vinaigrette.
12 cups mixed baby greens	
2 pounds boneless, skinless chicken breasts, grilled or sautéed until cooked through (see Note)	**5** Divide the greens among 6 plates; top with the fruit and walnut mixture.
	6 Slice each chicken breast diagonally, and serve with the salad.

Per serving: Calories 464 (From Fat 238); Fat 26g (Saturated 3g); Cholesterol 97mg; Sodium 289mg; Carbohydrate 23g (Dietary Fiber 4g); Protein 37g.

Note: This recipe is reproduced from www.blueberrycouncil.org. Reproduced with the permission of the U.S. Highbush Blueberry Council.

Improving your salad creations

When it comes to salads, there *is* such a thing as too much of a good thing. Many salads on the menus at your favorite restaurants may be slammed with calories and fat, mostly because they're laden with high-fat cheeses, dressings, and fried meats. Here are some tips to keep your salads delicious without sabotaging your healthy eating efforts:

✔ **When it comes to greens, the darker the better.** Try a variety of dark greens like arugula, endive, cabbage, spinach, kale, and Butterhead lettuce.

✔ **Steer clear of fried proteins and toppings.** Go for lean proteins like grilled chicken, turkey, hardboiled eggs, tofu, fish, and seafood.

✔ **Make your own salad dressing.** Preparing dressing from scratch may take a few extra minutes, but you'll know exactly what ingredients are in your dressing.

✔ **Add calorie-free toppings.** You can up the flavor while keeping calories in check with balsamic vinegar, white wine vinegar, citrus juices, and fresh herbs like cilantro, parsley, rosemary, and thyme.

✔ **Get inspired!** Try unique salad toppings such as avocado, chickpeas, asparagus, beets, broccoli, cottage cheese, nuts and seeds, quinoa, oranges, and pomegranate seeds. You have no excuse for getting bored when you're making a salad — the options are endless!

Chapter 11

Sides

When you think of side dishes, does your mind immediately go to the traditional, fat-laden, high-calorie sides that accompany a Thanksgiving dinner? If so, you may assume sides have no place in your Belly Fat Diet plan. But here's the good news: You can opt for light sides, sensibly seasoned and garnished with herbs and lemon zest, and misted with oils that bring out the natural flavor of the foods instead of weighing them down with all that butter and sauce.

"Sure," you're thinking, "I bet your idea of a healthy side is a bunch of steamed broccoli." Now, we're not ones to knock steamed broccoli, but in this chapter, we kick it up a notch (or ten!), giving you a variety of healthy recipes for sides that are sure to add interest and flavor to any meal.

Whole Grains and Starchy Vegetables

Sides based around starchy vegetables and whole grains (like the ones in this section) can be super-healthy, but you'll need to enjoy them in moderation because if you eat too much of them, your weight loss progress may slow to a crawl.

Spring Risotto

Prep time: 10 min • **Cook time:** 30 min • **Yield:** 4 servings

Ingredients	Directions
1 teaspoon olive oil	**1** In a large pot, heat the olive oil over medium heat.
1 medium yellow onion, diced	
2 cloves garlic, minced	**2** Add the onion, garlic, and salt, and sauté until tender.
¼ teaspoon kosher salt	
4 cups no-salt-added vegetable broth	**3** In a microwave-safe liquid measuring cup or bowl (preferably with a pour spout), add the vegetable broth. Heat on high for 3 to 4 minutes until steaming hot.
1 cup short-grain brown rice	
1 carrot, finely shredded	**4** Add the rice to the pot with the onion and garlic, and stir until it just begins to stick. Add one-quarter of the vegetable broth.
1 cup asparagus tips	
1 cup frozen peas	
1 tablespoon chopped parsley, for garnish	**5** Continue stirring the rice occasionally until almost all the broth has been absorbed. Add more broth in increments, allowing the broth to be absorbed before adding more.
1 tablespoon chopped mint, for garnish	
	6 When almost all the broth is absorbed, stir in the carrot until combined. Add the asparagus tips and continue cooking for a few minutes until they turn bright green. Gently stir in the peas.
	7 Garnish each serving of risotto with chopped parsley and mint.

Per serving: Calories 260 (From Fat 24); Fat 3g (Saturated 0g); Cholesterol 0mg; Sodium 443mg; Carbohydrate 53g (Dietary Fiber 5g); Protein 7g.

Tip: Slowly add the broth to ensure the starches are being released from the rice — this is what makes it creamy. Continue stirring to prevent the rice from sticking to the bottom of pan.

Tip: Make it a meal by stirring in chopped grilled chicken or serving it alongside a piece of baked salmon and a green salad.

Vary It! Mix up the veggies! You can add shredded zucchini instead of carrots, or broccoli instead of peas. Mushrooms and canned pumpkin are also delicious in risotto.

Curried Quinoa

Prep time: 5 min • **Cook time:** 35 min • **Yield:** 4 servings

Ingredients	*Directions*
1 medium sweet onion, diced	*1* In a saucepan, cook the onion, tomato, and bell pepper in the coconut oil and garlic over medium heat until tender.
1 medium tomato, diced	
1 green bell pepper, diced	
1 teaspoon coconut oil	
1 tablespoon minced garlic	*2* Add the coconut water, vegetable stock, pepper, and curry to the saucepan and bring to a simmer. Add the quinoa, reduce to a low heat, and cover. Let the quinoa cook for 15 minutes, or until the fluid is absorbed. Remove the saucepan from the heat and let stand for 10 minutes. Remove the cover and serve warm.
¾ cup ZICO Natural Pure Premium Coconut Water	
¼ cup vegetable stock	
½ teaspoon pepper	
1 tablespoon curry powder	
½ cup quinoa	

Per serving: Calories 138 (From Fat 24); Fat 3g (Saturated 1g); Cholesterol 0mg; Sodium 54mg; Carbohydrate 25g (Dietary Fiber 3g); Protein 4g.

Note: Curry and garlic are loaded with nutrition that helps to fight off inflammation.

Tip: This dish is a perfect side for a made-ahead lunch! Toss this grain over a bed of spinach and serve with shredded chicken or chickpeas to complete the meal.

Starchy vegetables?

Enjoy starchy vegetables, but just watch your portion sizes. The following vegetables fall into the starch category on the Belly Fat Diet plan (which is the same food group that contains breads, cereals, and pasta): beans, corn, lentils, peas, potatoes, sweet potatoes, winter squash (acorn, butternut, pumpkin, spaghetti), and yams.

Ginger Coconut Rice

Prep time: 5 min • **Cook time:** 1 hr • **Yield:** 4 servings

Ingredients	*Directions*
1½ cup ZICO Natural Pure Premium Coconut Water	*1* In a saucepan, bring the coconut water, water, salt, ginger, and shredded coconut to a boil.
¼ cup water	
½ teaspoon salt	*2* Add in the rice and stir. Reduce the heat to a simmer and cover the saucepan. Allow the rice to simmer approximately 45 to 50 minutes, or until the water is absorbed.
1 teaspoon minced ginger	
2 tablespoons unsweetened coconut, shredded	
1 cup brown rice	

Per serving: Calories 211 (From Fat 33); Fat 4g (Saturated 2g); Cholesterol 0mg; Sodium 310mg; Carbohydrate 41g (Dietary Fiber 2g); Protein 4g.

Note: Ginger has potent inflammation-reducing capabilities!

Healthy whole grains

What's the deal with whole grains? Simply put, a grain is a whole grain if it contains 100 percent of the nutrition that is naturally occurring in the grain. Whole grains are made up of the bran, germ, and endosperm. The bran and germ contain lots of nutrients that are taken away when processed into white flour, leaving only the endosperm behind. Whole grains have more fiber that can help reduce bad cholesterol, aid in maintaining healthy blood sugar levels, provide regularity to the digestive system, and promote fullness so you don't overeat and gain belly fat.

Here's a short list of whole grains commonly found in the grocery store that you should eat more of for wholesome nutrition: amaranth, barley, buckwheat, corn, couscous (whole grain), faro, millet, oats, spelt, quinoa, and rice (brown and wild). And don't forget 100 percent whole-wheat bread!

Sweet Potato and Carrot Bake with Pecan Crumble

Prep time: 10 min • **Cook time:** 10 min • **Yield:** 8 servings

Ingredients	Directions
2 sweet potatoes, peeled and diced	**1** Preheat the oven to 375 degrees.
2 carrots, finely shredded	**2** In a medium pot, place the sweet potatoes and fill with water. Bring to a boil and cook for 8 minutes, until the potatoes are softened.
2 tablespoons vanilla almond milk	**3** Toss the carrots into the water with the potatoes to blanch them; drain the excess liquid from the vegetables.
¼ teaspoon cinnamon	
⅓ cup pecans, crushed	**4** Mash the sweet potatoes and carrots together until combined.
⅓ cup graham crackers	**5** Stir in the almond milk and cinnamon.
1 teaspoon agave nectar	**6** In a small bowl, mix together the pecans, graham crackers, agave nectar, and coconut oil until crumbly.
1 tablespoon coconut oil	**7** Spray a 9-x-9-inch square baking pan with cooking spray.
	8 Add the sweet potato and carrot mixture to the pan and spread evenly.
	9 Top with the pecan crumble, and dust with a sprinkle of cinnamon.
	10 Bake for 10 minutes, until the crumble begins to turn golden.

Per serving: Calories 133 (From Fat 49); Fat 5g (Saturated 2g); Cholesterol 0mg; Sodium 58mg; Carbohydrate 20g (Dietary Fiber 3g); Protein 2g.

Note: This side dish is loaded with nutrition without all the fat that's in traditional sweet potato casserole! You fill up on vitamin A, vitamin C, the B vitamins, and fiber when you eat just one serving of this dish.

Tip: Don't have agave nectar on hand? You can use honey instead.

A Vegetable Free-for-All

Filling up on non-starchy vegetables is never a bad thing when trying to shred belly fat. Vegetables help to keep you full and increase your satisfaction, but they have only a few calories, which helps to promote weight loss. Vegetables are also packed full of powerful antioxidants, vitamins, minerals, and phytonutrients that support a healthy metabolism and reduce inflammation in the body.

Not all the nutrition you need for the day is in one vegetable, so you have to eat a variety of vegetables. One way of doing this is to focus on the different colors — orange, yellow, green, white, red, and purple! Aim to "eat the rainbow" by including all the different colors in your diet.

Keep your vegetables lean and belly-friendly by minimizing your use of oils, butter, and cream sauce and upping the flavor with vinegar, fresh and dried herbs, garlic, and citrus juices!

Unlike the starchy vegetables in the preceding section, the ones in this section you can have in unlimited quantities on the Belly Fat Diet plan. So, don't worry about portion sizes — fill up on these sides guilt-free! And if you're looking for more veggies to add to your diet, consider some or all of the following:

Asparagus	Cauliflower	Lettuce	Spinach
Beets	Eggplant	Mushrooms	Swiss chard
Broccoli	Green beans	Onions	Tomatoes
Brussels sprouts	Kale	Peppers	Zucchini

Get ready to unleash your inner veggie lover with the flavor-packed veggie sides in this section. They're finger-licking good! You may even surprise yourself with just how much you like vegetables when they're prepared in a new way.

Not all white is bad . . .

You know that you shouldn't eat white flour very often, so you may believe that white equals bad. You've also heard that the more vibrant the color, the more nutrients a vegetable contains, so you may forget the unique health benefits that white vegetables offer.

Potatoes are one of the best sources of potassium, a nutrient essential for maintaining healthy blood pressure. White vegetables also contain phytonutrients like flavonoids, indoles, and isthiocyanates, as well as organic sulfur compounds that help to reduce the risk of cancer and other diseases. For a list of more white vegetables (besides the tasty cauliflower in this recipe), refer to Chapter 6.

Cauliflower Bites

Prep time: 15 min • **Cook time:** 30 min • **Yield:** 4 servings

Ingredients	Directions
¾ **cup panko bread crumbs**	*1* Preheat the oven to 425 degrees.
1 teaspoon minced garlic	
¼ **teaspoon crushed red pepper flakes**	*2* In a large bowl, combine the bread crumbs, garlic, red pepper flakes, and cheese.
2 tablespoons grated parmesan cheese	*3* In a separate large bowl, whisk the eggs.
2 eggs	*4* Pour the cauliflower florets into the egg mixture and toss to coat evenly.
4 cups fresh cauliflower florets	
	5 Toss the coated cauliflower in the bread crumb mixture to coat. Line a baking sheet with parchment paper, and spread the florets evenly on the baking sheet.
	6 Bake for 30 minutes, until the cauliflower is crispy.

Per serving: Calories 68 (From Fat 12); Fat 1g (Saturated 1g); Cholesterol 2mg; Sodium 155mg; Carbohydrate 10g (Dietary Fiber 2g); Protein 5g.

Tip: Serve Cauliflower Bites with honey mustard dressing or ketchup for dipping if desired.

Note: These treats will be a big hit with kids and adults alike! Serve them as an appetizer or with fresh fish filet. People won't be able to keep their hands off them, so if serving a crowd, make a double batch!

Tip: Leftovers? No problem. When you're ready to reheat, slide them on a baking sheet and crisp them up for about 5 to 10 minutes in a 350-degree oven.

Green Bean Fries

Prep time: 5 min • **Cook time:** 25 min • **Yield:** 4 servings

Ingredients	Directions
4 cups fresh green beans, ends removed	*1* Preheat the oven to 450 degrees.
½ teaspoon fresh minced garlic	*2* In a large bowl, toss together all the ingredients.
¼ teaspoon kosher salt	*3* Line a baking sheet with parchment paper, and spread the prepared green beans evenly on the baking sheet.
1 tablespoon lemon juice	
1 tablespoon canola oil	*4* Bake for 25 minutes, or until the green beans are crispy and a little dehydrated.

Per serving: Calories 64 (From Fat 32); Fat 4g (Saturated 0g); Cholesterol 0mg; Sodium 152mg; Carbohydrate 8g (Dietary Fiber 4g); Protein 2g.

Note: Bean fries are a family favorite. Add them to your cookout in place of regular potato fries. Your family and dinner guests will love the crunch and flavor!

Vary It! This recipe is yummy with broccoli, too!

Roasting vegetables

Vegetables are oh-so-yummy when they're roasted! Roasting brings out the most amazing blend of flavors and sugars naturally in vegetables. Taste isn't the only benefit of roasting — it also reduces the size of the vegetable so you may find yourself eating more of them, enabling you to quickly reach your nutrient goals for potassium; magnesium; folate; vitamins A, C, and K; and fiber!

You may not think about sitting down and eating half a raw onion or a clove or two of garlic, but if you roast them with broccoli, carrots, or {insert favorite vegetable here}, you may be surprised by how scrumptious and easy it is to get more of the good stuff!

If you want to give roasting a try, turn your oven to 425 degrees, lightly toss vegetables with olive oil, place them on a parchment paper–lined baking sheet, and cook them until they begin to caramelize and turn brown, about 20 to 45 minutes depending on the vegetable. You may need to give the vegetables a little stir halfway through cooking.

Here are some of our favorite vegetables to roast: asparagus, broccoli, Brussels sprouts, carrots, cauliflower, garlic, green beans, mushrooms, and sweet potatoes.

Roasted Brussels Sprouts with Balsamic Glaze

Prep time: 10 min • **Cook time:** 18 min • **Yield:** 4 servings

Ingredients	Directions
4 cups Brussels sprouts, halved	**1** Preheat the oven to 450 degrees. Line a baking sheet with parchment paper.
1 tablespoon olive oil	
½ tablespoon minced garlic	**2** In a large bowl, toss the Brussels sprouts with the oil, garlic, salt, and pepper.
⅛ teaspoon kosher salt	
⅛ teaspoon pepper	**3** Spread the Brussels sprouts evenly on the baking sheet and bake for 18 minutes. Give the Brussels sprouts a stir halfway through to ensure even baking.
2 tablespoons sliced almonds	
2 tablespoons raisins	
1 tablespoon balsamic vinegar	**4** In a large bowl, mix the almonds, raisins, balsamic vinegar, and agave nectar until combined.
½ teaspoon agave nectar	**5** Toss the roasted Brussels sprouts in the bowl with the balsamic glaze.

Per serving: Calories 110 (From Fat 54); Fat 6g (Saturated 1g); Cholesterol 0mg; Sodium 89mg; Carbohydrate 13g (Dietary Fiber 4g); Protein 4g.

Vary It! Stir diced Granny Smith apples or dried tart cherries into the Brussels sprouts to add more variety.

Note: Don't have agave nectar on hand? You can use honey instead.

Chapter 12

Desserts and Snacks

In This Chapter

▶ Finishing off a meal with a satisfying and healthy dessert

▶ Snacking your way to a flat belly

You're trying to shrink your belly, and we bet the last thing you would think could help you do that is eating desserts and snacks! Many people swear off desserts and snacks because they feel that if they allow themselves to indulge, they won't be able to stop eating and they'll sabotage their health goals. The problem is, when you put a food on the "naughty" list, your cravings for that food intensify, which often leads to bingeing on the very food that you swore off.

Many desserts and snacks have a bad rap and are typically associated with lots of calories and fat. But they don't have to be high-fat calorie bombs. You may be thinking, "Healthy desserts? Isn't that an oxymoron? Aren't snacks supposed to be salty and come in a bag?" You may be conditioned to reach for the bag of cheesy puffs at snack time or picture chocolate lava cake when you dream of desserts, but you can work to reframe what snacks and desserts look like in order to enjoy them in a healthy way.

Desserts and snacks can be oh-so-satisfying and healthy at the same time! Your current late-night munchies and dessert indulgences may undo all your good exercise efforts, but you can alter them to support your healthy eating habits simply by changing the options you choose to munch on.

We don't believe you need to sacrifice desserts and snacks in the name of losing weight. In fact, it may just be quite the opposite! Including better-for-you desserts and snacks can actually help you achieve your goals without making you feel deprived and making your efforts more sustainable.

In this chapter, we show you how to satisfy your sweet tooth and salty cravings without adding all the extra calories and expanding your waistline!

Desserts to Die For

A sweet tooth is meant to be satisfied. And desserts shouldn't have to be off limits. Who's with us? Dessert is one of life's pleasures, so why do we think we need to deprive ourselves of all dessert when we try to get healthy. Is it because we're accustomed to very decadent sweets? Or maybe it has more to do with the portion distortion these days. We want huge milkshakes and often think that bigger equals better. It hasn't always been this way — desserts were once a very small treat.

If you find yourself at a fine-dining restaurant, order dessert and see what your server brings to your table. Often it's quite dainty and literally just a few bites. Those small bites are meant to be savored and to cleanse the palate after the meal.

You don't have to give up your favorite sweet treats when working to lose belly fat. Instead, you can focus on portions and finding ways to make your favorites healthier. In this section, we show you how to do just that.

Simple substitutions

You can transform your favorite desserts into healthier versions of their former selves with just a few simple switches:

✔ **Opt for natural sweetness.** Start by going for foods that are already naturally sweet. Instead of adding sugar to your plain Greek yogurt, mix in pureed banana, apricots, or applesauce for sweetness. One hundred percent fruit juice concentrate has a nice consistency and is a great way to up the sweet taste of fruit smoothies.

✔ **Spice it up!** Add cinnamon, nutmeg, pumpkin pie spice, and vanilla extract to your desserts for a subtle sweetness and zero calories. You'll get an antioxidant boost, too!

✔ **Build your dessert around fresh or frozen fruit.** Opt for a fruit smoothie or grilled pineapple. Or spread apple slices or strawberries with peanut butter and dark chocolate chips.

✔ **Make the switch to dark chocolate.** The antioxidants in cocoa are thought to improve blood flow by making the blood vessels more flexible, and dark chocolate has more of these healthful compounds than milk chocolate.

✔ **Substitute Greek yogurt for cream cheese, whipped cream, or butter for less fat and more nutrition.**

✔ **Instead of loading your baked goodies with white flour, substitute black beans (rinsed and drained, of course).** You'll get an added dose of protein!

Chocolate Peanut Butter Popcorn

Prep time: 5 min • **Cook time:** 3 min • **Yield:** 2 servings

Ingredients	Directions
3 cups air-popped popcorn	*1* Pop the popcorn according to package directions.
2 tablespoons natural creamy peanut butter	*2* Pour the popped popcorn into a large resealable plastic bag.
1 tablespoon butter-and-oil spread	*3* In a small bowl, combine the peanut butter and butter-and-oil spread; heat in the microwave for 15 seconds.
¼ cup chocolate protein powder	*4* Pour the softened peanut butter and butter mixture over the top of the popcorn, seal the bag, and shake until the popcorn is covered.
	5 Pour the protein powder into the bag with the popcorn, seal the bag, and shake to coat the popcorn.
	6 Serve immediately.

Per serving: Calories 272 (From Fat 152); Fat 17g (Saturated 3g); Cholesterol 5mg; Sodium 192mg; Carbohydrate 17g (Dietary Fiber 4g); Protein 16g.

Tip: If you have a peanut allergy, you can substitute the peanut butter in this recipe for another nut butter like cashew or almond.

Vary It! Make it into a snack mix by tossing in peanuts and whole-grain cereal.

Enjoying popcorn, guilt free

People often think of popcorn as a snack to indulge in when they're being naughty and falling off the wagon, but it can actually be quite nourishing if it's prepared correctly. Popcorn is a whole grain, making it a great source of complex carbohydrates and fiber for sustained energy. It's also very low in fat and calories — 1 cup of air-popped popcorn has only 30 calories!

Making air-popped popcorn at home is super-easy:

1. **Pour ¼ cup plain popcorn kernels into a small lunch-sack-size brown paper bag.**

2. **Fold down the bag about 4 or 5 times, leaving some room for the popcorn to grow.**

3. **Place the bag in the microwave and cook on high for 1 minute and 15 seconds.**

4. **Pour the air-popped popcorn into a bowl, and enjoy!**

Salted Caramel Apple Crisp

Prep time: 5 min • **Cook time:** 25 min • **Yield:** 4 servings

Ingredients	Directions
1 Honeycrisp apple, peeled, cored, and cut into small slices	**1** Preheat the oven to 375 degrees.
½ teaspoon cinnamon	**2** In a small bowl, combine the apple, cinnamon, and lemon juice until coated.
1 tablespoon lemon juice	
½ cup rolled oats	**3** In a separate bowl, mix together the oats, brown sugar, and salt. Cut in the butter with a fork or your hands until the mixture is crumbly.
2 tablespoons brown sugar	
⅛ teaspoon kosher salt	**4** Place 4 ovenproof ramekins on a baking sheet and coat them with cooking spray.
2 tablespoons butter	
4 teaspoons fat-free caramel syrup	**5** Evenly distribute the apples in the ramekins, and top each with 1 teaspoon of the caramel syrup.
	6 Place the crumbled oat mixture on top of the apples and bake the apple crisp for 25 minutes.

Per serving: Calories 190 (From Fat 58); Fat 6g (Saturated 4g); Cholesterol 15mg; Sodium 121mg; Carbohydrate 33g (Dietary Fiber 2g); Protein 2g.

Tip: For creamy decadence, serve this crisp with a scoop of nonfat vanilla Greek yogurt.

Ramekins and mini desserts: A match made in heaven

Desserts are much more fun and cute when they're miniature! Party guests love it when you serve them a personalized dessert — it makes them feel special. Not only do mini desserts sweeten the party, but serving individual-size desserts truly helps with portion control. Instead of making a full apple pie, piece it together using a miniature dish so you don't end up overindulging and swearing off sweets.

Some of our favorite mini dishes to bake with are ramekins — small, circular bowls that are not only stylish, but usually ovenproof. They're great for cold treats and snacks, like frozen yogurt or fresh fruit. Ramekins are very inexpensive and can be found near the kitchen dishes and housewares in department or discount stores.

Cinnamon Apple Butter Parfait

Prep time: 5 min • **Yield:** 2 servings

Ingredients	Directions
1 cup nonfat plain Greek yogurt	**1** In a small bowl, combine the yogurt, apple butter, and cinnamon.
¼ cup apple butter	
¼ teaspoon ground cinnamon	**2** Using two small dessert cups (preferably glass), pour ¼ cup of the yogurt mixture into each dish.
½ cup strawberries, sliced	
½ cup blueberries	**3** In a small bowl, combine the strawberries and blueberries. Layer each dish with ¼ cup of the mixed berries.
1 graham cracker square, crumbled	
Cinnamon, for garnish	**4** Repeat Steps 2 and 3. Top the final layer with graham crackers and dust with a sprinkle of cinnamon.

Per serving: Calories 159 (From Fat 6); Fat 1g (Saturated 0g); Cholesterol 0mg; Sodium 67mg; Carbohydrate 29g (Dietary Fiber 2g); Protein 10g.

Vary It! Make it a pumpkin parfait by stirring in ¼ cup pumpkin puree and replacing the cinnamon with pumpkin pie spice. Top with pumpkin seeds for extra crunch and pumpkin goodness!

What is apple butter?

Apple butter isn't as unhealthy as you may be thinking. It doesn't actually contain butter as the name implies. Instead, apple butter is made from cooked apples. It's very smooth and velvety, similar to butter (which is where the name comes from). Apple butter has a thinner consistency than jam or jelly.

You can use apple butter as a spread in the place of jelly or as a sweetener as we do in this recipe. Apple butter can be lower in calories than most jellies, too. This spread makes a yummy holiday treat because it's usually made with warm spices like cinnamon, cloves, and allspice.

If you've never tried apple butter, put it on your grocery list. You won't regret it!

Nutella Crepes

Prep time: 1 hr • **Cook time:** 10 min • **Yield:** 8 servings

Ingredients	Directions
½ cup fat-free milk	*1* In a blender, place the milk, egg, butter, and salt, and pulse until blended.
2 eggs	
1 tablespoon butter, melted	*2* Gently pour the flour into the blender in batches, and process until completely smooth.
¼ teaspoon kosher salt	
¼ cup whole-wheat flour	*3* Keeping the lid on the blender, place the batter in the refrigerator for 1 hour.
4 tablespoons Nutella	
2 cups fresh mixed berries	*4* Heat a 7-inch skillet over medium heat, and coat with cooking spray.
	5 Place 2 tablespoons of the batter into the skillet and tip the skillet to allow the batter to coat the pan. The crepes will be very thin.
	6 Cook for about 1 minute, until golden.

7	Flip the crepe over with a spatula and continue cooking for 30 seconds.
8	Transfer the crepe to a plate.
9	Repeat Steps 4 through 8 with the remaining batter to make a total of 8 crepes.
10	Place a crepe on a flat surface.
11	Spread ½ tablespoon of the Nutella evenly on the crepe.
12	Place ¼ cup of the berries in the center of the crepe.
13	Fold the crepe to form a long roll, and cut it in half.
14	Repeat Steps 10 through 13 with the remaining crepes.

Per serving: Calories 111 (From Fat 47); Fat 5g (Saturated 4g); Cholesterol 57mg; Sodium 101mg; Carbohydrate 14g (Dietary Fiber 2g); Protein 3g.

Vary It! You can fold any fruit into this recipe — it'll be delicious!

Tip: Serve these crepes for dessert at your next dinner party. They'll impress and please your guests!

Berry Baked Apples

Prep time: 10 min • **Cook time:** 8 min • **Yield:** 4 servings

Ingredients	*Directions*
4 baking apples, such as Rome Beauty, Fuji, or Northern Spy	*1* With a paring knife or apple corer, remove the cores from the apples.
½ cup dried fruit, such as blueberries, raisins, or cranberries	*2* With a knife, peel the top half of the apples.
1 teaspoon ground cinnamon	*3* In a small bowl, toss the dried fruit and cinnamon. Set aside.
½ cup frozen, fresh, or drained canned blueberries	*4* In each of four microwavable bowls (each large enough to hold one apple), place 2 tablespoons of the blueberries and 2 tablespoons of the apple juice.
½ cup apple juice	*5* Place the prepared apple on top of the blueberries, and evenly divide the dried fruit mixture into the cavities and around the apples.
	6 Loosely cover each apple with plastic wrap or wax paper.
	7 Microwave until the apples are tender, about 4½ to 5 minutes. Allow to cool.
	8 Cover and refrigerate, if desired.
	9 Serve warm or cold.

Per serving: Calories 172 (From Fat 4); Fat 0g (Saturated 0g); Cholesterol 0mg; Sodium 6mg; Carbohydrate 45g (Dietary Fiber 6g); Protein 1g.

Note: This recipe is reproduced from www.blueberrycouncil.org. Reproduced with the permission of the U.S. Highbush Blueberry Council.

Berry nutritious

Blueberries may be small in size, but when you look at all the nutrients they provide they pack a powerful punch. Here's the lowdown on why we think you should eat more blueberries:

✔ Blueberries are high in vitamin C, a nutrient that plays a key role in a healthy immune system and helps to promote iron absorption. If you aren't getting enough vitamin C in your diet, it may lead to fatigue and sickness.

✔ Blueberries are filled with manganese, which helps to convert proteins, carbs, and fats to energy. It's key in shredding belly fat.

✔ Anthocyanins are responsible for that beautiful blue hue. Not only do they look good, but they're mighty antioxidants that fight off stress and damage in the body.

Snack Attack

Snacking doesn't have to be a bad thing. The type of snacks you choose can make or break your healthy eating. In fact, eating healthy snacks in between meals is a great way to keep your metabolism going and burn those extra calories that help you lose belly fat (and prevent overeating from being too hungry at mealtime).

Snacks aren't meant to fill you up — they're just a bridge to your next meal. If you eat dinner late or work out at the end of the day, you may need two snacks between lunch and dinner. Getting hungry about every three hours is normal.

Frozen snacks

Some snacks are even tastier frozen, especially on a hot summer day! Don't worry that you're taking away nutrition by freezing your foods — frozen foods may be *better* for you than fresh produce sitting in the grocery store. Why? Because produce can often break down as it ages and nutrients can diminish. Frozen foods are frozen at their peak of ripeness, a time in which research has shown them to be the most nutrient packed.

Some great foods to freeze include: avocado slices, bananas, blueberries, dark chocolate, flavored ice cubes, grapes, Greek yogurt, kiwi, mango cubes, melon cubes, orange segments, pear slices, and watermelon.

Remember: Be sure to wash your produce before you freeze them to rinse off germs and debris.

It's all about stabilizing your blood sugar so you don't lose energy during the day. Like desserts, snacks should be around 100 to 300 calories — you don't want to blow your calorie budget at snack time. The goal is not to get full from a snack but to keep you from getting way too hungry. Reframing the role of snacks can help to keep portions in check.

Here are some 100-calorie snacks you can try:

- ✔ An apple with ½ tablespoon peanut butter or another nut butter
- ✔ ½ cup cottage cheese with sliced pears
- ✔ 1 ounce cubed cheese
- ✔ 3 cups air-popped popcorn
- ✔ 1 hardboiled egg
- ✔ 1 cup grapes
- ✔ ½ cup baby carrots and 3 tablespoons hummus
- ✔ 1 cup edamame in pods

Smart snacking can help you reach your Belly Fat Diet goals. With the recipes in this section, we prove that homemade snacks can be simple and tasty!

Frozen Yogurt Bites

Prep time: 10 min • **Freeze time:** 25 min • **Yield:** 4 servings

Ingredients	Directions
1 cup nonfat vanilla Greek yogurt	*1* In a large bowl, place the Greek yogurt.
2 bananas, sliced ½ cup blueberries ½ cup raspberries	*2* Toss the bananas, blueberries, and raspberries into the bowl of yogurt, and gently stir to coat.
	3 Line a baking sheet with parchment paper, and place each fruit piece individually on the baking sheet.
	4 Place the baking sheet in the freezer for 25 minutes or until completely frozen.
	5 Peel the frozen fruit from the parchment paper and transfer to a resealable freezer bag; store until ready to eat.

Per serving: Calories 104 (From Fat 3); Fat 0g (Saturated 0g); Cholesterol 0mg; Sodium 21mg; Carbohydrate 22g (Dietary Fiber 3g); Protein 6g.

Vary 1t! No fruit is off limits! We think mangoes, grapes, pineapples, and peaches would be amazing covered in frozen yogurt!

Cherry Pistachio Granola

Prep time: 15 min • **Cook time:** 25 min • **Yield:** 12 servings

Ingredients	*Directions*
½ cup shelled pistachios	*1* Preheat the oven to 300 degrees.
½ cup sliced almonds	
½ cup chopped pecans	*2* In a large bowl, combine the pistachios, almonds, pecans, oats, cherries, flaxseeds, pumpkin pie spice, and sea salt. Set aside.
2 cups old-fashioned oats	
½ cup dried tart cherries	*3* In a small pan over low heat, stir the sugar, coconut oil, and agave nectar until the sugar is dissolved. Remove from the heat and stir in the vanilla extract.
¼ cup golden flaxseeds	
½ teaspoon pumpkin pie spice	
¼ teaspoon sea salt	*4* Pour the sugar mixture into the large bowl with the dry ingredients, and stir until all the ingredients are coated evenly.
¼ cup brown sugar	
¼ cup coconut oil	*5* Line a rimmed baking sheet with parchment paper and coat with cooking spray. Arrange the granola mixture close together on the pan. (The granola may not cover the entire pan.)
¼ cup agave nectar	
1 teaspoon vanilla extract	
	6 Bake for 25 minutes, until the granola is slightly brown.
	7 Allow the granola to dry before breaking into chunks. Store in an air-tight container for up to 1 week.

Per serving: Calories 249 (From Fat 140); Fat 16g (Saturated 5g); Cholesterol 0mg; Sodium 74mg; Carbohydrate 24g (Dietary Fiber 4g); Protein 5g.

Vary It! You can use your favorite nuts and seeds in this recipe.

Note: For chewier bars, bake in a smaller square baking dish.

Smoked Chickpeas

Prep time: 2 min • **Cook time:** 20 min • **Yield:** 2 servings

Ingredients	Directions
One 15.5-ounce can low-sodium chickpeas, rinsed and drained	**1** Preheat the oven to 400 degrees.
½ tablespoon smoked paprika	**2** In a medium bowl, combine all the ingredients and coat the chickpeas.
⅛ teaspoon sea salt	
⅛ teaspoon cayenne pepper	**3** Line a rimmed baking sheet with parchment paper, and spread out the chickpeas on the baking sheet.
	4 Bake for 20 minutes. Allow the chickpeas to cool and serve. The chickpeas will become crispy as they cool.

Per serving: Calories 171 (From Fat 0); Fat 0g (Saturated 0g); Cholesterol 0mg; Sodium 515mg; Carbohydrate 33g (Dietary Fiber 8g); Protein 10g.

Vary It! Like it hot? Turn up the heat by adding more cayenne!

Vary It! Replace the spices in this recipe with pumpkin pie spice and vanilla extract for seasonal flavor.

Note: Smoked chickpeas are a yummy and nutritious snack filled with protein and fiber to keep you satisfied.

The benefits of chickpeas

Chickpeas, also called garbanzo beans, are a nutrient powerhouse. People often find more satisfaction from eating foods high in fiber, especially beans like chickpeas because they contain protein, too. Because too much belly fat can lead to an increased risk of heart disease, it's important to eat good-for-you foods like beans regularly, because they can help to lower your risk of heart disease, stabilize blood sugar, and control weight. One-half cup of chickpeas contains 150 calories, 6 grams of fiber, and 7 grams of protein! Chickpeas are also a great source of iron, folate, and manganese.

Blueberry Party Mix

Prep time: 5 min • **Yield:** 4 servings

Ingredients	Directions
1 cup dried blueberries	**1** In a large bowl, combine all the ingredients.
1 cup chopped walnuts	
1 cup thin pretzels, broken	**2** Store in an air-tight container for up to 1 week.
1 cup low-fat granola or other whole-grain cereal	

Per serving: Calories 416 (From Fat 161); Fat 18g (Saturated 2g); Cholesterol 0mg; Sodium 190mg; Carbohydrate 60g (Dietary Fiber 7g); Protein 7g.

Note: This recipe is reproduced from www.blueberrycouncil.org. Reproduced with the permission of the U.S. Highbush Blueberry Council.

Party snacking

Whether you have people over to watch the game or you're hosting a dinner party, planning your party snacks is important. Hungry party folk make for crabby houseguests. Having snackable items for your guests doesn't have to be elaborate or time consuming. You can actually throw together a healthy array of snacks in less than ten minutes. With these snack ideas you'll be sure to thrill your hungry crowd in minutes:

✔ **Tasty taco cups:** Fill whole-grain corn scoop chips with bean dip, cheese, and Greek yogurt, and top with salsa and an olive.

✔ **Mixed nuts:** Find a low-sodium or raw variety to reduce belly bloat.

✔ **Deviled eggs:** These little savory bites don't need to be fatty. Stir in fat-free Greek yogurt in place of the mayonnaise for a lightened-up party snack.

✔ **Veggie and mozzarella bites:** Thread cherry tomatoes, mozzarella, and basil together on skewers for a savory snack that will please your guests.

✔ **Turkey pinwheels:** Roll deli turkey, sliced cheese, and spinach in a whole-wheat wrap, and slice into even pinwheels.

Fruit Kebabs with Blueberry Dip

Prep time: 15 min • **Yield:** 8 servings

Ingredients	Directions
Blueberry Dip (see the following recipe) 1 cup fresh blueberries	**1** On 24 bamboo skewers (10-inch), alternate the blueberries with watermelon or pineapple pieces and apple pieces.
2 cups cubed watermelon or pineapple 2 apples, cored and cut into 24 pieces	**2** Serve the kebabs with the Blueberry Dip.

Blueberry Dip

2 cups fresh blueberries ⅓ cup light cream cheese	**1** In the container of a food processor or blender, place all the ingredients and whirl until smooth.
2 tablespoons apricot preserves	**2** Remove to a serving bowl, cover, and refrigerate until serving.

Per serving: Calories 107 (From Fat 15); Fat 2g (Saturated 1g); Cholesterol 5mg; Sodium 46mg; Carbohydrate 24g (Dietary Fiber 3g); Protein 2g.

Note: This recipe is reproduced from www.blueberrycouncil.org. Reproduced with the permission of the U.S. Highbush Blueberry Council.

How much is too much?

When it comes to desserts, people have the tendency to overdo it. Think hot fudge brownie sundae á la mode with whipped cream, nuts, and full-fat ice cream sitting atop a warm gooey brownie. Can you say sugar coma? Yes, a few bites may taste scrumptious. But be honest: If you ate the whole sundae, would you truly *taste* that very last bite, or would you be nauseated from all that sweetness?

Did you know that just a few bites can actually tame a sweet tooth. Give it a try! If you practice self-control and become more aware of portion sizes, having dessert doesn't have to blow your calorie budget. Depending on your body size and goals, a sensible dessert is anywhere from 100 to 300 calories.

If we're not feeling satisfied after a few bites or a sensible portion, something else is going on. If it's real hunger, eating a balanced meal is better than continuing to nosh on dessert.

Here are some ideas for tasty 100-calorie desserts:

- Eight strawberries and 2 tablespoons of dark chocolate chips
- One frozen banana pureed (tastes like frozen yogurt!)
- Skim milk with chocolate syrup
- Low-fat Greek yogurt with raspberries and mint
- Grilled pineapple
- Peaches with ¼ cup low-fat frozen yogurt
- 1 mango
- 1 cup low-fat chocolate pudding

Chapter 13

Smoothies and Cocktails

- -

In This Chapter

▶ Savoring belly-friendly smoothies

▶ Relaxing with a cocktail — without blowing your diet

- -

*I*f you've heard that beverages can be calorie laden, you've heard right! But when you're trying to lose weight and bust that belly fat, you don't have to stick just to water. Believe it or not, you can still enjoy beverages, including smoothies and cocktails (yes, cocktails!), without falling off the wagon. The smoothie and cocktail recipes in this chapter can help you maximize your belly-fighting efforts in a tasty and refreshing way.

Smooth Operator: Belly-Friendly Smoothies

Smoothies are a quick and delicious way to enjoy fruits and vegetables. These frozen treats are a favorite of picky eaters (we're lookin' at you, kids) and omnivores alike. We have yet to find someone who turns up her nose at a smoothie. And it's easy to see why. Smoothies can satisfy even the sharpest sweet tooth and make for a perfect breakfast as you're running out the door. (With the recipes in this chapter, you have no more excuses for skipping breakfast!)

The best way to get the flavor you want out of a smoothie is to begin with frozen fruits and vegetables. Why frozen, not fresh? Because frozen fruits and vegetables provide a better consistency. Plus, when you use frozen fruits and vegetables, you typically don't need to add ice. (Not having to add ice is a benefit, because ice tends to quickly water down a smoothie, which may tempt you to reach for sweetener to up the flavor.)

A common myth is that frozen fruits and vegetables are less nutritious than fresh, but that couldn't be further from the truth. The frozen fruits and vegetables you buy from your local grocery store are frozen almost immediately after being picked, so they hold onto all the nutrients, making them perfect to use in your favorite smoothie recipes.

You don't have to rely solely on the frozen fruits and vegetables you buy from your grocery store's freezer section. You can actually freeze your own. Here's how:

1. **When you get home from the grocery store, farmer's market, or roadside stand, wash or peel the fresh fruits or vegetables you've just bought.**

   You don't want to wait too long to freeze fresh fruits and vegetables, because the sooner you do it, the more nutrients they'll retain. You don't have to do it before you unload the rest of your groceries or anything, but try to do it the same day.

2. **Cut the fruits and vegetables into slices or pieces.**

   You don't have to worry about making the slices or pieces a certain size, especially if you plan to use the fruits or vegetables in smoothies.

3. **Lay the pieces on a baking sheet lined with parchment paper.**

4. **Freeze for four hours, or until frozen solid, and then transfer the pieces to a freezer bag or container and store them in the freezer until you're ready to use them.**

When you're freezing fruits and vegetables with a particular recipe in mind, you might want to freeze a specific amount and label the bag — for example, "1 kiwi" or "1½ bananas."

In this section, we share some of our all-time favorite smoothie recipes.

Water, water, everywhere: Why hydration matters

You don't have to restrict yourself to water in order to live a belly-blasting lifestyle. But that doesn't mean you can down a soda or root beer float and cheers to your health. However, incorporating in your diet better-for-you beverages (like the ones in this chapter) can keep you nourished and hydrated.

Why does hydration matter? For a variety of reasons, but here's a big one: It plays a key role in regulating appetite. If you drink water before, during, and after your meals, it can help to fill you up, enabling you to eat more slowly and regulate your portions. Plus, when you're dehydrated, the brain often confuses thirst for hunger, which means you may end up eating when you're really just thirsty.

If you're feeling thirsty, you're already dehydrated. The Institute of Medicine (www.iom.edu) recommends that women drink 90 ounces of fluids per day and men drink 120 ounces of fluids per day. The best way to tell if you're hydrated is to look at your urine. If it's pale yellow to colorless, you're well hydrated; if it's a definite yellow, you're not getting enough fluids.

Rainbow Green Smoothie

Prep time: 5 min • **Yield:** 2 servings

Ingredients	Directions
1½ frozen bananas, peeled	**1** In a blender, combine all the ingredients.
1 frozen kiwi, peeled and sliced	**2** Blend until smooth.
1½ cups chopped rainbow chard, stalk removed	**3** Pour into two chilled glasses, and serve each with a straw.
½ cup 100 percent orange juice	
6 ounces nonfat pear or pineapple Greek yogurt	

Per serving: Calories 183 (From Fat 0); Fat 0g (Saturated 0g); Cholesterol 0mg; Sodium 100mg; Carbohydrate 36g (Dietary Fiber 2g); Protein 11g.

Taste the rainbow (chard)

Rainbow chard is a leafy vegetable that gets its name from the multicolored stalk. It's packed with vitamins, minerals, and antioxidants that are extremely beneficial to your health and for fighting belly fat. If you can't seem to get enough greens in your diet, add rainbow chard to your fruit smoothie! The flavor of this leafy addition is tamed by the sweetness of fruit. So, drink up! Here are even more reasons to love chard:

- It regulates blood sugar levels.
- It's heart-healthy.
- It's an anti-inflammatory.
- It detoxifies the body.
- It's a great source of vitamins A, C, and K.
- It's packed with fiber, iron, and calcium.
- You can eat it raw, steam it, boil it, sauté it, or use it in smoothies.
- It's a nice replacement for spinach.
- You can easily grow it in your own garden!

Stress-Busting Smoothie

Prep time: 5 min • **Yield:** 1 serving

Ingredients	*Directions*
½ cup frozen strawberries	*1* In a blender, combine all the ingredients.
½ cup frozen blackberries	
¼ cup fresh spinach leaves	*2* Blend until smooth.
½ cup plain, low-fat Greek yogurt	
½ cup ZICO Passion Fruit Pure Premium Coconut Water	*3* Pour into a chilled glass, and serve with a straw.
½ cup ice	
1 tablespoon chia seeds	

Per serving: Calories 242 (From Fat 43); Fat 5g (Saturated 0g); Cholesterol 0mg; Sodium 90mg; Carbohydrate 36g (Dietary Fiber 11g); Protein 17g.

Tip: Finding it difficult to get your daily greens? Toss them into a smoothie! Spinach is a very mild-flavored green vegetable, so you won't even taste it in this drink!

Vary It! Mix it up by tossing in other greens, like Swiss chard or kale.

De-stressing away your belly

If your waistline seems to grow larger year after year, it may not just be your diet to blame. Day-to-day stressors can be just as damaging to your midsection as diet and inactivity. Although small amounts of stress are rarely harmful and can even be helpful at times, chronic stress, day in and day out, can have damaging effects on your health — increasing blood pressure, blood sugar, and even the storage of belly fat. When you experience stress, your body produces hormones such as cortisol and adrenaline, which mobilize fatty acid stores in your body for immediate energy to help you fight off stress. However, since most of our stress is mental as opposed to physical, we don't need excess energy to fight off stress. These fatty acids that have been mobilized aren't burned off, and your body needs to store them again. However, instead of returning the fatty acids to their original storage locations, your body takes the easy route and re-deposits them in the most convenient location: your belly!

Certain nutrients can actually *reduce* the amount of stress hormones circulating in your body. By reducing these hormones, you can reduce the amount of free fatty acids that are mobilized and repositioned into your midsection, helping to fight off stress-related belly fat. In our stress-busting smoothing, we include ingredients that are rich in potassium (coconut water), vitamin C (spinach and strawberries), and omega-3 fatty acids (chia seeds), which are all powerful stress fighters. Foods rich in potassium help to lower blood pressure and stabilize stress levels, reducing overall stress in your body. A diet rich in vitamin C has been associated with reducing circulating levels of stress hormones throughout your body. And omega-3 fatty acids keep stress hormones cortisol and adrenaline from peaking, meaning that less of these hormones will be circulating, reducing the amount of free fatty acids that are mobilized during stressful times. So, the next time you're facing a stressful day, pull out the blender and whip up our stress-busting smoothie for a delicious way to reduce stress hormones and shrink your waistline!

Berry, Rhubarb, and Ginger Smoothie

Prep time: 5 min • **Yield:** 2 servings

Ingredients	Directions
½ teaspoon freshly shredded ginger	*1* In a blender, combine all the ingredients.
1½ cups frozen strawberries	*2* Blend until smooth.
½ cup frozen rhubarb	
⅔ cup 100 percent pomegranate juice	*3* Pour into two chilled glasses, and serve each with a straw.
¼ cup nonfat plain Greek yogurt	
Dash of cinnamon	

Per serving: Calories 112 (From Fat 4); Fat 0g (Saturated 0g); Cholesterol 0mg; Sodium 23mg; Carbohydrate 25g (Dietary Fiber 3g); Protein 4g.

Note: Rhubarb is a tart and tangy fruit that balances out the sweetness of the strawberries.

Note: Ginger and cinnamon are two potent belly-blasting ingredients. They add a nice, spicy touch to this smoothie.

Fighting belly bloat with some key ingredients

The Berry, Rhubarb, and Ginger Smoothie is packed with foods that help to reduce belly bloat. Pomegranate, ginger, and cinnamon are filled with key nutrients that need to be in your weight loss arsenal:

✓ **Pomegranate:** This fruit contains some of the highest levels of antioxidants, specifically the polyphenol catechin. This chemical has been shown to increase your body's fat-burning potential and may actually help to boost metabolism. Catechins may also help to decrease appetite so that you don't find yourself overeating.

✓ **Ginger:** This spice has been found to have a *thermogenic* (heat-producing) effect and to aid in digestion.

✓ **Cinnamon:** This spice contains methylhydroxy chalcone polymer (MHCP), and studies have found it to make fat cells more responsive to insulin, helping to better regulate blood sugar levels.

Strawberry Milk

Prep time: 2 min • **Yield:** 2 servings

Ingredients	*Directions*
2 cups frozen strawberries	*1* In a blender, combine all the ingredients.
2 tablespoons creamy natural peanut butter	*2* Blend until smooth and creamy.
1 cup nonfat milk	*3* Pour into two chilled glasses, and serve each with a straw.

Per serving: Calories 188 (From Fat 75); Fat 8g (Saturated 2g); Cholesterol 2mg; Sodium 128mg; Carbohydrate 23g (Dietary Fiber 4g); Protein 9g.

Vary It! If you have a peanut allergy (or you just want to try something different), you can easily substitute almond or cashew butter for the peanut butter in this recipe.

Vary It! If you like grapes better than strawberries, replace the frozen strawberries with frozen red grapes instead.

Milk: It does a body good

Healthy forms of dairy can play a vital role in reducing belly fat. Particularly because dairy contains conjugated linoleic acid (CLA), which is thought to help trigger fat cells to shrink and die off and may also help to improve insulin resistance and lower blood sugar levels. Vanish your belly fat by following these dairy do's and don'ts:

✔ **Drink low-fat milk.**

✔ **If possible, choose organic milk that comes from grass-fed cows.** It's thought to have almost five times more CLA than the alternative!

✔ **Choose low-fat or fat-free yogurt over higher-fat varieties.**

✔ **Go for plain Greek yogurt.** Greek yogurt is thicker and higher in protein, which will fill you up.

✔ **Don't consume milk full of saturated fats, like whole milk or 2 percent milk.**

✔ **Don't choose milk substitutes that contain excess sugar or high fructose corn syrup.**

✔ **Watch out for flavored yogurts.** Although some of the sugars are natural, much of it is added. Aim for a yogurt with no more than 15 g of sugar per 8-ounce serving.

Shaken, Not Stirred: Cocktails That Are Easy on the Waistline

A cocktail can help you unwind after a long day, make dinner with friends a little more special, or be refreshing on a hot summer day. Most people love a good cocktail now and then, but often they're packed with calories and sugar, neither of which is good for your waistline. So, what's a cocktail lover to do?

The good news is, there are ways to make lighter cocktails that taste great, which means you can fight off belly fat even when you're splurging. Here are some tips for enjoying your favorite cocktails without paying the price:

- **Try a low-calorie mixer.** Here are some great options:

  - Lemon juice
  - Lime juice
  - Light cranberry juice
  - Light lemonade
  - Club soda
  - Sparkling wine
  - Diet soda
  - Brewed coffee
  - Coconut water

- **Make it virgin.** The recipes in this section taste just as yummy without alcohol, and going alcohol-free lowers the calorie count.

- **When you're drinking, try alternating between an alcoholic beverage and water or a nonalcoholic beverage.** Switching back and forth between the two helps keep calories in check.

- **Eat about an hour before sipping on drinks.** This will keep you from filling up on drinks just because you're hungry.

- **Garnish your drink with an orange or lime wedge or maybe even olives or fresh mint.** This will give you an extra burst of flavor but few calories — a big bang for your buck!

The cocktail recipes in this section are healthier and belly friendly. Whatever your taste, you're bound to find a drink you can enjoy while trimming your midsection.

Chocotini

Prep time: 2 min • **Yield:** 1 serving

Ingredients	Directions
⅓ cup ZICO Chocolate Premium Coconut Water (plus 1 ounce for rimming glass)	**1** Saunter and shake ⅓ cup of the coconut water, the vodka, and the coffee over the ice.
¼ cup Van Gogh Dutch Chocolate Vodka	**2** Wet the rim of a martini glass with the remaining ounce of coconut water.
½ teaspoon instant coffee (optional)	
½ cup ice	**3** Gently cover a small plate with the cocoa powder and swizzle the glass.
Cocoa powder, for rimming the glass	
Finely chopped toasted coconut, for garnish	**4** Garnish with the shredded coconut and cocoa nibs.
Cocoa nibs, for garnish	

Per serving: Calories 142 (From Fat 0); Fat 0g (Saturated 0g); Cholesterol 0mg; Sodium 12mg; Carbohydrate 4g (Dietary Fiber 0g); Protein 0g.

Note: This recipe is reproduced from `www.zico.com`. Reproduced with the permission of ZICO Pure Premium Coconut Water.

What is coconut water?

Not to be confused with coconut milk, coconut water is a sweet, clear liquid that has a refreshing flavor and is found in green coconuts. Look for all-natural, unflavored coconut water, and be sure to check the label to make sure it doesn't contain added sugar or dyes.

Active people often drink coconut water because it's a good source of potassium, an electrolyte lost in sweat. Here are even more reasons to drink coconut water:

✔ **It's hydrating.** Tired of plain water? One cup of plain 100 percent pure coconut water has a yummy taste for only 45 calories.

✔ **It's heart-healthy.** Coconut water is fat- and cholesterol-free and loaded with potassium, which has been shown to reduce the risk of hypertension and stroke.

✔ **It contains natural sugars.** The calories from coconut water are all natural from the sugars present naturally in the coconut — a definite upgrade from sports drinks that contain added sugars!

✔ **It's convenient.** Grab coconut water, and drink to your health while you're on the go!

Blueberry and Mint Spritzer

Prep time: 20 min • **Cook time:** 5 min • **Yield:** 8 servings

Ingredients	Directions
3 cups fresh or frozen blueberries	**1** In a small saucepan, combine the 3 cups of blueberries, simple syrup, lime juice, and lemon zest, and bring to a boil.
1 cup simple syrup	
½ cup lime juice	
2 teaspoons lemon zest	**2** Remove from the heat, and add the 1 cup of torn mint leaves.
1 cup torn mint leaves	
4 cups ice cubes	**3** Stir with a wooden spoon to release the mint aromas.
8 fluid ounces vodka (optional)	**4** Chill completely in the refrigerator.
4 cups club soda	**5** Transfer the blueberry mixture to a strainer over a large bowl. Push on the blueberries in the strainer, to extract as much juice as possible.
1 cup fresh blueberries, for garnish	
8 mint leaves, for garnish	**6** For each drink, combine 3 ounces of the chilled blueberry base in a shaker with ½ cup ice cubes.
	7 Add 1 ounce vodka per drink (if using) and shake; strain into a chilled glass.
	8 Add 4 ounces club soda.
	9 Garnish each drink with a few blueberries and a mint leaf.

Per serving: Calories 151 (From Fat 3); Fat 0g (Saturated 0g); Cholesterol 0mg; Sodium 28mg; Carbohydrate 22g (Dietary Fiber 2g); Protein 1g.

Note: This recipe is reproduced from www.blueberrycouncil.org. Reproduced with the permission of the U.S. Highbush Blueberry Council.

Note: Simple syrup, also known as sugar syrup, is a common ingredient in many cocktails. You can buy simple syrup in liquor stores, or even better, make your own! Simply combine equal parts sugar and water in a bottle and shake until the sugar is completely dissolved. Store it in a well-sealed container in the refrigerator up to six months.

Tropicolada

Prep time: 2 min • **Yield:** 2 servings

Ingredients	*Directions*
1 cup frozen mango	*1* In a blender, combine all the ingredients except the coconut.
1 cup frozen pineapple	
½ cup light coconut milk	*2* Blend until smooth and creamy.
¾ cup nonfat milk	
¼ cup coconut-flavored rum	*3* Pour into two chilled glasses, top each drink with coconut flakes, and serve each with a straw.
½ teaspoon pure coconut extract	
2 teaspoons unsweetened flaked coconut, for topping	

Per serving: Calories 259 (From Fat 78); Fat 9g (Saturated 7g); Cholesterol 1mg; Sodium 33mg; Carbohydrate 30g (Dietary Fiber 3g); Protein 4g.

Note: Coconut extract offers all the flavor of coconut without all the calories of sweetened coconut milk.

Vary It! Make it virgin! Blend in an additional ¼ cup nonfat milk to take the place of the rum but still give it the creamy texture you're after.

Mango madness

Mango has a unique scent, taste, and flavor — it takes you straight to the tropics in your mind, no matter where you are. This succulent and juicy fruit is packed with nutrition! A large mango is loaded with fiber and vitamin A, and it gives you 100 percent of the vitamin C you need every day. A mango gives you more than 20 different vitamins and minerals, all for only 100 calories!

Part IV

Flat Belly Recipes for Special Situations

Daily-Free Calcium Sources

Food Source	Serving Size	Calcium (mg)
Turkey breast, boneless, skinless	1 cup	450
Cod	1 cup	349
Tuna, light, canned in water	1 cup	301
Halibut	2 ounces	217
Pork tenderloin	2 tablespoons	176
Chicken breast, boneless, skinless	3 ounces	175
Beef, eye round roast and steak	1 cup cooked	154
Beef, top round roast	½ cup	121
Beef, top sirloin steak	1 cup raw	104

Find belly-flattening foods for the whole family, in a free article at www.dummies.com/extras/flatbellycookbook.

In this part . . .

✔ Save time with slow-cooker meals.

✔ Find yummy meat-free and dairy-free meals that can help to fight belly fat.

✔ Prevent nutrient deficiencies on a vegan or vegetarian diet.

✔ Get the whole family involved and eat healthy on the Belly Fat Diet plan.

Chapter 14

Vegetarian and Vegan Meals

In This Chapter

▶ Turning to tofu

▶ Doing without dairy

▶ Buying into beans

*W*ell-planned vegetarian and vegan diets put the focus on balancing whole grains, vegetables, fruits, plant proteins, and calcium-rich foods to provide the body with the essential nutrients needed for health and well-being. Whether you live a completely vegetarian or vegan lifestyle, or you just incorporate vegetarian or vegan meals into your diet from time to time, you can reap the rewards of this healthy way of eating.

If you're not exactly clear on what a vegetarian is versus a vegan, check out this handy list of definitions:

✔ **Vegetarian:** Someone who doesn't eat meat.

✔ **Lacto vegetarian:** Someone who eats dairy products (milk, cheese, yogurt, butter, and so on) but doesn't eat meat or eggs.

✔ **Ovo vegetarian:** Someone who eats eggs, but doesn't eat meat or dairy.

✔ **Lacto-ovo vegetarian:** Someone who eats dairy and eggs, but doesn't eat meat.

✔ **Pescetarian:** Someone who eats fish and seafood, but doesn't eat meat.

✔ **Vegan:** Someone who consumes absolutely no animal products. Some vegans also avoid foods that are processed using animal products, such as refined sugar and some wines.

✔ **Flexitarian:** Often referred to as a *semi-vegetarian,* someone who eats a diet based on meatless items, but eats meats on an occasional basis. There is no set standard for how often "occasional" is — it's really up to each individual.

Reducing or eliminating animal products in the diet can lead to nutritional deficiencies and poor health. If you're a vegetarian or vegan, you need to pay particular attention to getting a balanced diet. You may become deficient in nutrients such as iron, zinc, vitamin B12, calcium, and protein. Talk to your doctor if you have any concerns about nutritional deficiency.

This chapter is filled with delicious, all veggie recipes for breakfast, lunch, or dinner. The meals are balanced with key vitamins, minerals, protein, and fiber. This chapter provides tofu, bean, and dairy-free recipes. And you don't have to be vegetarian to enjoy these dishes. Give new textures and flavors a chance — the carnivore in you may be surprised how much you love them!

Tofu-Based Meals

Tofu is coagulated soybeans that are pressed into the bricklike shapes you can find at the grocery store. It's a great meat substitute for vegetarians because of its high protein content — it contains about 10 g of protein per ½ cup serving.

Unlike animal meats, tofu has a generous amount of calcium, 227 mg per ½ cup of firm tofu — almost as much calcium you would get from drinking a cup of milk! This makes tofu an excellent calcium source for the dairy-free diet. It's also a good source of B vitamins and iron, and is naturally low in saturated fat, cholesterol, and sodium, providing heart-healthy benefits.

Tofu comes in many varieties and the variability depends on the texture, from silken or soft to firm. Silken tofu has a much softer consistency than regular tofu and contains more liquid. It's ideal in smoothies, puddings, and baked dishes. Other textures include light firm, firm, extra firm, and super firm. All textures of tofu are made from the same ingredients — they're just processed slightly differently. When experimenting with tofu recipes, stick with the recommended texture — sometimes one texture can't be substituted for another in a recipe.

How to press tofu

Be sure to drain and press your tofu before cooking it. This way all the excess moisture is removed and the tofu can absorb more flavor from the rest of the dish. To press tofu, follow these steps:

1. **Place two layers of paper towel in a bowl and set the tofu on top.**

2. **Put two more layers of paper towel on top of the tofu and press down gently.**

3. **Drain the moisture from the bowl and repeat with clean paper towels as needed, until minimal moisture is released from the tofu.**

Tofu Scramble

Prep time: 10 min • **Cook time:** 10 min • **Yield:** 4 servings

Ingredients	Directions
1 teaspoon olive oil	**1** In an extra-large nonstick skillet, heat the olive oil over medium-high heat.
½ red onion, diced	
1 clove garlic, minced	**2** Sauté the onion and garlic until fragrant, about 2 minutes.
½ cup carrot sticks	
½ cup sliced mushrooms	**3** Add the carrots, mushrooms, zucchini, and pepper and sauté until softened, about 8 minutes.
½ medium zucchini, chopped	
½ red bell pepper, diced	
12 ounces lite, firm, low-calorie tofu, drained	**4** Crumble the tofu over the vegetables and stir to incorporate. Stir in the turmeric, paprika, salt, and cumin.
½ teaspoon turmeric	
½ teaspoon paprika	**5** Stir in the rainbow chard and serve.
¼ teaspoon kosher salt	
¼ teaspoon cumin	
1 cup rainbow chard	

Per serving: Calories 61 (From Fat 18); Fat 2g (Saturated 0g); Cholesterol 0mg; Sodium 249mg; Carbohydrate 5g (Dietary Fiber 1g); Protein 6g.

Vary It! This recipe is very versatile. If you have other veggies on hand, throw them in!

Tip: This colorful dish is great for breakfast, lunch, or dinner. Prepare this easy meal and heat it up any time of the day!

Note: The crumbled tofu is an easy way to include added protein and calcium in this dish.

Note: Serve this with whole-grain nutty seed bread to provide a full meal's worth of nutrition.

Vegetable Paella

Prep time: 10 min • **Cook time:** 10 min • **Yield:** 4 servings

Ingredients	Directions
1 teaspoon olive oil	**1** In a large skillet, heat the olive oil over medium-high heat. Sauté the onion, garlic, and mushrooms until softened, about 3 minutes.
1 sweet onion, diced	
1 clove garlic, minced	
½ cup mushrooms, chopped	**2** Stir in the paprika, turmeric, salt, and cayenne pepper, and crumble the tofu over the vegetable mixture. Mix to incorporate the tofu and coat it with seasonings.
½ teaspoon paprika	
½ teaspoon turmeric	
¼ teaspoon kosher salt	**3** Stir in the brown rice, vegetable broth, peas, tomato, kale, and parsley. Cook for 5 minutes until heated through and the liquid is absorbed.
¼ teaspoon cayenne pepper	
6 ounces extra-firm tofu, drained	
2 cups cooked brown rice	
½ cup low-sodium vegetable broth	
½ cup peas	
1 tomato, diced	
3 cups kale, chopped	
½ cup parsley, chopped	

Per serving: Calories 233 (From Fat 46); Fat 5g (Saturated 1g); Cholesterol 0mg; Sodium 224mg; Carbohydrate 39g (Dietary Fiber 5g); Protein 11g.

Vary It! Are you a seafood lover? Mix shrimp, scallops, and mussels into this dish.

Tip: You can spice up this dish with more cayenne pepper, red pepper flakes, Sriracha hot sauce, or jalapeños.

Green Curry Tofu

Prep time: 10 min • **Cook time:** 1 hr • **Yield:** 4 servings

Ingredients	Directions
1 butternut squash	*1* Preheat the oven to 400 degrees. Cut the butternut squash lengthwise into two even sections, discarding the seeds.
1 teaspoon olive oil	
½ yellow onion, diced	*2* Place the squash on a lined baking sheet, and coat gently with cooking spray.
1 red bell pepper, diced	
1 cup shredded carrots	
½ teaspoon cinnamon	*3* Roast the squash in the oven for 45 minutes or until softened. Allow the squash to cool, and remove the skin by scooping the squash out with a spoon. Dice the squash.
2 tablespoons green curry paste	
3 tablespoons low-sodium soy sauce	*4* In a large Dutch oven or medium soup pot, heat the oil over medium-high heat.
6 ounces extra-firm tofu, drained and cubed	
One 13.5-ounce can light coconut milk	*5* Sauté the onion, bell pepper, and carrots for 5 minutes.
3 cups broccoli florets	*6* Stir in the cinnamon, green curry, soy sauce, and salt until combined.
1 cup low-sodium vegetable broth	
	7 Toss in the tofu, coconut milk, broccoli, and vegetable broth. Gently mix, taking care not to break the tofu, and cook until heated through.

Per serving: Calories 212 (From Fat 80); Fat 9g (Saturated 5g); Cholesterol 0mg; Sodium 768mg; Carbohydrate 28g (Dietary Fiber 5g); Protein 10g.

Tip: Serve this recipe over a bed of brown rice or quinoa.

Going Dairy-Free

Calcium is a key nutrient that plays a vital role in maintaining bone integrity, muscle contraction, nerve impulses, and hormonal and enzymatic activity. It may also play a crucial role in regulating how fat is stored and broken down in the body. Researchers think that the more calcium a fat cell has, the more fat it will burn. A diet high in calcium may help to promote weight loss and burn belly fat.

How much calcium you need depends on your gender and stage of life. Calcium needs increase from birth through the teenage years, with kids 9 to 18 years old needing 1,300 mg per day. From the ages of 19 through 70, men need 1,000 mg per day; from 71 on, men need 1,200 mg per day. From the ages of 19 through 50, women need 1,000 mg per day; from 51 on, women need 1,200 mg per day. (For a full breakdown, go to http://ods.od.nih. gov/factsheets/Calcium-HealthProfessional/.)

If you go dairy-free, make sure you aren't just removing milk, but replacing it with calcium-rich food sources, like the ones in Table 14-1.

Table 14-1   Calcium-Rich Non-Dairy Foods and Beverages

Food or Beverage	Serving Size	Calcium
Almond milk	1 cup	450 mg
Calcium-fortified 100 percent orange juice	1 cup	349 mg
Fortified soymilk	1 cup	301 mg
Sesame seeds	1 ounce	280 mg
Sardines	2 ounces	217 mg
Firm tofu	3 ounces	175 mg
Baked beans	1 cup cooked	154 mg
Dried figs	½ cup	121 mg
Turnip greens or kale	1 cup raw	104 mg

Quinoa Stuffed Peppers

Prep time: 15 min • **Cook time:** 30 min • **Yield:** 4 servings

Ingredients	Directions
1 teaspoon olive oil	*1* Preheat the oven to 450 degrees. Line a baking sheet with aluminum foil, and coat it with cooking spray.
¼ red onion, diced	
1 clove garlic, minced	*2* In a skillet, heat the olive oil over medium heat. Sauté the onions, garlic, and mushrooms until softened.
1 cup mushrooms, chopped	
½ cup reduced-sodium black beans, rinsed and drained	*3* Stir in the black beans, Swiss chard, and basil and sauté until chard is wilted; remove from the heat.
1 cup chopped Swiss chard	
¼ cup basil	*4* Mix in the quinoa and tofu.
1½ cups cooked quinoa	
½ cup crumbled tofu	*5* Place the bell pepper halves on a baking sheet and stuff them evenly with the quinoa mixture.
1 yellow bell pepper, halved and seeds removed	
1 red bell pepper, halved and seeds removed	*6* Bake in the oven for 20 minutes. With 5 minutes remaining, top with the cheddar cheese.
¼ cup shredded vegan cheddar cheese	

Per serving: Calories 203 (From Fat 55); Fat 6g (Saturated 1g); Cholesterol 0mg; Sodium 248mg; Carbohydrate 29g (Dietary Fiber 7g); Protein 10g.

Vary It! Mix it up by stuffing this quinoa mixture into zucchini, eggplant, or acorn squash.

Note: You can serve this dish as an appetizer or side by stuffing baby bell peppers.

Baked Falafel

Prep time: 10 min • **Cook time:** 15 min • **Yield:** 4 servings

Ingredients	*Directions*
1 large clove garlic, peeled	*1* Preheat the oven to 400 degrees.
¼ red onion, peeled	
One 14.5-ounce can garbanzo beans	*2* In the bowl of a food processor, process the garlic and onion until minced.
¼ cup parsley, roughly chopped	*3* Add the garbanzo beans and process until combined, leaving the beans a little chunky.
½ teaspoon cumin	
¼ teaspoon coriander	*4* Pour the mixture into a large bowl, and add the parsley, cumin, coriander, red pepper flakes, and lemon juice.
⅛ teaspoon red pepper flakes	
2 tablespoons lemon juice	
Four 4-inch whole-grain pitas	*5* Line a baking sheet with parchment paper, and coat with cooking spray.
4 tablespoons hummus	*6* Roll the chickpea mixture into 8 even balls, and flatten slightly. Spray the tops of the chickpea patties with cooking spray.
½ cup cucumber, chopped	
½ cup tomato, chopped	
½ cup carrot sticks	*7* Bake for 15 minutes.
	8 To serve, cut warmed chickpea patties in half. In the bottom of each pita, stuff with half of the cucumbers, tomatoes, and carrots; then fill each with 4 chickpea patty slices, and top with the other half of the veggies and a dollop of hummus.

Per serving: Calories 242 (From Fat 30); Fat 3g (Saturated 0g); Cholesterol 0mg; Sodium 505mg; Carbohydrate 46g (Dietary Fiber 8g); Protein 9g.

Tip: Impress your friends! These bite-size portions can also serve as the perfect appetizer for any party or get-together.

Note: The simplicity of this recipe makes it an easy, all-in-one way to create a meal without a lot of effort and avoid the excess cleanup.

Red Lentil Dal

Prep time: 10 min • **Cook time:** 20 min • **Yield:** 8 servings

Ingredients	*Directions*
1 teaspoon olive oil	**1** In a large Dutch oven, heat the olive oil over medium-high heat. Add the onion and celery and cook for 2 to 3 minutes to soften.
1 yellow onion, diced	
4 stalks celery, chopped	
1 large clove garlic, peeled and minced	**2** Add the garlic and ginger and cook until fragrant.
¼ teaspoon fresh ginger, minced	**3** Stir in the cumin, turmeric, and lentils.
1½ teaspoons cumin	**4** Add the tomatoes and vegetable broth to deglaze the pan, picking up the browned bits at the bottom and stirring to incorporate. Stir in the cilantro.
½ teaspoon turmeric	
2 cups split red lentils	
One 14.5-ounce can diced tomatoes, with juices	**5** Bring the lentils to a boil and cover. Reduce the heat to medium and cook for 20 more minutes, until the lentils are softened. Stir often.
5 cups low-sodium vegetable broth	
⅓ cup cilantro, chopped	

Per serving: Calories 208 (From Fat 16); Fat 2g (Saturated 0g); Cholesterol 0mg; Sodium 196mg; Carbohydrate 35g (Dietary Fiber 7g); Protein 13g.

Tip: Lentil dal is delicious served over spiced rice or quinoa. Add a side of steamed broccoli for extra veggies.

Note: Lentils are a type of bean that are relatively quick and easy to prepare. In addition to being high in fiber, they absorb all the delicious flavors of the foods and seasonings they're cooked in.

Beans, Beautiful Beans

We don't care if you call yourself a vegan, vegetarian, flexitarian, or meat eater — in our opinion, beans should be a staple of your diet. Beans are one of the best sources of lean protein, fiber, complex carbs, and phytochemicals, along with a host of other minerals like iron, zinc, and magnesium. They've also been shown to protect against heart disease and lower cholesterol levels. In fact, the U.S. Department of Agriculture recommends people eat about 1 to 2 cups of beans per week!

Here are the benefits beans provide:

- **Fiber:** Depending on the type of legume, they can vary from 10 g to 16 g of fiber per cup. That's almost half your daily fiber quota! The fiber in beans helps you to feel fuller longer, so you don't eat too much, promoting a reduction in belly fat. Adding beans to the diet helps cut calories without feeling deprived.

- **Protein:** One cup of cooked beans contains about 12 g to 18 g of muscle-building protein.

- **Simplicity:** Canned beans are a really easy and fast option for every kitchen pantry. To keep sodium in check, purchase reduced-sodium varieties, and rinse canned beans before using. You'll cut the sodium by about 30 percent.

- **Cheap:** When beans are on your plate, proteins couldn't get any more economical! If you want to save even more money, use dried instead of canned.

- **Diversity:** Beans are extremely diverse, so you can find them for almost any cooking need. Some of the most common types of beans and legumes include black, navy, pinto, kidney, garbanzo or chickpeas, white, lima, lentils, black-eyed peas, and soybeans and edamame.

- **Gluten-free:** Because beans are gluten-free, they're an important part of a gluten-free diet to obtain adequate fiber. They're also ground into flours, and become a helpful ingredient in gluten-free cooking or if you want to experiment with new flours. For more information on gluten-free eating, check out *Living Gluten-Free For Dummies,* by Danna Korn (Wiley).

In this section, we provide bean-based recipes you'll love!

Skillet Eggplant Gnocchi

Prep time: 15 min • **Cook time:** 30 min • **Yield:** 6 servings

Ingredients	Directions
2 tablespoons olive oil	**1** In a large nonstick skillet, heat 1 tablespoon of the oil over medium heat. Add the gnocchi and cook, stirring often, about 5 to 7 minutes. Transfer to a bowl and set aside.
One 16-ounce package shelf-stable gnocchi	
1 small eggplant, trimmed and cut into ½-inch cubes	**2** Add the remaining tablespoon of oil to the skillet. Add the eggplant, onion, garlic, and herbs. Cook over medium heat, stirring frequently, about 5 to 7 minutes, or until the eggplant and onions are soft.
1 medium onion, peeled and diced	
4 cloves garlic, minced	
1 tablespoon dried Italian herbs	**3** Add the kale and cook until wilted, about 2 to 3 more minutes.
3 cups fresh kale, stems removed and chopped	
12 ounces no-salt-added tomato sauce	**4** Add the tomato sauce, beans, and tomatoes and cook another 2 to 3 minutes.
One 15-ounce can white beans, drained and rinsed	**5** Stir in the gnocchi and sprinkle with the mozzarella and Parmesan cheeses. Cover and cook until the cheeses are melted and the sauce is bubbling, about 3 to 5 minutes.
½ cup sundried tomatoes, not in oil	
½ cup shredded part-skim mozzarella cheese	
¼ cup shredded Parmesan cheese	

Per serving: Calories 363 (From Fat 128); Fat 14g (Saturated 6g); Cholesterol 28mg; Sodium 519mg; Carbohydrate 46g (Dietary Fiber 9g); Protein 16g.

Vary It! This one-skillet dish makes it easy to incorporate all the vegetables you may already have on hand. Try zucchini, broccoli, butternut squash, or any vegetables you like!

Tip: Serve with a salad and a delicious homemade bread for a traditional Italian meal.

Pumpkin Enchiladas

Prep time: 10 min • **Cook time:** 15 min • **Yield:** 8 servings

Ingredients	*Directions*

Ingredients

1 teaspoon canola oil

1 yellow onion, peeled and diced

1 cup corn

One 14.5-ounce can low-sodium pinto beans

4 tablespoons low-sodium taco seasonings

¼ teaspoon cinnamon

One 15-ounce can pumpkin puree

1 cup tomato sauce

½ cup no-salt-added vegetable broth

1 cup cheddar cheese

Eight 6-inch whole-wheat tortillas

¼ cup scallions, chopped, for topping

¼ cup cilantro, chopped, for topping

4 cups baby spinach greens

Directions

1 Preheat the oven to 375 degrees.

2 In a large saucepan, heat the oil over medium-high heat. Sauté the onion until softened.

3 Add the corn, pinto beans, 2 tablespoons of the taco seasonings, and cinnamon. Stir until incorporated and warmed through.

4 Fold in 1 cup of the pumpkin puree.

5 In a small bowl, mix the tomato sauce, vegetable broth, the remaining pumpkin, and the remaining 2 tablespoons of taco seasonings. Stir until combined to make the enchilada sauce.

6 In a large baking dish, spread half of the enchilada sauce on the bottom.

7 Reserve ½ cup of the cheddar cheese and set it aside for topping.

8 Soften the tortillas in the microwave on high for 20 seconds. Form the enchiladas by layering the remaining cheddar cheese and the pinto bean mixture on each of the tortillas; roll them up. Place each enchilada in the pan, side by side.

9 Top the enchiladas with enchilada sauce and the remaining cheddar cheese. Bake for 15 minutes, and serve warm.

10 Top the enchiladas with scallions and cilantro and serve on top of a bed of spinach.

Per serving: Calories 245 (From Fat 57); Fat 6g (Saturated 7g); Cholesterol 15mg; Sodium 693mg; Carbohydrate 40g (Dietary Fiber 8g); Protein 12g.

Note: Never used pumpkin in a savory dish before? Pumpkin is a low-calorie addition that is rich in fiber, antioxidants, vitamins, and minerals. It can add a deliciously sweet flavor to a savory dish!

White Bean and Tomato Pesto Pizza

Prep time: 15 min • **Cook time:** 15 min • **Yield:** 6 servings

Ingredients	Directions
16 ounces whole-grain pizza dough	**1** Preheat the oven to 450 degrees.
½ cup cannellini beans	**2** Spray a baking sheet or pizza pan with cooking spray.
3 tablespoons sundried tomato pesto	**3** Roll the dough into a thin circle. Transfer the rolled dough onto the baking sheet.
½ cup chopped fresh broccoli florets	**4** In a food processor or blender, puree the beans and pesto. Spread the bean and pesto mixture on top of the dough.
½ cup thinly sliced mushrooms	
2 ounces goat cheese, crumbled	**5** Top the pizza with broccoli, mushrooms, and goat cheese.
	6 Bake for 18 minutes or until crispy and the cheese is melted.

Per serving: Calories 293 (From Fat 96); Fat 11g (Saturated 4g); Cholesterol 8mg; Sodium 480mg; Carbohydrate 41g (Dietary Fiber 8g); Protein 13g.

Note: Pizza often gets a bad rap, but adding lots of vegetables and beans along with a whole-wheat crust can provide a nutritious and balanced meal.

Vary It! Get creative! Switch up the cheese, beans, or vegetables to find your unique flavor combination.

Mango Quesadillas

Prep time: 15 min • **Cook time:** 20 min • **Yield:** 6 servings

Ingredients	Directions
½ **jalapeño, seeded**	**1** In a food processor or blender, process the jalapeño and garlic. Add the crushed tomatoes and lime juice and mix until smooth.
1 clove garlic	
½ **cup canned no-salt-added crushed tomatoes**	**2** On a nonstick grill pan, heat the oil over medium heat and sauté the mushrooms, onion, and bell pepper.
½ **lime, juiced**	
1 teaspoon canola oil	
½ **cup mushrooms**	**3** Stir in the black beans and kale and cook until heated. Remove the vegetables and beans from the pan and set aside in a bowl.
½ **red onion, peeled and diced**	
1 yellow bell pepper, thinly sliced	**4** Place a tortilla on the grill pan, and layer one-quarter of the cheese, sautéed vegetables and beans, mango, avocado, and cilantro.
1 can low-sodium black beans, rinsed and drained	
1 cup kale, chopped	**5** Fold the tortilla in half, gently pressing down to form a quesadilla.
Six 6-inch whole-wheat tortillas	
4 ounces pepper jack cheese, shredded	**6** Allow the quesadilla to get crispy on one side and flip to toast the other half.
1 mango, thinly sliced	**7** Cut the tortilla into three even triangles and serve hot.
1 California (Hass) avocado, thinly sliced	
¼ **cup cilantro, chopped**	**8** Repeat Steps 4 through 7 with each of the remaining tortillas.

Per serving: Calories 275 (From Fat 109); Fat 12g (Saturated 4g); Cholesterol 17mg; Sodium 314mg; Carbohydrate 35g (Dietary Fiber 8g); Protein 12g.

Vary It! Mix it up by opening the tortilla to make it a pizza. Or skip the tortilla, add a few greens, and create a colorful salad.

Chapter 15

Slow-Cooker Meals

In This Chapter

▶ Waking up to a warm breakfast

▶ Coming home from work to a ready-to-eat dinner

We're big believers that it shouldn't take hours of slaving away in the kitchen to get a meal on the table. You may be thinking that slow cookers are the exact opposite of fast. But when it comes to effortless cooking and cleanup, the slow cooker has no match. The amount of time it takes to prepare ingredients for the slow cooker is minimal. Then you "set it and forget it" until you're ready to eat.

Not only do slow cookers make life easier in our hectic and busy lives, but they're also a belly-friendly way to cook. The low cook temperatures of the slow cooker are a nutritional benefit because they help to prevent nutrient loss. Cooking with a slow cooker is a moist heat method, making meats fall-off-the-bone tender and allowing you to choose healthier, leaner cuts while still enjoying moist and succulent meats. Raw vegetables are even more delicious in the slow cooker because their water content provides a healthy cooking liquid and helps to moisten meat. Enjoy vegetables in a new way — in the slow cooker!

In this chapter, we show you how slow cookers provide new and appealing ways to spice things up in your kitchen along with belly-friendly slow-cooker recipes for any time of the day. Using your slow cooker will leave you more satisfied and more energized, and give you more time to hit the gym and get rid of belly fat.

Breakfast in the Slow Cooker

You've probably heard that breakfast is the most important meal of the day, but while you're dragging yourself out of bed, getting yourself and the kids ready to leave the house, and running out the door, sometimes breakfast is the last thing on your plate.

But we have great news: Making breakfast can be as easy as skipping it! Using a slow cooker saves you time in the morning, and eating breakfast will curb your appetite and help you burn belly fat throughout the day. The sugar- and calorie-laden snacks in your line of sight at the office will be less of a threat, and you'll feel more energized. Starting out with the right breakfast leads to better meal decisions later in the day, too — in fact, research suggests that breakfast eaters weigh less than those who skip it!

Slow-cooked meals are easier than you may think. Here are some tips to get the most out of your slow-cooking experience:

- ✔ **Explore your options.** You can make so many breakfast recipes in the slow cooker! We've included our favorite breakfast slow-cooker recipes in this section.

- ✔ **Prepare your breakfast the night before.** While you sleep, let your slow cooker do the work for you. This keeps you from scrambling to pull something together in the morning.

- ✔ **Have family members serve themselves.** This is one of our favorite benefits of a slow-cooker breakfast. Family members have the convenience of serving themselves whenever they're ready to eat, which means less morning stress for you!

- ✔ **If your slow cooker has one, use a liner.** This minimizes your breakfast cleanup, so you don't come home from work to a mess.

- ✔ **Save yourself a trip to the fast-food drive-through by quickly turning your slow-cooked meal into a breakfast on the go.** Simply pack your breakfast in an air-tight container, and you're out the door!

In this section, we give you fun and satisfying slow-cooker breakfast recipes to prove how easy breakfast can be!

Cinnamon Applesauce

Prep time: 10 min • **Cook time:** 8 hr • **Yield:** 6 servings

Ingredients	*Directions*
8 Honeycrisp apples	*1* Peel and core the apples.
1 teaspoon cinnamon	*2* Cut the apples into cubes, and place them in a slow cooker.
2 tablespoons orange juice	
	3 Add the cinnamon and orange juice.
	4 Cover the slow cooker and cook on low heat for 8 hours.
	5 Mash the apples to reach the desired consistency.
	6 Serve hot or chilled.

Per serving: Calories 141 (From Fat 3); Fat 0g (Saturated 0g); Cholesterol 0mg; Sodium 0mg; Carbohydrate 37g (Dietary Fiber 4g); Protein 1g.

Vary It! Mix up the spices. Try ginger, pumpkin pie spice, or cardamom for a twist.

Vary It! Go with a different apple variety! You can use Granny Smith, Gala, or Red Delicious in this recipe.

Tip! Serve this Cinnamon Applesauce with our Greek Yogurt Banana Pancakes (see Chapter 6) or with your favorite omelet. Applesauce also provides a natural and yummy sweetness mixed into your morning oatmeal or atop low-fat cottage cheese.

An apple a day

Apples are rich in the flavonoid quercetin, which has been shown to block fat cells from maturing and helps to fight inflammation. This antioxidant makes apples a great metabolism booster and belly blaster. Here are some fun facts about apples:

✔ One medium apple contains 4 g of fiber and only 95 calories!

✔ Apples are a member of the rose family.

✔ There are more than 7,500 apple varieties worldwide.

✔ Apples contain both types of fiber — soluble and insoluble — both of which are important in preventing disease and reducing belly fat.

✔ Apples keep you satisfied and fuller for longer so you don't gain weight.

Cherry Almond Steel-Cut Oatmeal

Prep time: 5 min • **Cook time:** 8 hr • **Yield:** 4 servings

Ingredients	*Directions*
1 cup steel-cut oats	**1** Liberally coat a slow cooker with cooking spray.
3 cups unsweetened almond milk	**2** In the slow cooker, combine the oatmeal, almond milk, applesauce, almond extract, and tart cherries.
½ cup unsweetened applesauce	
¼ teaspoon almond extract	**3** Cover the slow cooker and cook on low heat for 8 hours.
¼ teaspoon vanilla extract	
⅓ cup dried tart cherries, unsweetened	**4** To serve, top with sliced almonds.
⅓ cup sliced almonds	

Per serving: Calories 224 (From Fat 92); Fat 10g (Saturated 0g); Cholesterol 0mg; Sodium 140mg; Carbohydrate 28g (Dietary Fiber 5g); Protein 7g.

Note: Steel-cut oats are a high-fiber food, which keeps you satisfied and may help to lower cholesterol and regulate blood sugar.

Vary It! Stir in pumpkin puree or applesauce before cooking for a unique flavor and nutrition blast.

Pretty please, with (tart) cherries on top?

Tart (or Montmorency) cherries are different from raw cherries and are typically found either dried or frozen because they're so delicate and high in water that they can't withstand transport. Aside from their oh-so-scrumptious flavor, there are so many more reasons to top your oatmeal with tart cherries:

✔ Tart cherries contain the highest amount of anti-inflammatory properties of any food.

✔ They're a natural source of melatonin, which can help you sleep longer and feel more rested to conquer your belly-blasting workouts!

✔ They contain anthocyanins, which are unique compounds that help to reduce muscle soreness and speed recovery.

Egg, Spinach, and Mozzarella Casserole

Prep time: 10 min • **Cook time:** 8 hr • **Yield:** 4 servings

Ingredients	*Directions*
8 eggs	*1* Coat a 4-quart oval slow cooker with cooking spray.
1 cup skim milk	
1 cup plain, frozen hash browns	*2* In the slow cooker, whisk the eggs, milk, hash browns, spinach, tomato, ½ cup of the mozzarella, salt, and pepper.
2 cups baby spinach	
1 tomato, diced	*3* Top with the remaining ¼ cup of mozzarella cheese.
¾ cup mozzarella	
⅛ teaspoon kosher salt	*4* Cover the slow cooker with the lid and cook on low heat for 7 to 8 hours.
Pepper, to taste	

Per serving: Calories 283 (From Fat 132); Fat 15g (Saturated 6g); Cholesterol 436mg; Sodium 373mg; Carbohydrate 16g (Dietary Fiber 2g); Protein 22g.

Tip: This beautiful dish looks lovely served on a tray at a brunch or holiday get-together.

Vary It! Add turkey sausage, Canadian bacon, or ham for an even heartier casserole.

We love eggs!

It's been said that eating eggs for breakfast leaves people feeling more satisfied for longer than they do after eating other common breakfast items. One egg contains all nine essential amino acids and is a great source of protein for only 70 calories! You can enjoy eggs any time of day. Pack a hard-boiled egg in your lunchbox for a filling snack. Make an egg salad for lunch. Or toss some eggs into your slow cooker and gobble them up for breakfast. Bottom line: We love eggs and hope you do, too!

Gluten-Free Banana Nut Bread

Prep time: 15 min • **Cook time:** 2 hr • **Yield:** 8 servings

Ingredients	Directions
3 tablespoons melted butter	**1** In a medium bowl, combine the butter and brown sugar, and whisk in the eggs.
½ cup brown sugar, unpacked	
3 eggs	**2** Stir in the applesauce, buttermilk, and bananas.
¼ cup unsweetened applesauce	
½ cup reduced-fat buttermilk	**3** In a large bowl, whisk together the brown rice flour, millet, baking soda, baking powder, allspice, and salt.
3 bananas, mashed (about 1½ cups)	
1½ cups brown rice flour	**4** Pour the banana mixture into the flour mixture, and stir just until combined, taking care not to overmix. Fold in the walnuts.
½ cup whole millet, crushed	
1 teaspoon baking soda	**5** Coat a round 6-quart slow cooker with cooking spray. Pour the batter into the slow cooker, cover the slow cooker, and cook on high for 2 hours, until a toothpick inserted in the center comes out clean.
1 teaspoon baking powder	
1 teaspoon allspice	
½ teaspoon kosher salt	**6** Run a flat spatula around the edges of the slow cooker to ensure the bread has released from the pan. Cool on a baking rack until ready to cut. Store in an airtight container in the refrigerator for up to 3 days.
½ cup chopped walnuts	

Per serving: Calories 361 (From Fat 116); Fat 13g (Saturated 4g); Cholesterol 92mg; Sodium 440mg; Carbohydrate 55g (Dietary Fiber 4g); Protein 8g.

Tip: Pair a slice of this bread with a whole fruit smoothie for breakfast. Or spread nut butter on top and drink a glass of milk for added protein.

Note: The applesauce in this recipe allowed us to trim the fat while still keeping the bread moist!

Tip: Prepare this Gluten-Free Banana Nut Bread recipe at night so you have it ready when you wake up.

Dinner in the Slow Cooker

After a long day with the kids or at the office, having to continue working, in the kitchen, isn't always fun. Being exhausted after a long day may lead you to call your local pizza place for takeout, and that doesn't help your Belly Fat Diet plan.

Plus, coming home to the enticing aroma of your ready-to-serve dinner is a great feeling. No hungry kids asking, "Is dinner ready yet?" You can sit back and relax, enjoying quality time with your family without having to be in the kitchen.

A slow cooker is an efficient way to enjoy a healthy meal. Here are some foolproof tricks for getting dinner on the table when using the slow cooker:

- ✔ **Use a liner.** You can make breakfast and dinner in your slow cooker, if you use liners. All you have to do is remove the used liner and replace it with a fresh one, instead of having to clean the slow cooker by hand.

- ✔ **Keep the lid on.** Resist the urge to open the lid to check on your dinner. This causes heat and steam to escape, which slows cooking time.

- ✔ **Upgrade to a new model if you want to treat yourself.** Your decades-old slow cooker may still work like a charm, but newer slow cookers have fancy bells and whistles that will save you time and trouble. For example, you can program your slow cooker for a set time, and then keep the food warm and at a safe temperature until you're ready to eat. No more overcooked slow-cooked meals!

- ✔ **Prep ingredients before you need them.** If you're making dinner in a slow cooker, the night before, get your ingredients ready. That way, in the morning, all you have to do is put the ingredients in the pot and turn it on!

Store any leftovers in an airtight container for lunch the next day! Put your slow cooker to work for you, and you'll be eating healthy 'round the clock in no time.

Balsamic Glazed Meatloaf

Prep time: 15 min • **Cook time:** 3 hr • **Yield:** 6 servings

Ingredients	Directions
½ cup diced red onion	*1* In a large bowl, combine the onion, mushrooms, bell pepper, and zucchini.
1 cup chopped mushrooms	
½ cup chopped green bell pepper	*2* Stir in the Italian seasoning, salt, garlic, red pepper flakes, and oats.
¾ cup shredded zucchini	
¼ teaspoon Italian seasoning	*3* Gently mix in the beef, cheese, and egg.
⅛ teaspoon kosher salt	
½ teaspoon minced garlic	*4* Form the meat mixture into a flattened loaf, about 1½ inches thick, and place it in a slow cooker.
⅛ teaspoon red pepper flakes	
½ cup old-fashioned oats	*5* In a separate bowl, stir together the balsamic vinegar, ketchup, and honey.
1 pound extra-lean beef	
3 ounces reduced-fat cheddar cheese, cubed	*6* Spread the balsamic glaze on top of the meatloaf.
1 egg, beaten	*7* Cover the slow cooker and cook on low heat for 4 to 5 hours, until cooked through.
1 tablespoon balsamic vinegar	
¼ cup ketchup	
½ tablespoon honey	

Per serving: Calories 197 (From Fat 56); Fat 6g (Saturated 3g); Cholesterol 85mg; Sodium 288mg; Carbohydrate 12g (Dietary Fiber 2g); Protein 23g.

Vary It! Add shredded carrots instead of zucchini, or toss in a spicy jalapeño cheese to mix it up.

Tip: Many grocery stores sell pre-chopped onions and bell peppers. If you're really short on time, take advantage of these convenient options!

Note: Oats replace breadcrumbs in this recipe for a higher fiber content.

Philly Cheese Steak Salad

Prep time: 10 min • **Cook time:** 2 hr • **Yield:** 6 servings

Ingredients	Directions
1 teaspoon olive oil 1 sweet onion, thinly sliced	**1** In a large sauté pan, heat the olive oil and sauté the onion, pepper, and mushrooms until softened.
1 green bell pepper, thinly sliced	**2** Pour the vegetables into a round 6-quart slow cooker, and place the steak on top.
1 cup baby bella mushrooms, thinly sliced	
1 pound top sirloin steak	**3** Season with salt, pepper, and balsamic vinegar.
⅛ teaspoon kosher salt	**4** Layer with provolone cheese.
⅛ teaspoon pepper	**5** Cover the slow cooker and cook on low heat for 2 to 3 hours, until the steak is medium-well done.
2 tablespoons balsamic vinegar	
4 slices provolone cheese, reduced fat	**6** Remove the steak from the slow cooker, and thinly slice.
6 cups romaine lettuce	**7** Place the romaine lettuce in a serving bowl, and top with the vegetables and steak.

Per serving: Calories 283 (From Fat 128); Fat 14g (Saturated 6g); Cholesterol 61mg; Sodium 252mg; Carbohydrate 9g (Dietary Fiber 2g); Protein 29g.

Tip: Cooking the vegetables in the sauté pan first helps to develop and intensify the flavors. If you're short on time, just toss it all into the slow cooker — the flavors will be slightly different, but it still tastes delicious!

Asian BBQ Pulled Pork

Prep time: 10 min • **Cook time:** 8 hr • **Yield:** 6 servings

Ingredients	*Directions*
1 yellow onion, diced	*1* In a slow cooker, place the onions, bell pepper, and carrots.
1 red bell pepper, diced	
½ cup shredded carrots	*2* Pour in the soy sauce, vinegar, ketchup, and molasses and stir to combine.
2 tablespoons low-sodium soy sauce	
2 tablespoons rice vinegar	*3* In a small bowl, combine the Chinese five-spice powder, garlic, and sesame seeds.
¼ cup ketchup	
1 tablespoon molasses	*4* Rub the spice mixture onto the pork and place it in the slow cooker on top of the vegetables.
1 pound pork tenderloin	
¼ teaspoon Chinese five-spice powder	*5* Cover the slow cooker and cook on low for 8 hours.
1 teaspoon minced garlic	*6* Remove the meat from the slow cooker, and shred the meat into a large bowl.
1 tablespoon sesame seeds	
	7 Strain the vegetables from the liquid and add the vegetables to the meat mixture.
	8 Moisten the meat mixture with enough of the liquid BBQ sauce mixture to coat but not overwhelm the meat.

Per serving: Calories 144 (From Fat 23); Fat 3g (Saturated 1g); Cholesterol 49mg; Sodium 343mg; Carbohydrate 13g (Dietary Fiber 2g); Protein 17g.

Note: Serve pulled pork on whole-wheat slider buns topped with broccoli slaw and pickles.

Vary It! Instead of shredding the meat, slice it and put it over a bed of steamed rice and broccoli for an Asian-inspired pairing!

Turkey Lasagne

Prep time: 15 min • **Cook time:** 3½ hr • **Yield:** 6 servings

Ingredients	Directions
12 ounces ground turkey breast	*1* In a large skillet, brown the turkey breast. After cooking, combine the turkey with 1½ cups of the tomato sauce.
2 cups no-salt-added tomato sauce	*2* In a small bowl, mix together the cottage cheese, ricotta cheese, egg, and Italian seasonings.
½ cup low-fat reduced-sodium cottage cheese	*3* Coat a 5-quart oblong-shaped slow cooker with cooking spray. Place the remaining ½ cup tomato sauce in the slow cooker.
½ cup part-skim reduced-sodium ricotta cheese	
1 egg	*4* Break the lasagna noodles to fit the bottom of the cooker.
½ teaspoon Italian seasonings	*5* Layer the noodles with the cheese mixture and the meat sauce.
¾ cup part-skim reduced-sodium mozzarella cheese	*6* Repeat with noodles, cheese, and meat sauce with two additional layers.
8 whole-grain no-boil lasagna noodles	*7* Top with mozzarella cheese.
	8 Cover the slow cooker and cook on low for 3½ hours.

Per serving: Calories 318 (From Fat 77); Fat 9g (Saturated 4g); Cholesterol 87mg; Sodium 412mg; Carbohydrate 33g (Dietary Fiber 4g); Protein 29g.

Note: Cottage cheese replaces some of the ricotta cheese in this recipe, giving this dish less fat and extra protein. Whole-grain noodles are substituted for white noodles for extra fiber. Ground turkey breast replaces ground beef to reduce the fat content even more! This dish is a comfort food made healthy.

Tip: Sauté mushrooms, spinach, olive oil, salt, and pepper for a quick and healthy side dish, or pair with a side salad for a dose of leafy greens!

Jambalaya

Prep time: 15 min • **Cook time:** 8 hr • **Yield:** 8 servings

Ingredients	*Directions*
1 onion, peeled and diced	**1** In a slow cooker, place the onion, garlic, celery, bell peppers, and tomatoes.
3 cloves garlic, minced	
3 stalks celery, diced	
1 red bell pepper	**2** Stir in the Italian seasoning, chicken stock, wild rice, and kidney beans.
1 green bell pepper	
1 cup no-salt-added crushed tomatoes	
2 teaspoons Italian seasoning	**3** Cover the slow cooker and cook on low for 8 hours. With 15 minutes remaining, add the sausage and shrimp to the pot and stir.
3 cups low-sodium chicken stock	
1 cup wild rice	
One 15-ounce can low-sodium kidney beans, rinsed and drained	
6 ounces precooked spicy chicken sausage, cubed	
12 ounces precooked shrimp	

Per serving: Calories 254 (From Fat 36); Fat 4g (Saturated 1g); Cholesterol 94mg; Sodium 602mg; Carbohydrate 34g (Dietary Fiber 6g); Protein 23g.

Tip: Turn up the heat with a drop or two of Sriracha hot sauce.

Note: Jambalaya transports and reheats well, so bring it along in your lunchbox!

Tex-Mex Chicken Nachos

Prep time: 15 min • **Cook time:** 8 hr • **Yield:** 8 servings

Ingredients	Directions
1 pound chicken breast	*1* In a slow cooker, place the chicken, black beans, corn, salsa, and taco seasoning.
One 15-ounce can reduced-sodium black beans, rinsed and drained	*2* Cover the slow cooker and cook the chicken over low heat for 8 hours.
One 15-ounce can no-salt-added yellow sweet corn	*3* Shred the chicken, and mix to combine with the other ingredients in the slow cooker.
½ cup medium salsa	
3 tablespoons low-sodium taco seasoning	*4* Preheat the oven to 350 degrees.
8 ounces blue corn chips	*5* Line a baking sheet with parchment paper, and spread the chips onto the baking sheet.
1 cup shredded reduced-fat cheddar cheese	*6* Top the chips with the shredded chicken breast mixture and cheddar cheese. Bake for 8 minutes, until the cheese melts.
3 cups shredded romaine lettuce	
1 avocado, diced (refer to Figure 7-1)	*7* Top the nachos with shredded lettuce and avocado.
1 lime	*8* Squeeze lime juice on top of the nachos and serve immediately.

Per serving: Calories 364 (From Fat 120); Fat 13g (Saturated 2g); Cholesterol 39mg; Sodium 516mg; Carbohydrate 43g (Dietary Fiber 8g); Protein 23g.

Vary It! Not a black bean lover? You can use pinto beans in this recipe instead.

Tip: This dish is a great appetizer for any get-together! Simply transfer baked nachos onto a plate and pass around the party!

Note: Avocados are high in monounsaturated fats, making them a good belly fat fighter.

How to mince garlic

Garlic helps to shrink belly fat by controlling blood sugar and protecting against insulin spikes that trigger the storage of belly fat. For more health benefits, use fresh garlic.

Mincing fresh garlic may seem a little tricky, but with these step-by-step instructions, you'll be all set. You can also purchase fresh minced garlic at the grocery store for weeknight convenience.

1. Free the individual clove from the bulb.

2. Smash the clove to crush.

3. Peel the outer coating off the clove.

4. Chop the hard end off the clove.

5. Thinly slice the garlic clove lengthwise and crosswise until you form a very small dice.

Chapter 16

Kid-Friendly Meals

In This Chapter

▶ Whipping up sandwiches and snacks

▶ Packing in the protein for the whole family

"*O*h, my kid would never eat that." We hear this comment way too often from parents. It's true that feeding kids foods they already enjoy and challenging them with new foods once in a while can be difficult. Our society doesn't make it any easier: The foods targeted toward children are often filled with fat, sugar, and sodium, which doesn't exactly set them up for lifelong health.

If you have kids and you're embarking on a Belly Fat Diet plan, you don't have to cook one meal for you and another for your little ones. Make it a family affair! A healthy diet is key for children as they grow and develop, so why not begin by sharing healthy meals together as a family? The dinner table may also be a place where you can share with them why you're working on your health and explain that trying new foods is part of the process.

While you're developing healthy habits, your kids will be sure to notice your new choices. And you know what they say: "Monkey see, monkey do." You're the best example for your kids to follow, so if you eat vegetables, your kids will be more likely to take their first bite and follow in your footsteps.

As parents, it's our responsibility to teach our kids to like healthy foods, and to prepare them in a way that they'll love. Not everyone is a fan of raw baby carrots, but you can cook them in a new and exciting way such as roasting them to bring out their delicious taste!

In this chapter, we offer up recipes that will expose your kids to new flavors, textures, and foods, in a healthy, delicious way. These recipes are ones you can enjoy as a family, without blowing your Belly Fat Diet plan.

The Five-Finger Discount: Sandwiches and Snacks

Kids (and adults) love sandwiches any time of day! They're great for breakfast, lunch, dinner, and snacks. Cold sandwiches are perfect for packed lunches, and warm sandwiches can make a hearty dinner meal. Cut sandwiches into a fun shape, like pinwheels or sticks, and you have a kid-appealing snack!

When we say "sandwiches," we're talking about more than the beloved PB&J. We're talking about sandwiches getting a makeover, turned into wraps, grilled, and baked, in a kid-friendly way! In this section, we show you how to reinvent the sandwich to make mealtime and snack time fun for your kids!

How to make over the basic sandwich

You can make over any sandwich with the following tips:

✔ **Serve it warm.** Give your sandwich a makeover by serving it warm. For an example, try the Pear and Cheddar Grilled Cheese and Baked Egg-in-a-Hole recipes in this chapter.

✔ **Shape up!** Kids love fun shapes. Try the Peanut Butter and Banana Honey Sticks and Ham and Cheese Pinwheels.

✔ **Add fruit.** We let real food — such as bananas, cherries, pears, and pineapples — shine in the recipes in this chapter. Fruit adds a natural sweetness without adding processed sugar!

✔ **Veggify it!** Add lots of veggies to the sandwich to up the vitamins, minerals, and fiber content!

✔ **Give it a protein pump!** Protein is a key ingredient for sandwiches, but keep your kids interested by using proteins in new ways like our Baked Egg-in-a-Hole and Ham and Cheese Pinwheels.

✔ **Go light.** Light on the sauce and light on the cheese, please. Don't smother your sandwich in high-fat spreads and cheeses. There are plenty of reduced-fat cheeses that taste fabulous and have the same amount of bone-building calcium, just less fat. Fill your sandwich with healthy fats like avocado, light mayo, or even Greek yogurt!

Baked Egg-in-a-Hole

Prep time: 5 min • **Cook time:** 5 min • **Yield:** 1 serving

Ingredients	Directions
1 slice whole-grain bread	*1* Preheat the oven to 450 degrees. Place a baking sheet in the oven to heat.
1 egg	
1 tablespoon shredded reduced-fat cheddar cheese	*2* Using a cookie or round biscuit cutter, cut a shape into the center of the bread and reserve the cut-out piece.
Pepper, to taste	*3* Remove the baking sheet from the oven, lightly coat it with nonstick spray, and arrange the bread pieces on the pan.
	4 Crack an egg in the center of the bread with the hole.
	5 Sprinkle the egg with cheese and top it with pepper.
	6 Bake for 5 minutes until the egg white is set and the yolk is the desired firmness.

Per serving: Calories 152 (From Fat 57); Fat 6g (Saturated 2g); Cholesterol 231mg; Sodium 244mg; Carbohydrate 12g (Dietary Fiber 2g); Protein 12g.

Note: Serve with a side of grapes and fresh cut strawberries to make this a balanced breakfast. Also, you can toss the cut-out piece of bread if you want. But especially if you use a cookie cutter with a fun shape, kids like eating this tiny piece of toast!

Tip: Egg yolks are good for your eyes! They contain antioxidants that have been shown to ward off loss of vision.

Brain food

"You are what you eat." We bet you've heard that saying before. But surprise, surprise, it doesn't pertain only to us humans! You may have noticed that some eggs have the term *omega-3* on the label, and this is largely due to the diet that the hens receive. Hens that are fed a veg-etarian diet supplemented with flaxseed naturally produce eggs rich in omega-3s! This is great news because many people, especially kids get far too little omega-3s in their diet. And this fatty acid is so important for brain development and eye health. If you choose the right eggs, you can get almost 25 percent of your recommended daily intake of omega-3s in just one egg! Every little bite counts!

Peanut Butter and Banana Honey Sticks

Prep time: 5 min • **Cook time:** 1 min • **Yield:** 4 servings

Ingredients	Directions
2 slices whole-grain bread	**1** Toast the bread; then spread peanut butter evenly on top of the bread.
2 tablespoons natural crunchy peanut butter	
1 banana	**2** Slice the banana lengthwise, creating 4 long slices, and place them on top of the peanut butter.
1 teaspoon honey	
½ teaspoon cinnamon	**3** Drizzle honey and sprinkle cinnamon over the banana slices.
	4 Cut the bread in between the bananas, creating easy-to-grab "sticks."

Per serving: Calories 115 (From Fat 41); Fat 5g (Saturated 1g); Cholesterol 0mg; Sodium 105mg; Carbohydrate 16g (Dietary Fiber 2g); Protein 4g.

Note: Serve sticks with refreshing blueberries and a glass of milk.

Vary It! Use almond butter as a substitute for peanut butter. Or try grilling your sandwich so it's crunchy on the outside and gooey in the middle!

Nut-rition

Nuts are a rich source or protein and heart-healthy monounsaturated fats. Most important, they're a healthy kid favorite! Kids are most familiar with peanut butter, but if you like to mix it up or your child has a peanut allergy, we have some other nutty ideas! These days it's easy to find a variety of nut butters in the supermarket, so we've compiled a list of our favorite nut butters that your kids will love:

✔ **Almond butter:** Almonds are loaded with more calcium and fiber than any other nut!

✔ **Cashew butter:** This nut is high in zinc and iron, both important nutrients for keeping energy up.

✔ **Hazelnut butter:** Hazelnuts are filled with folic acid, which is needed to help make DNA.

✔ **Pistachio butter:** Pistachios are packed with potassium. Say that three times fast!

✔ **Sunflower butter:** It's not technically a nut, but it sure does taste nutty! Sunflower butter is creamy and made from sunflower seeds.

Rotisserie Chicken Salad Cups

Prep time: 5 min • **Yield:** 4 servings

Ingredients	Directions
2 cups diced rotisserie chicken	*1* In a large bowl, combine the chicken, blueberries, celery, lemon juice, yogurt, and chives.
½ cup dried blueberries	
½ cup celery, thinly chopped	*2* Spoon the chicken salad inside the tortilla chips and top with avocado.
1 teaspoon lemon juice	
¼ cup nonfat Greek yogurt	*3* Serve immediately.
2 tablespoons chopped chives	
4 cups baked corn tortilla chip scoops	
1 avocado, diced (refer to Figure 7-1)	

Per serving: Calories 418 (From Fat 111); Fat 12g (Saturated 2g); Cholesterol 62mg; Sodium 218mg; Carbohydrate 49g (Dietary Fiber 7g); Protein 27g.

Vary it! Serve inside a whole-wheat pita or with toasted pita chips.

Note: Greek yogurt makes a delicious and low-fat substitute for mayo that your kids will enjoy!

Teach a child to cook . . .

At a young age, children develop their eating habits. Teaching them how to cook healthy can impact their lives forever. Getting your children involved with meal prep has many benefits for you and for them:

- When kids prepare food, they become invested in the outcome and more interested in new foods and taking a bite.

- Cooking is a life skill, and you don't have to be a master chef to teach it! If you're still learning how to cook yourself, that's okay — just let your kids join in on the process.

- Cooking together is a bonding experience that creates lasting memories and may also help improve your kids' self-esteem.

- Cooking with children may slow you down in the beginning, but it can save you preparation and cooking time down the road as they learn new skills!

Pear and Cheddar Grilled Cheese

Prep time: 5 min • **Cook time:** 5 min • **Yield:** 2 servings

Ingredients	Directions
1 teaspoon butter	*1* Coat a griddle or grill pan with butter and heat over medium heat.
2 tablespoons fig preserves	
4 slices whole-grain bread	*2* Spread the fig preserves on one side of the bread.
1 pear, sliced very thin	*3* Place the bread on the hot pan, fig side up.
3 ounces reduced-fat sharp cheddar cheese	*4* Begin layering the bread with cheddar cheese, pear slices, and spinach.
½ cup raw spinach	
	5 Sandwich two slices of bread together, and press together to form grilled cheese.
	6 Continue cooking until the bread is toasted on both sides.
	7 Remove from the pan and slice.

Per serving: Calories 311 (From Fat 62); Fat 7g (Saturated 3g); Cholesterol 14mg; Sodium 550mg; Carbohydrate 44g (Dietary Fiber 6g); Protein 18g.

Vary it! Replace the pears with Granny Smith apples for a tangy twist. For an extra protein kick, add a slice of deli ham or turkey!

Note: A great side to this meal would be sliced cucumber and carrots with a light yogurt-based ranch dressing. Or simply steam up some broccoli and season with salt and pepper.

Ham and Cheese Pinwheels

Prep time: 5 min • **Yield:** 2 servings

Ingredients	Directions
¼ cup light whipped cream cheese	*1* In a small bowl, mix the cream cheese and pineapple together.
¼ cup crushed pineapple, drained (packed in juice)	*2* Spread the cream cheese mixture on the tortilla, making sure to spread it thinly to the edges of the tortilla.
1 large whole-wheat tortilla	
4 ounces sliced deli ham	*3* Layer the tortilla with ham, carrots, and lettuce.
¼ cup shredded carrots	
¼ cup shredded romaine lettuce	*4* Roll the tortilla tightly together to form a long log.
	5 Cut the tortilla into 1-inch rounds to form bite-size pinwheels.

Per serving: Calories 226 (From Fat 75); Fat 8g (Saturated 4g); Cholesterol 43mg; Sodium 970mg; Carbohydrate 25g (Dietary Fiber 3g); Protein 14g.

Vary it! Instead of pineapple, mix cut peaches into the cream cheese! Swap the shredded carrots for thinly sliced celery.

Tip: Whole wheat is important. Due to the fiber content, whole-grain products can aid in weight management for both children and adults. To ensure that you're getting 100 percent whole grains, check the ingredients list to make sure that the first ingredient is "100 percent whole wheat."

The Clean Your Plate Club: Steer clear

In case you haven't heard, don't join the Clean Your Plate Club, and please don't force your kids to either! Research shows that people who lick their plates clean consume about 35 percent more calories than those who don't clean their plates. Here are a few things to keep in mind when you find yourself tempted to clean your plate (or when you're tempted to tell your kids to do the same):

✔ Stop eating when you're satisfied, not stuffed.

✔ If you're tired of fighting your kids at the dinner table about eating enough, start by serving them kid-friendly portion sizes. *Remember:* Kids don't need to eat much as you do.

✔ If you don't clean your plate, you're not *wasting* food. But overeating adds food to your growing *waistline!* Eating out? Grab a to-go box and eat it later! Think about how much money you could save if you stopped overeating.

Half-Pint–Pleasing Proteins

As a parent, the last thing you want to hear after you've been cooking is "Ew, gross!" Picky eating can easily add stress to mealtime that isn't helpful for you or your little ones. You want to be on your kiddos' team, but one of the worst things you can do is fall into the pattern of being a short-order cook. Feeding your kids only what they want to eat and not challenging their palates with new foods isn't a good idea.

Your role is to provide your kids with structured meal timing and a balanced plate. You don't need to force your kids or fight with them to eat their broccoli and salmon. But you'd be surprised that when the atmosphere is neutral, it gives them an opportunity to decide if they want to eat it or not. When they're hungry, they'll eat!

It takes no time at all for kids to develop a liking for sweets, cookies, crackers, candies, breads, and pasta. But when you present veggies and proteins to them, it can be more difficult (and scary) for a child to learn how to eat and enjoy them.

Your child's pediatrician may be stressing how vital it is for you to feed your little one protein to support growth, but you may be at your wits' end with picky eating. In this section, you find tried-and-true, kid-pleasing proteins that the whole family will enjoy!

TIP

Making protein appealing to kids

Sometimes all it takes is a little creativity to get your kids interested. Here are some tips for getting kids to eat enough protein:

✔ **Mix it!** Make mealtime a success by mixing a liked food with something more challenging. Give our Pumpkin Mac 'n' Cheese a whirl!

✔ **Crunch, crunch.** Kids are big on texture, as well as fans of crunchy foods. Let them munch on our Salmon Nuggets and Crispy Coconut Shrimp.

✔ **Dip it.** Who doesn't like a yummy sauce? Kids love the sweetness or creaminess that dip provides proteins. Try our sweet and tangy dip paired with the Crispy Coconut Shrimp!

✔ **Kid-size!** Get on their level, and make it mini. Our Mini Chicken Mozzarella Meatballs, Salmon Nuggets, and Mini Spinach Cheeseburger Pizzas are just the right size for little fingers.

Mini Chicken Mozzarella Meatballs

Prep time: 10 min • **Cook time:** 15 min • **Yield:** 5 servings

Ingredients	*Directions*
1 pound extra-lean ground chicken breast, 98 percent lean	*1* Preheat the oven to 400 degrees.
¼ cup whole-grain breadcrumbs	*2* Mist a nonstick 24-count mini muffin pan with cooking spray.
2 tablespoons minced onion **2 tablespoons chopped parsley**	*3* In a large bowl, combine all the ingredients except the mozzarella.
¼ cup marinara sauce **¼ teaspoon Italian seasonings**	*4* Roll the chicken mixture into 20 uniform meatballs and place them in the muffin pan.
¼ teaspoon fennel seeds, crushed	*5* Bake for 10 minutes; remove from the oven.
¼ teaspoon crushed red pepper flakes **¼ teaspoon garlic powder**	*6* Top each meatball with a sprinkle of mozzarella and continue baking for 5 minutes.
½ cup shredded part-skim mozzarella cheese	

Per serving: Calories 144 (From Fat 28); Fat 3g (Saturated 1g); Cholesterol 66mg; Sodium 197mg; Carbohydrate 3g (Dietary Fiber 0g); Protein 25g.

Tip: Serve the meatballs over warmed marinara sauce, cooked spinach, and whole-wheat noodles.

Vary It! Serve meatballs as an appetizer on toothpicks.

Note: This recipe is a timesaver! Make the meatballs ahead and store on a bed of marinara sauce in an airtight container or freezer bag. Reheat and eat well, even on a weeknight!

Salmon Nuggets

Prep time: 5 min • **Cook time:** 10 min • **Yield:** 6 servings

Ingredients	*Directions*
1 cup panko breadcrumbs	*1* Preheat the oven to 400 degrees; line a baking sheet with parchment paper and coat with cooking spray.
1 egg	
1½ teaspoons minced garlic	*2* Place the breadcrumbs into a small bowl.
1½ teaspoons lemon pepper	
½ cup flour	*3* In a separate bowl, whisk the egg.
12 ounces salmon filet, skin removed	*4* In another bowl, combine the garlic, lemon pepper, and flour.
Ketchup, for dipping, if desired	
	5 Cut the salmon into uniform 1-inch bite-size pieces.
	6 Dip each salmon piece in the flour mixture, shaking off the excess. Dip it in the egg, and then roll it in the breadcrumbs.
	7 Lay the salmon on the baking sheet and spray the tops with cooking spray.
	8 Bake for 10 minutes. Serve the salmon nuggets with a side of ketchup if desired.

Per serving: Calories 188 (From Fat 79); Fat 9g (Saturated 2g); Cholesterol 66mg; Sodium 96mg; Carbohydrate 12g (Dietary Fiber 0g); Protein 14g.

Vary it! Mix up the spices! Add Italian seasonings or lime zest instead of lemon pepper.

Tip: Salmon is a great source of omega-3 fatty acids, which are important for brain development and protect against heart disease.

Note: Complement the salmon with a yummy salad. Toss romaine lettuce, croutons, Parmesan cheese, and a light yogurt-based Caesar dressing together and serve.

Pumpkin Mac 'n' Cheese

Prep time: 10 min • **Cook time:** 8 hr • **Yield:** 8 servings

Ingredients	Directions
8 ounces quinoa pasta shells	**1** Preheat the oven to 400 degrees. Spray a square 8-x-8-inch baking dish with cooking spray.
⅛ teaspoon kosher salt	
½ cup canned pumpkin	**2** Cook the pasta in salted water according to package directions. Rinse and drain.
½ cup plain Greek yogurt	
¼ cup skim milk	**3** In a large bowl, mix the pasta, pumpkin, yogurt, and milk together. Stir to combine.
¼ teaspoon ground mustard	
⅛ teaspoon paprika	**4** Stir the ground mustard, paprika, 1 cup of the cheese, and the chicken into the pasta mixture.
1½ cups shredded, reduced-fat cheddar cheese	
1 cup shredded rotisserie chicken breast	**5** Pour the macaroni mixture into the prepared baking dish and top with the remaining ½ cup of cheese.
	6 Bake for 20 minutes, until the cheese is melted.

Per serving: Calories 141 (From Fat 19); Fat 2g (Saturated 1g); Cholesterol 19mg; Sodium 228mg; Carbohydrate 16g (Dietary Fiber 2g); Protein 14g.

Vary It! Try a different type of squash instead of pumpkin, such as butternut.

Tip: Pumpkins contain an extremely high amount of vitamin A, which is a powerful antioxidant and is essential for good eyesight.

Treat with love, not food

Your kids need love and affection, and it's best to show them your love with hugs and kisses, not food. Parents often treat a good grade or behavior with a food reward, like candy or ice cream. Rewarding your kids with sweets may confuse them, making them think that desserts are better than other foods.

Instead, give them a hug or praise them for good behavior. If you treat good behavior with food, it teaches kids that food is comfort or reward. Later in life, this pattern may cause them to reach for food to make themselves happy.

Mini Spinach Cheeseburger Pizzas

Prep time: 10 min • **Cook time:** 10 min • **Yield:** 6 servings

Ingredients	Directions
2 cups spinach	*1* Preheat the oven to 400 degrees.
1½ tablespoons pesto	
Six 4-inch whole-wheat pita rounds	*2* In a food processor or blender, blend the spinach and pesto together until incorporated.
¾ cup tomato sauce	*3* Place the pitas on a baking sheet, and lightly cover with tomato sauce.
½ pound lean ground beef, cooked	
½ cup part-skim mozzarella cheese, shredded	*4* Top each pita with spinach pesto, beef, and mozzarella cheese.
	5 Bake for 10 minutes, until the cheese is melted.

Per serving: *Calories 183 (From Fat 58); Fat 6g (Saturated 2g); Cholesterol 29mg; Sodium 426mg; Carbohydrate 18g (Dietary Fiber 3g); Protein 14g.*

Vary It! Instead of ground beef, try ground turkey breast.

Slip 'em a mickey: Getting your kids to eat their vegetables

Do you ever hear kid squeals of "Ew, gross!", "It's crunchy," or "I'm not eating that"? It's common for kids to speak their minds when it comes to the foods on their plate. It can take 15 to 20 attempts at trying a food before a child (or adult) decides he likes it! So, don't give up! But in the meantime, while you work on teaching your kids to like their Brussels sprouts, here are a few things you can do to sneak a little extra nutrition into their bellies:

✔ Puree veggies — such as bell peppers, carrots, cauliflower, celery, onions, spinach, and zucchini — and add them to pasta sauces, casseroles, and even desserts.

✔ Puree beans, and add them to brownies or lasagne.

✔ Swap half of the all-purpose flour called for in recipes for whole-grain flour. You can also hide wheat germ and flax in oatmeal, pancakes, and smoothies!

Remember: These tricks aren't an excuse to stop challenging your little ones with new tastes and textures, but they do allow you to feel more at ease with their nutrition while your kids are experimenting with their likes and dislikes.

Crispy Coconut Shrimp

Prep time: 10 min • **Cook time:** 10 min • **Yield:** 4 servings

Ingredients	Directions
1 cup bran cereal flakes	*1* Preheat the oven to 400 degrees. Place the bran flakes in a food processor. Spin until roughly chopped, place in a bowl, and mix with the coconut flakes.
⅓ cup sweetened coconut flakes	
½ cup whole-grain flour	*2* In a separate bowl, place the flour.
1 egg	
½ teaspoon water	*3* In a separate bowl, whisk the egg and water.
1 pound large shrimp, deveined and tail on (refer to Figure 8-1)	*4* Line a baking sheet with parchment paper, and coat with cooking spray.
¼ cup orange marmalade	*5* Dip the shrimp into the flour, then the egg, and then the coconut mixture, and place on the cooking sheet.
1 tablespoon white wine vinegar	
2 teaspoons olive oil	*6* Coat the tops of the shrimp with cooking spray, and bake for 10 minutes.
2 to 3 drops Sriracha hot sauce, for heat if desired	*7* In a small bowl, whisk together the orange marmalade, vinegar, olive oil, and hot sauce (if desired) to form a dipping sauce.

Per serving: Calories 351 (From Fat 89); Fat 10g (Saturated 4g); Cholesterol 278mg; Sodium 317mg; Carbohydrate 38g (Dietary Fiber 4g); Protein 30g.

Note: Shrimp is low in saturated fat and high in iron, protein, and selenium. Iron is important for healthy blood to transport oxygen. Protein is required for proper muscle development. Selenium is essential for a healthy metabolism.

Tip: Serve with a fresh fruit salad for a great summer meal!

Part V
The Part of Tens

the
part of
tens

For a list of ten belly-bloating foods to avoid, head to www.dummies.com/
extras/flatbellycookbook.

In this part . . .

✔ Incorporate belly-friendly seasonings into your favorite foods to maximize your belly-burning results.

✔ Find the top spices that burn off belly fat and boost metabolism.

✔ Find the top kitchen gadgets to save you time and energy when preparing belly-friendly meals and snacks.

✔ Use timesaving kitchen gadgets to make you look like an expert chef in no time.

Chapter 17

Ten Belly-Flattening Spices and Seasonings

In This Chapter

▶ Determining the best seasonings and spices for slimming the waistline

▶ Understanding how seasonings and spices can promote the loss of belly fat

▶ Incorporating belly fat–burning seasonings into your meal plan

*I*f you want to maximize the power of your Belly Fat Diet plan, look no further than your spice rack. Many common seasonings and spices are actually loaded with health properties! For example, some spices can help better regulate insulin in your body, while another can actually boost your metabolism, helping you to torch more calories throughout the day!

Even better, seasonings and spices are often loaded with disease-fighting antioxidants, provide little to no calories, and are a great way to add additional flavor and variety to your meals. Spices can jazz up even the dullest dish or snack, making your taste buds sing! In addition, seasonings and spices make a great way to flavor a dish with less sodium, a belly bloater!

Throughout this chapter, we list the top ten spices and seasonings you want to incorporate in your diet on a regular basis to help boost metabolism, decrease inflammation, and burn belly fat. We also tell you where to find these seasonings, what foods they work best with, and how much you need to gain the benefits they provide.

So, get ready to get spicy! Losing weight and shrinking your waistline never tasted so good!

Black Pepper

One of the most commonly used spices has a hidden secret: It may actually help you shed additional pounds and belly fat! Black pepper contains a substance called *piperine,* which is what gives it its strong taste and smell. A recent study published in the American Chemical Society's *Journal of Agricultural and Food Chemistry* found that piperine may actually stop the formation of new fat cells. Although scientists aren't yet sure of the exact mechanism in piperine that allows it to stop fat cells from forming, this study provides exciting new information in the link between seasonings and belly fat.

Black pepper isn't just good for your waistline, it can also be good for your overall health. Pepper is rich in antioxidants and has been found to help aid digestion and may even help to decrease fat-storing inflammation in your body. In addition, pepper makes a great alternative to salt when you reach to shake a seasoning on your food. Because too much salt can lead to belly-bloating water retention, using pepper as an alternative is a great way to add flavor without adding to the bloat.

 You can buy black pepper as whole peppercorns or ground pepper in any supermarket. For maximum flavor and aroma, choose whole peppercorns and grind them in a pepper grinder just before using. Black pepper is quite versatile and can be added to many recipes, spice blends, and sauces. Try adding it to salads, marinades, meats (as a rub before cooking), egg dishes, baked goods, dressings, sauces, gravies, and even vegetables such as tomatoes!

Cayenne Pepper

If you're serious about slimming your waistline and dropping those last stubborn pounds, start thinking *hot!* Hot and spicy cayenne powder is rich in *capsaicin,* a compound shown to have *thermogenic* (heat-producing) properties that help to boost metabolism, allowing you to burn more calories throughout the day and, therefore, lose weight and body fat.

And that's not all this amazing seasoning can do. In parts of the world where cayenne is used regularly, there is less incidence of high blood pressure. It appears that the capsaicin in cayenne can help to relax arterial muscles, allowing blood to flow more easily and, therefore, reducing blood pressure. In addition, animal studies have also indicated that capsaicin may decrease insulin resistance, helping to improve blood sugar control and reducing the risk of type 2 diabetes.

To start making cayenne a regular part of your diet, stock up on cayenne pepper, which you can find in the seasoning aisle at your local grocery store. You can sprinkle cayenne pepper into any recipe that can use a bit of a kick. This spicy pepper works great in Mexican and Cajun recipes and can even be used to heat up rice and quinoa dishes. You can even try sprinkling cayenne onto popcorn for a spicy snack!

Cinnamon

Just because you've made a commitment to burn off belly fat once and for all doesn't mean you have to give up sweets. If you have a sweet tooth, you're in luck! Not only does cinnamon help to curb sweet cravings, but it can actually help you to shed belly fat in the process.

Studies have found that an active compound in cinnamon, methylhydroxy chalcone polymer (MHCP), can actually help to make your fat cells more receptive to insulin. So, what does that mean exactly? Well, when cells are more receptive to insulin, they let insulin transport sugar into the cells for energy without resistance, helping to keep both sugar and insulin levels in the bloodstream stable, preventing rapid spikes and crashes. Because elevated levels of insulin in your bloodstream trigger your body to store more fat (specifically, belly fat), consuming a seasoning like cinnamon, which helps to lower circulating insulin levels, can help to protect against insulin-related fat storage. The result: Eating cinnamon on a regular basis can be a great way to help ward off belly fat!

Less belly fat isn't the only benefit this sweet spice provides. Cinnamon has also been shown to lower post-meal blood sugar levels and may help to decrease insulin resistance, protecting against type 2 diabetes.

You can buy cinnamon from almost any food market or grocery store. If you store it properly (in an airtight container, away from heat and light), ground cinnamon can last up to three years and cinnamon sticks can last up to four years. If your cinnamon begins to fade in color or has a diminished taste or aroma, replace it to gain the most health benefits.

Cinnamon is very versatile. You can use it in many foods and beverages. For example, you can add cinnamon on top of cereals and yogurts, use it to season fruits and vegetables, and even add it to beverages such as coffee and tea for a delicious, sweet treat that will help shrink your waistline!

Cloves

Cloves, which are the unopened flower buds of the *Syzygium aromaticum* tree, provide a sweet and spicy flavor and can be used in a variety of foods and recipes. Cloves are rich in several vitamins and minerals, including vitamin C and omega-3 fatty acids — two potent stress fighters that help to reduce the levels of belly fat–building stress hormones such as cortisol.

In addition, research has shown that diets that include cloves on a regular basis for 30 days can provide a significant reduction in blood sugar levels. This can help to protect against type 2 diabetes, as well as insulin resistance, a condition that can promote an increase in belly fat.

 You can buy cloves in both whole and ground forms, but the whole form provides the most significant health benefits. If you store them in an airtight container, ground cloves will remain good for up to six months; whole cloves, up to one year.

 You can use cloves in combination with other seasonings and spices in many recipes and marinades. They're commonly found in Asian, Middle Eastern, and African dishes. In fact, cloves are actually one of the main ingredients in Worcestershire sauce! You can incorporate cloves into your cooking by following these tips:

- ✔ Add a few cloves to a piece of meat or poultry before cooking.
- ✔ Add cloves to the pot when making homemade sauces and marinades, such as homemade barbecue sauce.
- ✔ Add cloves to soups, rice dishes, and even bread dough.
- ✔ Add cloves to sweet dishes, such as applesauce, mashed sweet potato, or even fruit stew.

Coriander

Found mainly as dried cilantro seeds, coriander brings a spicy and citrusy flavor to the dishes it's added to. This spice is rich in potassium, a mineral that helps to expel excess water weight, which can lead to bloating of the belly.

If you struggle with an expanding waistline due to gas and bloat, coriander may be your answer. It has been found to help aid in digestion and can fight bloating, excess gas, and even symptoms of irritable bowel syndrome (IBS).

In addition, some research points to coriander helping to raise HDL ("good") cholesterol levels while lowering LDL ("bad") cholesterol levels, improving heart health.

If you struggle with insomnia, you'll appreciate this tidbit: Coriander has been shown to promote better sleep. Inadequate sleep and slow metabolism can cause an imbalance in appetite-regulation hormones, which can lead to weight gain (specifically, gains in belly fat). By incorporating coriander into your diet on a regular basis, you may improve your sleep quality, helping to trim your waistline.

You can buy coriander fresh or dried. Fresh coriander lasts about three days after purchase. If you opt for dried coriander, store it in an airtight container, and it will remain good for six months to a year. Try incorporating coriander into your meal plan on a regular basis by using it to season salads; flavor soups and homemade breads; add flavor to stir-fried vegetables; or garnish meats, poultry, and seafood.

Cumin

Cumin seeds add a rich nutty, peppery flavor to any dish. These seeds are commonly found in Indian, Middle Eastern, and Mexican cuisines. In addition to their pleasant flavor, cumin seeds have another benefit: They may help shrink belly fat. Cumin seeds attack unwanted belly fat stores from two angles: They help regulate blood sugar and insulin levels, and they help fight stress.

Some research suggests that cumin may help improve blood sugar control in people with diabetes or at risk for developing diabetes. These wonder seeds help keep blood sugar levels consistent, allowing insulin levels to remain consistent as well.

Spikes in insulin can not only increase appetite and trigger cravings, but also cause your body to pack more belly fat. Maintaining healthy insulin levels without peaks and spikes can prevent your body from storing additional fat around your midsection.

When your body is under a state of stress, stress hormones such as cortisol peak. These stress hormones mobilize free fatty acids in your body. When not used, those free fatty acids may be repositioned right in your belly, creating an ever-expanding waistline. Cumin helps to reduce circulating stress hormones in the body, reducing belly fat storage. In addition, cumin has been found to aid digestion and expel excess gas from the body, helping to protect against belly bloat.

You can buy cumin in whole and ground forms in your local grocery store or in Indian or Middle Eastern groceries. Try adding it to rubs for meats, as well as marinades, salad dressings, and even chilies. You can even incorporate cumin into stir-fries, casseroles, soups, and stews. Try to consume 1 teaspoon of cumin two to three times per week for maximum belly fat–burning effectiveness!

Fennel Seeds

The bloat you can experience by chewing gum or drinking carbonated beverages can actually increase your waistline so much that you may go up one whole size in less than an hour! Now, before you panic, this isn't real weight that you're gaining — it's bloat due to swallowing or ingesting air into your stomach rather than your lungs. When this happens, it causes your midsection to look distended — the exact opposite of the flat abs you're aiming for!

To expel and eliminate this excess gas, look no further than fennel seeds. These seeds are powerful digestive aids that help to rid you of unwanted gas. These seeds can also help aid the good bacteria in your gastrointestinal (GI) tract digest and break down food while inhibiting the growth of bad bacteria.

For the greatest benefit for beating gas and bloat, consume a small handful (about 1 tablespoon) of fennel seeds after meals, especially when eating gas-producing foods such as cruciferous vegetables.

You can find fennel seeds in most supermarkets, as well as in markets that specialize in Indian and Chinese cuisines. You can buy seeds in their whole form or ground. The whole seeds have a longer shelf life, so if you buy them whole, store them whole and grind them as needed. Store fennel seeds in an airtight glass container, away from direct sunlight. Seeds are best used within six months.

Garlic

Love the taste of garlic? You're in luck! This pungent seasoning is packed full of health benefits that can shrink your belly. For starters, garlic has been shown to aid blood sugar control, helping to maintain consistent levels of insulin in the bloodstream and protecting against spikes that can trigger your body to begin storing more belly fat. In addition, garlic may help you to burn more calories and boost metabolism, thanks to its thermogenic properties.

But your waistline isn't all that will thank you for adding more garlic to your meal plan. Diets rich in garlic have been linked with lower cholesterol and lower blood pressure, helping to decrease your risk of heart disease. In addition, animal studies have found that garlic may help to kill off cancer cells, making it a potentially potent cancer fighter!

 You can buy fresh garlic in the form of cloves in any grocery store. You can also find fresh garlic available minced and jarred, as well as dried and powdered varieties. To maximize the health and weight benefits of garlic, opt for fresh garlic over dried (the drying processes can diminish some of the health benefits). You can incorporate garlic into your meal plan in many ways. For example, you can sauté vegetables in minced garlic and oil. You can use garlic in marinades, in salad dressings, in pureed veggie soups, and even sprinkled onto whole-grain pastas. Finally, you can roast or bake meats, poultry, and fish with minced or sliced garlic on top to enhance flavor.

Ginger

If you're looking for a spice packed full of antioxidant power, look no further than ginger! This pungent seasoning is commonly found in many Asian dishes and has been shown to improve digestion, relieve nausea, and even relieve cold and flu symptoms. But as if that weren't enough, ginger may also play an important role in the fight against belly fat.

Ginger has been found to contain strong anti-inflammatory properties, and inflammation plays a large role in causing your body to work against you to store more and more fat in your midsection. Incorporating powerful anti-inflammatory spices can help to cool body-wide inflammation, helping your body to focus on burning belly fat instead of storing it. In addition, ginger may also contain thermogenic properties, helping to boost metabolism and further slimming your waistline.

But that's not all that ginger provides. Recent research also points to ginger's ability to help decrease arthritis-related joint pain, as well as reduce the risk of heart attack and stroke while helping to reduce blood pressure levels.

Add ginger to your meal plan by dicing it and adding it to stir-fries; pureeing it into salad dressings, marinades, and even soups; or even using as a flavoring in smoothies.

 You can buy ginger at your local grocery store, as well as in Asian food markets. This spice comes in many forms — fresh, dried, powdered, and even pureed.

You may see two types of ginger on your supermarket shelves:

- **Old ginger:** Has a firmer skin and needs to be peeled before using. This form of ginger is mainly found in Asian groceries.

- **Young ginger:** Has a softer skin and can be used in recipes and seasonings without peeling.

Turmeric

If you've never heard of turmeric, you're missing out! Part of the ginger family, turmeric is an Indian spice that is used in many recipes and spice blends as a coloring agent and flavoring. The flavor can be described as somewhat buttery and slightly bitter, with a hint of a mustard.

Turmeric contains the compound *curcumin,* which is a powerful anti-inflammatory. In fact, the anti-inflammatory and antioxidant properties of turmeric are so powerful that some research even suggests this spice may have cancer-fighting properties!

The curcumin in turmeric has been found to help reduce blood sugar levels and prevent insulin resistance. This means that turmeric may help to protect against high levels of circulating insulin in your bloodstream, which can help to fight off the storage of belly fat. The strong anti-inflammatory properties of turmeric may also help to reduce inflammation markers and stress hormones in your body, which, when elevated, can cause your body to store belly fat instead of fighting it.

Turmeric is available for purchase in the spice aisle of most grocery retailers and is most commonly found in powdered form. This spice can be incorporated into many foods and recipes. It's used as an essential ingredient in many dishes, especially curry dishes. In addition, turmeric can be used to boost the flavor of sides such as rice and couscous dishes, meat and poultry dishes, and even vegetables and salad dressings. You can even sprinkle a small amount of turmeric into yogurts, egg dishes, or marinades for an additional health and flavor kick.

Chapter 18

Ten Timesaving Kitchen Gadgets

When you cook at home, you know what you're eating and you can cut down on ingredients and additives that can bloat your belly (such as excess sodium, sugars, and trans fats). All that is great, but when it comes down to it, the number-one reason most people eat out or grab takeout on the go is time. And that's where this chapter comes in!

Many products on the market today can simplify the cooking process. These products can save time, make cooking easier, and even make it more fun — which, in the end, will help you to prepare and create more belly-friendly meals and snacks at home. You can find gadgets for every budget — from dollar-store options to gadgets that may break the bank. But in this chapter, we show you our top ten favorite gadgets that are truly worth the cost. These gadgets are sure to save you time, leaving you more time for everything else!

Box Grater

Box graters are different from typical flat graters because they can handle a variety of foods. Box graters can do everything from grate cinnamon to shred cheese, shave chocolate, and even slice vegetables. And all this without your having to worry about an electronic motor or power cords! A box grater has four sides, which provide four functions: slicing, small-hole shredding, large-hole shredding, and grating. The versatility of a box grater allows you to prep many foods in little time, and best of all, you don't have to go searching for four different tools. Instead, the box grater is four tools in one.

You can buy box graters at home-goods store. They range in price from about $10 to $30.

Flexible Cutting Board

How can a cutting board possibly save time? Well, when it's a *flexible* cutting board, it can. Sure, you still have to spend time slicing and dicing food, but think about the last time you used a standard cutting board to chop up vegetables. To transfer the vegetables from the cutting board into the pan, bowl, or dish, you had to scrape them off the board and into the pan — and we're willing to bet some pieces dropped onto the countertop and floor.

With a flexible cutting board, after you finish chopping and cutting your vegetables, fruits, or herbs, you simply lift up the board, bend it, and pour the contents directly into the pan, bowl, or dish you're using. Being able to bend the board prevents the spillage that typically occurs with standard cutting boards. Spillage not only wastes time, but typically leads to waste (because you end up throwing out the food that falls onto the floor). Plus, when you're all done, just put your flexible cutting board into the dishwasher — they're dishwasher safe!

Flexible cutting boards are available in most home-goods and cookware stores and can range in price from $5 to $20, depending on their size and what they're made of.

Food Processor

Have you ever looked at a recipe that called for grating, chopping, or dicing and decided not to make it because it would be too time consuming? If so, you may want to consider investing in a food processor — it can make cooking a breeze! Food processors allow you to slice, shred, grate, chop, dice, and even puree in no time.

So, is a food processor the same as a blender? The two gadgets are similar, but they aren't quite the same. Food processors typically come with interchangeable blades instead of a blender's fixed blade. Food processors also have shorter and wider bowls than blenders have, making them more appropriate for working with solid and semisolid foods. Unlike blenders, which require some liquid to move food around the blades, little to no liquid is required when using a food processor. This allows you to knead dough, shred cheese, and even grind nuts, which may break a typical blender or burn out the motor.

When you're shopping for a food processor, consider what you'll use it for most often. Do you need one that can handle very large volumes of food at once, or do you just need one that can handle 2 to 4 cups of food at a time? Depending on the size and function, food processors can cost as little as $25 or as much as a few hundred dollars.

Immersion Blender

Also known as a *stick blender* or a *wand blender,* an *immersion blender* is an appliance that allows you to blend or puree foods and ingredients right inside the container in which you're preparing them. These blenders are fantastic for making soups and sauces, and some can even be used in pans while they're on the stove. Immersion blenders differ from hand mixers in that they're able to chop food while blending.

So, what makes an immersion blender such a timesaver? Traditional blenders can be bulky, and if you need to blend soups and sauces, you have to transfer the ingredients (possibly hot ingredients) to the blender and back to the pot, which can be messy and time consuming and increases the amount of dishes and utensils you have to clean. With an immersion blender, you just stick it in the pot and blend away! When you're done, just rinse it off in soapy water and that's it — it's that easy.

Immersion blenders can range in price from as little as $25 to as much as several hundred dollars, depending on whether you're looking for a home model or a professional model.

Kitchen Shears

Kitchen shears may *seem* like just another pair of scissors, but they're so much more! Instead of slowly chopping and cutting everything from chicken breasts to herbs and spices with a knife, which can be quite time consuming, with kitchen shears you can butcher meat and snip through spices much more rapidly than you can with any knife.

Kitchen shears are much sharper than office scissors. You can be buy them at most home-goods stores. They range in price from about $15 to $50.

Be sure to properly wash and disinfect kitchen shears after each use, especially when using them to cut animal proteins such as chicken and pork.

Mandoline

A *mandoline* is used for slicing and cutting (typically, vegetables and fruits). Getting enough vegetables every day is essential not only for good health, but also for slimming your waistline. Adding vegetables to soups and stews and topping salads with freshly sliced veggies are great ways to boost your intake. Many people stop short of making dishes that are heavy in vegetables because all that washing and chopping is time intensive.

That's where a mandoline comes in. This gadget consists of two parallel working surfaces, which can be adjusted in height. You simply slide a food along the adjustable surface until it reaches the blade on the fixed surface. This blade then slices the food and allows it to fall onto the plate below. Depending on the height and setting, you can cut everything from thick slices, to thin chips, and even crinkle-cut shapes.

When shopping for a mandoline, look for one with a good blade, which allows for easier slicing. Pricing can range from approximately $15 to over $100, depending on the brand and slicing options.

Prep Bowls

Sometimes the simplest gadget is the biggest timesaver. *Prep bowls* (small glass bowls in varying sizes) can actually help you prepare a meal much quicker. Have you ever watched cooking shows on TV and wondered why the chefs have so many little bowls cluttering their workspace? These little bowls full of various ingredients really aren't clutter at all. In fact, they can actually help you stay more organized, allowing you to set out all your ingredients so they're ready when you need them. You can prepare all your ingredients in advance, place them in the prep bowls, and then start cooking. You'll find that cooking will go much quicker when you have everything you need on hand — and you won't realize halfway through the cooking process that you forgot to mince the garlic or chop the onion.

Don't let the cleanup scare you off of using prep bowls. If you're using prep bowls to hold simple ingredients such as sliced vegetables, all they need is a simple rinse under running water to clean off. Otherwise, put them in the dishwasher.

Prep bowls are typically sold in sets (for example, sets of 8) and can range in price from $10 to $25 per set, depending on the size of the bowls, the number of bowls, and what the bowls are made of.

Salad Spinner

Have you ever been in the mood for a salad, only to wash your lettuce, wait for it to dry, and nibble on something else instead because you were too hungry to wait? It can happen. But here's the good news: A salad spinner can rapidly dry lettuce (and any leafy vegetable, such as spinach leaves, collards, kale, and even herbs), making them ready to eat in no time.

The spinner, which is also referred to as a *salad tosser,* removes excess water from leafy greens by using centrifugal force to separate the leaves from the water. This allows the leaves to be dried without leaving them limp. These products are typically made from plastic and consist of an outer bowl with an inner strainer or colander basket that can be removed. The cover of the salad spinner fits snuggly onto the outer bowl and contains a spinning mechanism, which when pressed, causes the food inside to spin rapidly, expelling excess water.

Salad spinners are typically inexpensive. They can range in price from as little as $5 to as much as $35.

Slow Cooker

Have you ever wished you could just walk in the door after work to a delicious, hot meal? Well, you can make this dream a reality with a slow cooker (often referred to by the brand name Crock-Pot). Slow cookers are great for many reasons, but our favorite is that all you have to do is toss in a few simple ingredients (typically a meat, seasonings, and some vegetables) and then turn it on. Four to eight hours later, your meal is cooked and ready to eat, with no additional effort on your part.

Slow cookers come with multiple cooking settings, including low, high, and warm. For the slowest cooking option, select the low setting, which will cook meats in six to eight hours. On the high setting, meats can usually cook in about four hours. Cooking on low allows you to set up your slow cooker in the morning, turn it on, and leave for the day. Then, when you return home, the meal is ready to eat.

Look for a slow cooker with a programmable timer. This will allow it to switch from the cook mode to a warming mode when the meal is done. That way, if you have to be gone for more than eight hours, the food won't overcook.

Slow cookers can range in size and price. Smaller ones with fewer features can sell for as little as $25; higher-end, larger slow cookers cost as much as $100. In general, when shopping for a slow cooker, look for one that's sized right for the meals you want to make.

For a variety of slow-cooker recipes, check out Chapter 15.

T-fal ActiFry

One of our favorite kitchen appliances is the T-fal ActiFry. This product may be a bit on the pricey end of home appliances, but in our opinion, it's completely worth it! The ActiFry is a low-fat cooker that allows you to make dishes such as french fries and stir-fries with a minimal amount of oil. The dishes taste just as delicious as if they were prepared the traditional way, but they have much less fat and calories — making them a perfect addition to your Belly Fat Diet plan.

One of the best timesaving features of the ActiFry is its ability to work as a stir-frier. If you've ever made a stir-fry, you know that slaving over the stove constantly stirring the food to make sure it cooks evenly and consistently can be tedious and time consuming. With the ActiFry, you simple toss in your ingredients, add about 1 tablespoon of oil, and turn it on. It stirs and cooks food on its own, with no assistance. You can simply set the timer, and when it goes off, you know your food is hot and ready to enjoy. You can cook vegetable dishes, chili, gumbo, and even dessert with barely any effort.

The T-fal ActiFry is available in many home-goods stores. As of this writing, the retail price is $249.99, but you may be able to find it for less if you shop around.

Appendix

Metric Conversion Guide

· ·

*N*ote: The recipes in this book weren't developed or tested using metric measurements. There may be some variation in quality when converting to metric units.

Common Abbreviations	
Abbreviation(s)	**What It Stands For**
cm	Centimeter
C., c.	Cup
G, g	Gram
kg	Kilogram
L, l	Liter
lb.	Pound
mL, ml	Milliliter
oz.	Ounce
pt.	Pint
t., tsp.	Teaspoon
T., Tb., Tbsp.	Tablespoon

Volume

U.S. Units	Canadian Metric	Australian Metric
¼ teaspoon	1 milliliter	1 milliliter
½ teaspoon	2 milliliters	2 milliliters
1 teaspoon	5 milliliters	5 milliliters
1 tablespoon	15 milliliters	20 milliliters
¼ cup	50 milliliters	60 milliliters
⅓ cup	75 milliliters	80 milliliters
½ cup	125 milliliters	125 milliliters
⅔ cup	150 milliliters	170 milliliters
¾ cup	175 milliliters	190 milliliters
1 cup	250 milliliters	250 milliliters
1 quart	1 liter	1 liter
1½ quarts	1.5 liters	1.5 liters
2 quarts	2 liters	2 liters
2½ quarts	2.5 liters	2.5 liters
3 quarts	3 liters	3 liters
4 quarts (1 gallon)	4 liters	4 liters

Weight

U.S. Units	Canadian Metric	Australian Metric
1 ounce	30 grams	30 grams
2 ounces	55 grams	60 grams
3 ounces	85 grams	90 grams
4 ounces (¼ pound)	115 grams	125 grams
8 ounces (½ pound)	225 grams	225 grams
16 ounces (1 pound)	455 grams	500 grams (½ kilogram)

Length

Inches	Centimeters
0.5	1.5
1	2.5
2	5.0
3	7.5
4	10.0
5	12.5
6	15.0
7	17.5
8	20.5
9	23.0
10	25.5
11	28.0
12	30.5

Temperature (Degrees)

Fahrenheit	Celsius
32	0
212	100
250	120
275	140
300	150
325	160
350	180
375	190
400	200
425	220
450	230
475	240
500	260

Index

• N •

Notes

Notes

About the Authors

Erin Palinski-Wade, RD, CDE, LDN: Erin is a nationally recognized nutrition and fitness expert, spokesperson, and author of *Belly Fat Diet For Dummies* (Wiley), as well as the 2 Day Diabetes Diet (Reader's Digest), Healthy 'n Fit Pediatric Weight Management Program, and the Healthy Resolutions Weight Management Program. She has contributed her expertise to national media outlets such as *The Early Show* (CBS), *The Doctors,* ABC News, CBS News, News 12, Fox News, *Fitness, Consumer Reports, Glamour,* and *Prevention.* She runs a private practice in northern New Jersey and frequently serves as a media spokesperson, nutrition consultant, and speaker. Erin is a Registered Dietitian, Certified Personal Trainer, and Certified Diabetes Educator who currently serves on the Dietetic Advisory Board for the College of Saint Elizabeth. She is also a featured nutrition expert for KnowMoreTV.

Tara Gidus, MS, RD, CSSD, LDN: Tara is a nationally recognized expert and spokesperson on nutrition, fitness, and health promotion. Tara is quoted in a variety of media including television, radio, newspapers, magazines, and websites and is a past National Media Spokesperson for the Academy of Nutrition and Dietetics. She appears regularly as the "Diet Diva" on the national morning television show, *The Daily Buzz.* Tara is currently the Team Dietitian for the Orlando Magic NBA team and Nutrition Consultant for the University of Central Florida (UCF) Athletics, as well as the "official nutritionist" for runDisney endurance events. She is the nutrition advisor for *American Baby* magazine and the Healthy Eating Expert and blogger on Healthline. Tara is the author of *Pregnancy Cooking & Nutrition For Dummies* (Wiley). She helps senior executives from Fortune 100 companies manage their energy in her role as a nutrition and movement coach at the Human Performance Institute.

Kristina LaRue, RD, LDN, CLT: Kristina writes the food and fitness blog Love & Zest (www.loveandzest.com), where she shares recipes, life, and nutrition. She believes healthy food should be delicious and hopes to inspire people to get in the kitchen and cook! She is a registered dietitian in Orlando, Florida, specializing in food sensitivities, sports nutrition, and eating disorders. Kristina is the sports dietitian for the University of Central Florida Athletics program, works for Tara Gidus Nutrition Consulting, and works with Joyful Nutrition in the treatment of eating disorders. She is an avid runner and enjoys competing in triathlons and marathons.

Dedication

This book is dedicated to everyone who believes that being healthy doesn't mean having to deprive yourself or give up great-tasting food.

This book is also dedicated to our loving and supportive families and friends, without whose constant support and belief in us, this book would not have been possible.

Authors' Acknowledgments

Special thanks to everyone who made this book possible, including our literary agent, Margot Hutchison; our acquisitions editor, Tracy Boggier; our project editor and copy editor, Elizabeth Kuball; our technical editor and nutrition analyst, Rachel Nix; and our recipe tester, Emily Nolan. We can't tell you how much we've appreciated all your support, patience, and knowledge.

Erin Palinski-Wade: I could not have written this book without the incredible love and support from those around me. I want to thank my amazingly wonderful husband, without whose support and confidence in me I would not have been able to achieve what I have, as well as my incredible family. I can't put into words how thankful and blessed I am to have each of you in my life. Your constant encouragement and confidence in me has made me who I am today. I also thank all the wonderful nutrition professionals whom I've had the pleasure to work with, for your guidance, advice, and support, especially my wonderful co-worker Susan Gralla, as well as my coauthors, Kristina and Tara, with whom it was a pleasure to work on this project.

Tara Gidus: A hearty thanks to my precious boys, Basil and Levi, and to my parents, Don and Jean Timpel, for their unending support and dedication to both me and their grandsons. Without you, Mom and Dad, I wouldn't be able to juggle my hectic work and home schedule. Thanks to all my RD buds — you know who you are — for paving the way for all dietitians to be seen as *the* nutrition experts. Of course, thanks to my coauthors, Kristina and Erin. We pulled together, tested and tasted, and bounced many e-mails back and forth!

Kristina LaRue: I would like to thank my sweet husband, Eric, for his patience and gentleness, and for inspiring me daily to be my best self. Thank you to my loving parents, Dwight and Becky, and siblings, Lauren, DJ, and Tyler, for all the encouragement, love, and support you've always given me. I am truly grateful for my wise mentors, Tara Gidus and Alice Baker; I know I would not be the dietitian I am today without you pouring into me. Many thank-yous to my wonderful coauthors, Erin and Tara, and all the interns who have helped us create and test recipes. We sure had a blast, and I appreciate every one of you! Above all, I give the praise and honor to my Lord and Savior Jesus Christ who has blessed me immensely, far more than I deserve.

Publisher's Acknowledgments

Senior Acquisitions Editor: Tracy Boggier

Project Editor: Elizabeth Kuball

Copy Editor: Elizabeth Kuball

Technical Editor: Rachel Nix

Recipe Tester: Emily Nolan

Nutrition Analyst: Rachel Nix

Art Coordinator: Alicia B. South

Project Coordinator: Patrick Redmond

Illustrator: Elizabeth Kurtzman

Cover Images: T. J. Hine Photography

le & Mac

d For Dummies,
Edition
-1-118-49823-1

one 5 For Dummies,
Edition
-1-118-35201-4

Book For Dummies,
Edition
-1-118-20920-2

X Mountain Lion
Dummies
-1-118-39418-2

gging & Social Media

ebook For Dummies,
Edition
-1-118-09562-1

n Blogging
Dummies
-1-118-03843-7

erest For Dummies
-1-118-32800-2

dPress For Dummies,
Edition
-1-118-38318-6

ness

modities For Dummies,
Edition
-1-118-01687-9

sting For Dummies,
Edition
0-470-90545-6

Personal Finance For Dummies, 7th Edition
978-1-118-11785-9

QuickBooks 2013 For Dummies
978-1-118-35641-8

Small Business Marketing Kit For Dummies, 3rd Edition
978-1-118-31183-7

Careers

Job Interviews
For Dummies,
4th Edition
978-1-118-11290-8

Job Searching with
Social Media
For Dummies
978-0-470-93072-4

Personal Branding
For Dummies
978-1-118-11792-7

Resumes For Dummies,
6th Edition
978-0-470-87361-8

Success as a Mediator
For Dummies
978-1-118-07862-4

Diet & Nutrition

Belly Fat Diet For Dummies
978-1-118-34585-6

Eating Clean For Dummies
978-1-118-00013-7

Nutrition For Dummies, 5th Edition
978-0-470-93231-5

Digital Photography

Digital Photography
For Dummies,
7th Edition
978-1-118-09203-3

Digital SLR Cameras &
Photography For Dummies,
4th Edition
978-1-118-14489-3

Photoshop Elements 11
For Dummies
978-1-118-40821-6

Gardening

Herb Gardening
For Dummies,
2nd Edition
978-0-470-61778-6

Vegetable Gardening
For Dummies,
2nd Edition
978-0-470-49870-5

Health

Anti-Inflammation Diet
For Dummies
978-1-118-02381-5

Diabetes For Dummies,
3rd Edition
978-0-470-27086-8

Living Paleo For Dummies
978-1-118-29405-5

Hobbies

Beekeeping
For Dummies
978-0-470-43065-1

eBay For Dummies,
7th Edition
978-1-118-09806-6

Raising Chickens
For Dummies
978-0-470-46544-8

Wine For Dummies,
5th Edition
978-1-118-28872-6

Writing Young Adult Fiction
For Dummies
978-0-470-94954-2

Language & Foreign Language

500 Spanish Verbs
For Dummies
978-1-118-02382-2

English Grammar
For Dummies,
2nd Edition
978-0-470-54664-2

French All-in One
For Dummies
978-1-118-22815-9

German Essentials
For Dummies
978-1-118-18422-6

Italian For Dummies
2nd Edition
978-1-118-00465-4

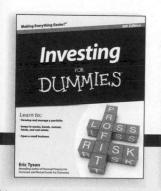 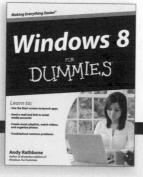  

Available in print and e-book formats.

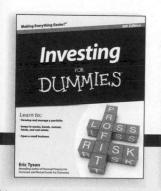

Math & Science

Algebra I For Dummies,
2nd Edition
978-0-470-55964-2

Anatomy and Physiology
For Dummies,
2nd Edition
978-0-470-92326-9

Astronomy For Dummies,
3rd Edition
978-1-118-37697-3

Biology For Dummies,
2nd Edition
978-0-470-59875-7

Chemistry For Dummies,
2nd Edition
978-1-1180-0730-3

Pre-Algebra Essentials
For Dummies
978-0-470-61838-7

Microsoft Office

Excel 2013 For Dummies
978-1-118-51012-4

Office 2013 All-in-One
For Dummies
978-1-118-51636-2

PowerPoint 2013
For Dummies
978-1-118-50253-2

Word 2013 For Dummies
978-1-118-49123-2

Music

Blues Harmonica
For Dummies
978-1-118-25269-7

Guitar For Dummies,
3rd Edition
978-1-118-11554-1

iPod & iTunes
For Dummies,
10th Edition
978-1-118-50864-0

Programming

Android Application
Development For
Dummies, 2nd Edition
978-1-118-38710-8

iOS 6 Application
Development For Dummies
978-1-118-50880-0

Java For Dummies,
5th Edition
978-0-470-37173-2

Religion & Inspiration

The Bible For Dummies
978-0-7645-5296-0

Buddhism For Dummies,
2nd Edition
978-1-118-02379-2

Catholicism For Dummies,
2nd Edition
978-1-118-07778-8

Self-Help & Relationships

Bipolar Disorder
For Dummies,
2nd Edition
978-1-118-33882-7

Meditation For Dummies,
3rd Edition
978-1-118-29144-3

Seniors

Computers For Seniors
For Dummies,
3rd Edition
978-1-118-11553-4

iPad For Seniors
For Dummies,
5th Edition
978-1-118-49708-1

Social Security
For Dummies
978-1-118-20573-0

Smartphones & Tablets

Android Phones
For Dummies
978-1-118-16952-0

Kindle Fire HD
For Dummies
978-1-118-42223-6

NOOK HD For Dummies,
Portable Edition
978-1-118-39498-4

Surface For Dummies
978-1-118-49634-3

Test Prep

ACT For Dummies,
5th Edition
978-1-118-01259-8

ASVAB For Dummies,
3rd Edition
978-0-470-63760-9

GRE For Dummies,
7th Edition
978-0-470-88921-3

Officer Candidate Tests
For Dummies
978-0-470-59876-4

Physician's Assistant E
For Dummies
978-1-118-11556-5

Series 7 Exam
For Dummies
978-0-470-09932-2

Windows 8

Windows 8 For Dumm
978-1-118-13461-0

Windows 8 For Dumm
Book + DVD Bundle
978-1-118-27167-4

Windows 8 All-in-One
For Dummies
978-1-118-11920-4

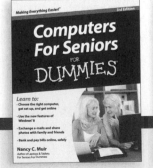

Available in print and e-book formats.

Take Dummies with you everywhere you go!

Whether you're excited about e-books, want more from the web, must have your mobile apps, or swept up in social media, Dummies makes everything easier .

Visit Us

Like Us

Follow Us

Watch Us

Join Us

Pin Us

Circle Us

Shop Us

Dummies products make life easie

- DIY
- Consumer Electronics
- Crafts

- Software
- Cookware
- Hobbies

- Videos
- Music
- Games
- and More!

For more information, go to **Dummies.com®** and search the store by categor

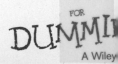

FOR
DUMMI
A Wiley